French Entrée

Calais, Boulogne and the North of France

Independent reviews of the best restaurants and hotels in the area

second edition

French Entrée

Calais, Boulogne and the North of France

Independent reviews of the best restaurants and hotels in the area

second edition

Patricia Fenn

Aspect Guides

Aspect Guides
Second edition published in Great Britain 2002
First published in 2000

Published by Aspect Guides, an imprint of Peter Collin Publishing
32-34 Great Peter Street, London, SW1P 2DB

British Library Cataloguing-in-Publication Data
A catalogue record for this book is available from the British Library
ISBN 1-904012-03-5

Design and production by Book Production Services, Norfolk
Printed and bound in Italy by Legoprint

Every effort has been made to ensure that the information in this guide is
accurate and up-to-date and the advice is given in good faith. However,
neither the publisher nor the author is responsible for any problems or
disappointments encountered before or during your travels.

Contents

The French Entrée Difference

This book is part of the French Entrée series of guide books that provide individual and personal reviews of restaurants and hotels in a particular region of France.

Unlike many of our competitors, we do not make any charge nor accept money to include establishments. This might seem like financial suicide, but it does ensure that you get a true review of the restaurant and, most importantly, the choice of restaurants and hotels is ours. Many of the best restaurants and hotels are not featured in other guides because the owners are already very busy and don't need to pay to get extra custom. But you'll find them in these guides – because they offer great food.

You can blame Patricia Fenn for having the original idea for this series of guides. And 20 years ago, this was an inspirational idea! Still, Pat and the fellow editors who compile these guides travel thousands of kilometres every year in search of great food and a great atmosphere. We hope you'll find the guide useful, or simply enjoy reading their travels around France.

www.aspectguides.com

Introduction

To Calais, Boulogne and the North

This guide to Calais and its surrounding areas came about thanks to your comments on my previous French Entrée guides.

Looking through my files it became obvious that the area you are primarily concerned with is quite compact and near the Channel-crossing ports. Some of you explore further inland from the coast – a great idea because there is much to see in this tourist-neglected hinterland. But the vast majority use a guide to help them find somewhere to eat or sleep just across the Channel. You don't spend a fortnight here, but rather a long weekend or even a day.

In this new edition, you'll find updates on favourite places and new entries to tempt you. As always, if you have comments about these entries, or suggestions for as-yet-undiscovered gems, please let me know (the address details are on page 25).

The first book, 20 years ago, was written to introduce the Brits to the pleasures that lay so near, but previously so far. I remember that many were nervous of driving on the wrong side of the road or having to speak French. It's hard to believe now that second holidays, short breaks abroad, were something new. The area covered by these first guides was immediately round the Channel ports. This subsequently expanded to one hundred kms inland, and that is exactly the same area in this latest book. Restricting the limits has enabled me to spend the same amount of time researching a smaller area more intensively, so that I can safely say that I know virtually every village in its confines and every restaurant and hotel. I have been able to add details, like walks, excursions and attractions, for which there was previously neither time nor space.

Because the area is smaller, it is definitely not less interesting nor varied. I continue to be amazed at the variety on offer. Look at the one-offs: **Cassel**, a hilltop fortress in the middle of the Flanders plain, and it's hard to believe that not so very far away is the sophisticated **Le Touquet-Paris-Plage**, all 1930s nostalgia. Look at the old ramparted town of **Montreuil** in its new guise as a gastro-centre, with Michelin stars competing with rustic contenders. Look at **St Valery**, at the vast estuary of the Somme, oozing history and salty charm, then consider **Arras**, with one of the biggest and most beautiful squares in Europe at its heart, and several others besides. **St Omer** is unique, with its rivers, canals, locks, market gardens and misty moistness, **Bergues** is a pleasant surprise, like a mini Bruges, **Hesdin** too has water running through its centre, a charming town well worth a visit, and **Rue** deserves better recognition for its historical connections and lack of tourists. Even familiar **Boulogne** keeps some surprises up its sleeve for those who have never climbed up to the old town. I still discover something new on every visit. Last time it was **Gravelines**, which I had never got around to before. Fascinating and, like all the others mentioned, completely different from anywhere else.

The scenery too is greatly under-estimated. It may not be the Alps but it's certainly not all flat, as so many sceptics claim. Only a few kilometres drive from Boulogne are the Boulonnais hills, green and unspoiled, sheltering time-warped villages and a degree of rusticity that is rare in England's over-crowded acres. The estuary of the Somme is vast and magnificent, with the opalescent light that has delighted artists for many years and which gave the area its name: the Côte d'Opale. There are forests and many rivers, with strange monosyllabic names like the Slack, the Hem, and the Aa. The valleys of the Course, the Canche and the Authie are all demanding to be explored.

As for the beaches, they are incomparable. They stretch the entire way from the Belgian border to the Somme, broken at the two Caps, Gris and Nez, by high chalk cliffs, but otherwise offering miles of firm sand and dunes.

Sadly this gateway to France has predictably been the scene of centuries of bloody conflicts. War and territorial acquisitions, with the aggression and tragedies that accompany them, have always been part of the area's heritage. The bloodshed in this century among the Flanders poppies and the cornfields of the Somme and the subsequent alien occupation of the whole region are a contemporary reminder of its vulnerability. For those who are remotely interested in the past there are plenty of memorials.

Entrée to the Entrées

Symbols

This is a chatty book, not a concise set of symbols. That said, there are times when symbols come in useful as space-saving shorthand. Here is the French Entrée code:

Hotels and restaurants are categorised in three groups. 🛏 is hotel, and ⊠ restaurant. In three cases there will be 'Ch d'H', which stands for Chambres d'Hôtes, or bed and breakfast. (See the *French Entrée Bed and Breakfast* guide for a greater range of independent reviews of the best bed and breakfast establishments in the area; because of this companion guide, chambre d'hôtes have been generally excluded from this guide, but these three are exceptional for various reasons.)

Closed: Refers to weekly and annual closing days. Ignore these at your peril. There can be nothing more frustrating than arriving after a long drive, with a hearty appetite and thirst, to find the door firmly barred and the whole establishment so shuttered and uncaring that you wonder if it's lost and gone forever. By far the most popular closing days are Sunday dinner and Monday all day; some entries are in the Otherwise section solely because they are the only restaurants open on the dread Sunday and Monday.

o.o.s. (out of season). 'Season' is loosely interpreted as Easter to October, but if in doubt it is always best to check first, because it could refer only to July and August.

So, to translate a typical entry, 'Closed: Sun. p.m.; Mon; Thurs. o.o.s., 15-Jul. to 14-Aug., fêtes' would indicate that the place is closed every Sunday evening, all day Monday, Thursday out of season, from 15th July to 14th August, and on fête days (list opposite).

The ☆ symbol indicates a specially recommended entry. A list of stars and the reasons for their selection is on p.10.

The next symbols are the style of establishement: L for Luxury, **M** for Medium and **S** for Simple.

The L Group

If you are planning a celebration (or are plain rich) this is the group to look for, and you will find great value, compared with prices for similar standards back home. I find myself apologising when I have to write that a top of the range French hotel room costs 112€, but the equivalent £70-odd doesn't go far for two persons' accommodation on this side of the Channel. Luxuries might include marble bathrooms with power showers and fleecy bathrobes hanging behind the door, a swimming pool, tennis courts, spacious 'parcs' dotted with recliners, elegant public rooms, and immaculate service. There will certainly be a complementary smart restaurant. Expect to pay between 80 and 160€ for a double room and 8-12€ for breakfast. The latter sum is actually better value than some of the cheaper *petits déjeuners* in the other categories, because the orange juice will be freshly squeezed, the croissants will be home-baked not dry and leathery, the preserves will be in pots not foil, the butter will be *doux*, and it will probably include a buffet style choice of eggs, ham, fish, yoghurts, cereals and fruit, from which you can fill up until dinner time.

There are some bargains too amongst L restaurants. The economic necessity of seeing bums on chairs for every meal means that chefs will offer rock-bottom (excuse the pun) priced menus for the less popular meals like lunch and mid-week dinners. There are several Michelin-starred nominations in the guide where you can eat like a lord on a three course 21€ menu. The most expensive is the only two-starred restaurant, Marc Meurin in Béthune, where the cheapest evening menu clocks in at 48€, but even here there is a lunchtime not-to-be missed menu at 35€ Compare these prices with a two-star Michelin restaurant in the U.K. and you will immediately understand why it makes good sense to do your celebrating in France. (In fact, in the L range, the highest price you will find is 67€ for a menu). Head here if you want your meal to be a memorable one, with chefs realising that if they want to hang on to hard-earned, fiercely competitive awards, standards must never never slip. At long last the more enlightened French cooks are beginning to admit that there is something new under the sun and that traditional French cuisine is not the only one. It is in this category that you will taste new flavours and combinations, with influences from all over the world, not just la Belle France. Beware the wine prices. They are often higher than at home and can transform a bargain into a financial crisis. On the other hand, you are more likely to be able to buy a glass of decent wine here, rather than a whole bottle, an important consideration at lunchtime, with driving in mind.

The M Group

The most numerous group in both hotels and restaurants. The hotels are nearly all owner-managed, and will have upgraded their rooms to make sure that they are all en suite. They will be well-equipped, with English television channels, good bathrooms, and plenty of extras and prices between 64-96€. The chain hotels would come into this group but you will not find them here. I know that they can be useful at times when all that is required is a convenient bed for the night, but my reasoning is that I personally would not choose them for any other reason, they are more or less predictably the same, and that readers can perfectly well find them for themselves, without any help from me. Old readers will know by now that this is a totally subjective guide and I am allowed prejudices.

M restaurants range from brasseries to comfortable bourgeois establishments, archetypally French with their tapestry chairs and velvet curtains, full of *hommes d'affaires* at lunchtime and families on Sundays. Chefs sometimes aspire to Michelin accolades, not quite there yet. These are the ones to spot while you can still afford them. Some are chosen because they are in especially attractive sites, overlooking water perhaps. Fish restaurants will probably come in this category, because fresh fish, however simply cooked, is basically expensive and cannot be included in the S group. Prices for the cheapest menu will be around 13-22€.

The S Group

The S hotels and restaurants are the ones that give me most pleasure and most pain. If I discover a really good one, like the Restaurant de la Gare at Les Attaques or le Cerisier at Laventie, I am mightily chuffed and enjoy the readers' letters congratulating me. On the other hand, these are the ones that so easily go wrong. They change hands more frequently than the others do, and the *patron/chefs* seem to have more marital disasters, leading to disruption in the kitchen and accueil as well as in the home. Understandably corners are cut to keep prices down, and sometimes this shows, disastrously. The S hotels are even more worrying than the S restaurants because you can forgive an indifferent meal but a bad night's sleep is not easily forgotten. There aren't many of them in the guide; use them by all means but read my caveats before you commit yourself. They will cost between 43 and 64€

for a double room, and breakfast (don't expect too much) will be around 35€.

S restaurants are another proposition. I use them frequently at lunchtime when, in order to appreciate properly my forthcoming evening meal, all I want is a plate of cheese with a salad, or *terrine*, or *crudités*, or an omelette, or a bowl of mussels. For those of sterner stuff the *plat du jour* is the dish to head for. It will change every day, to cater for the locals who eat at their favourite restaurant every lunchtime. Around 12.5€ will buy a three course *menu fixe*. Bistros and brasseries feature here, so all tastes and pockets are catered for. As a general rule I would caution against spending a large sum in an S restaurant. The kitchens just do not have the scope nor the chef the expertise to do justice to the more expensive menus, which can shoot up to the 29€ mark and are based on the like of bought-in *foie gras*. Desserts are often a disappointment - crème caramel, commercial ice cream, chocolate mousse and indifferent apple tart is about the range.

Otherwise...

This indicates those establishments which do not qualify for inclusion in the main headings but are worth a mention. It may be that I have inadvertently missed them on my round-ups (not often, I am happy to say), or that a reader has recommended them too late for inspection, or that their claim to distinction is an unusually attractive site, or more frequently that there is nothing better in that particularly area.

Prices

Compiling this new edition coincided with the change in currency in France from French Francs to Euros. By December 2001, just a month before the change of currency and publication of this book, many of the smaller restaurants and hotels had still not set their new price-structure in Euros. Others had used the change to convert and round-up their prices to the nearest Euro (or five), giving an often unnoticed price increase.

Throughout this book, we have included prices in Euros but, where the establishment had not set a Euro price, we have converted the latest prices from French Francs at the current rate of exchange. This will give you a good idea of the expected price, but you should expect some adjustment as the owners (and consumers) adapt to the new currency.

Star Recommendations

☆ The stars are to direct you towards the best, the trusted and true. The attributes for which they receive the star accolade are: good value, extra good food, good welcome and even good situations. The stars have all of these, but the stars all have at least one to make them stand out from the crowd.

Sometimes stars have to be deleted because readers have not agreed with my judgement, or I have revisited and been disappointed, or perhaps simply because there is just not enough information available to warrant certainty. If you have any views, and are good enough to pass them on to me, they will be put in the pool of wisdom and re-cycled in time for the next edition.

Obviously the standards by which the S establishments are judged are very different from the Ls. When reviewing the latter it is quite justifiable to be extremely picky. You are paying for nothing but the best, and second best is not acceptable.

The fact that there are rather a lot of stars in this relatively small area is an indication of the amount of time spent there and information collated over the years, both by myself and by faithful readers. I view them all with great affection for not having let me down.

The best establishments in this guide:

Aire sur la Lys:
Les Trois Mousquetaires 🛏 ☒ M-L. Comfortable hotel within easy reach of port, excellent cooking.

Arques:
La Grande Ste. Cathérine 🛏 ☒ S. Good value, good welcome.

Arras:
Les Trois Luppars 🛏 S. Good value, good situation.
La Faisanderie ☒ M-L. Excellent cooking.

Les Attaques:
Restaurant de la Gare ☒ S. Good value

Attin:
Au Bon Acceuil ☒ S-M. Excellent value, popular choice.

Auchy-les-Hesdin:
Auberge de la Monastère 🛏 ☒ S-M. Cheerful good value.

Bergues:
Le Berguenard ☒ M-S. New and interesting. Good value.
Le Pont Tournant ☒ S-M. Local favourite.

Béthune:
>   *Marc Meurin* 🛏 ☒L. Best cooking in the book. Comfortable rooms.

Beussent:
>   *Chez Barsby* (Ch d'H)L. Superb chambres d'hôtes.

Bollezeelle:
>   *St Louis* 🛏 ☒ M. Convenient, welcoming.

Bournonville:
>   *Le Moulin* ☒ S. Quantity.

Boulogne:
>   *Chez Jules* ☒ M-S. Best brasserie.
>   *La Coquillette* ☒ S. Good value, best Italian.

Calais:
>   *Le Channel* ☒ M. Consistent good value. Very popular.
>   *Aquar'Aile* ☒ M. Best fish.
>   *Le Grand Bleu* ☒ M. Good value fish

Cassel:
>   *l'Estaminet T'Kastell* ☒ S. Delightful eccentricity.

Le Crotoy:
>   *Les Tourelles* 🛏 ☒ M. Chic seaside hotel

Dèsvres:
>   *Agriculture* ☒ S. Home cooking.

Dunkerque: (Tétéghem)
>   *La Meunerie* ☒ L. Best cooking in le Nord.

Favières:
>   *Le Clé des Champs* ☒ M. Unusually good cooking.

Hallines:
>   *Hostellerie St. Hubert* 🛏 ☒ M. Stylish, peaceful.

Laventie:
>   *Le Cerisier* ☒ M-S. Outstanding cooking at bargain prices.

La Madelaine-sous-Montreuil:
>   *La Grenouillère* ☒ L. Outstanding cooking.

Maintenay:
>   *Le Moulin* ☒ S. Rustic charm.

Molinghem:
>   *Le Buffet* ☒ M. Good cooking.

Montreuil:
>   *Château de Montreuil* 🛏 ☒ L. Old favourite, luxurious, superb cooking. *Hotel de France* 🛏 M. Lots of character.
>   *Le Clos des Capucins* 🛏 S ☒ M. Affordable hotel, good cooking.

Le Coquempot ☒ M. Excellent value, good welcome.

Quend:

Le Fiacre 🛏 ☒ M. Inexpensive luxury.

St Josse:

Auberge du Moulinel ☒ M-S. Outstanding cooking and value.

Saulchoy:

Val d'Authie ☒ S-M. Great value.

Le Touquet:

Flavio ☒ L. Consistently high standards

Wimereux:

l'Atlantic 🛏 M-S ☒ M-L. Prime site, excellent fish.

L'Epicure ☒ M. Interesting cooking

La Goëlette (Ch d'H)M. Outstanding chambres d'hôte.

French Public Holidays

New Year's Day
Easter Sunday and Monday
Labour Day, 1st May
VE Day, 8th May
Ascension Day
Whit Sunday and Monday
France's National Day, 14th July
The Assumption, 15th August
All Saints' Day, 1st November
Armistice Day, 11th November
Christmas Day

Many travellers are now older and wiser having previously ignored the above fêtes and been forced to sleep in the car. Check that they are not part of your holiday; if they are book well ahead for both bed and board. The same applies to Sunday lunch when generations of French families settle down soon after mid-day to enjoy an orgy of eating, drinking, conversation and baby-worship that can easily last till teatime. Don't imagine you can squeeze in for a second sitting. There is no such thing.

And don't rely on eating at lunchtime after 1.30 in any case. "Finis" is a word that the waiters really enjoy. If your French is non-existent, make use of the local tourist bureaux, usually prominently lodged in the best building in the town centre, who will make the booking for you. Pick up local maps and advice while you're at it.

Shopping Hours

Most shops close for a lengthy lunch break at 12.30. Don't bank on them re-opening for a couple of hours. Some supermarkets stay open, but by no means all, and it is sometimes impossible to buy even petrol during the sacred lunch-time. On the plus side it is a joy to find shops open until 7 in the evening. Ingredients for the evening meal, and particularly freshly baked bread, are shopped for in the late afternoon. How sensible.

A list of the main local supermarkets and their opening hours is on p.24.

Another hazard is the Monday closing. There is no absolute rule about this but many smaller shops stay shuttered all day on

Monday as well as Sunday. Some on the other hand open up after lunch. If you're thinking of adding an extra day to the weekend, make it Friday, when you will be able to shop and eat.

Markets too snap shut for lunch. Most of them pack up for the day then. (See list on p. 22.)

What to buy

Every year there are fewer items to bring home that are not available in this country; it is just a question of comparing prices now. Best buy of course is wine and beer. See some suggestions where to buy under 'Calais' and throughout the book where applicable. A list of hypermarkets and their closing times are on p.24.

I always stock up on pure Arabica coffee, which is better and considerably cheaper in France, as is top-quality chocolate. You save a bit on preserves like Bonne Maman jams, and with the exchange rate so favourable an average weekly shopping list would undoubtedly cost less in France than in England. It's all a question of how much you want to lug around. I would prefer to spend the time in the markets, finding seasonal produce, like mushrooms, or olives, or asparagus, or strawberries, which may not be any cheaper but are a whole lot fresher than I can buy back home. Cheeses are definitely on my list, just because it is a pleasure to have so much variety and such high quality. Saucissons are a good buy for summer lunches or picnics. Don't be tempted to buy any more bread,however delicious, than you can consume immediately; it will go stale very quickly simply because it doesn't have any preservatives incorporated.

Maps and Guides

I must stress that the maps on pages 26-27 are intended only as indications of the location of the entries. They should be used in conjunction with the appropriate Michelin map, 236. I find the French Michelins a pleasure to use, so reliable and all-encompassing are they. Navigating even the delightfully rural white roads with their help is a doddle.

The red Michelin book, quite apart from all its other virtues, has excellent town maps. Gault Millau gives more specific detail and is better for spotting newcomers, but you do have to understand French and it is useless for the S grades. It's expensive too. The Logis de France do a useful guide to their chain of hotels, including the name of the patron (in Michelin you have to be a rosette-holder before this accolade is granted). You can buy this at the French Government Tourist Office at 178 Piccadilly, London W1, the source of all manner of helpful advice and literature, before you set off. There are two French guides, whose red badges are worth looking out for in the windows of their favoured establishments: Le Petit Futé, from which I have stolen some winners, and Le Routier, which is best for S choices.

However, the best guide of all is always word of mouth, or a car park full of French cars.

Getting there

The area is generously served with cross-Channel transport facilities. The choice between conventional ferry, tunnel or Hoverspeed must be a personal one. Each has its advantages and I am happy to mix and match. It would be futile to try and list the prices, since they vary so much from week to week, with special offers, especially on the ferries, making the prospect of a quick hopover extremely tempting.

For those passengers who have already had a long car journey to Kent, need the opportunity to stretch legs, gulp some fresh air and enjoy a leisurely meal the answer will be to choose the P&O Stena Line ferries. The ships have been regularly improved throughout the years and I can recommend their facilities as comfortable, going on luxurious, especially if you make the extra small investment for Club Class, which guarantees peace and quiet along with the free coffee and newspapers. Their journey time is around 75 minutes, with frequent crossings. Booking number is 0990 980980. If you like to feel French the moment you leave Dover try SeaFrance 0990 711711.

The tunnel is perhaps the most hassle-free, the quickest (journey time around 35 minutes) but the least agreeable. If your priority is to get there quickly, if you suffer from seasickness (but not claustrophobia) this is the one to go for, especially if your main reason for travelling is to visit the Cité Europe which is immediately at the mouth of the tunnel. Departures are very frequent. You don't have to book but it is always prudent to do so. If you arrive early or late for your reservation, they will allow you to take the most convenient train, subject to availability. Many people allow an extra half-hour to visit the duty free shop, which along with the cafés and other shops is the most agreeable of the three outlets. Le Shuttle: 0990 353535.

Hoverspeed has its fans, me among them, because of its speed – 45 minutes – and French port Boulogne. Given fair weather, it is a very smooth and comfortable crossing, though you have to forego the fresh air. The obvious disadvantage is that The Seacat does not enjoy extremely rough weather, and is sometimes cancelled if the forecast looks too dire. Not for those with delicate stomachs but otherwise a good choice. Hoverspeed 0990 240241.

Food and drink

This part of France is farming land. Rich and fertile soil yields gratifying crops, fat pigs and cows munch contentedly, lambs graze on the salt marshes. Hearty appetites pay little attention to *nouvelle cuisine*. The air is often chilly and damp, a problem eased by the consumption of substantial peasant food. This is not a region known for its sophisticated gastronomy, but for traditional home-cooked fare that has changed little over the centuries.

As in most regions of France, la chasse is a preoccupation. Particularly in the Somme area you can be sure to find dishes that have evolved from a surplus of hare, venison, wild boar, pigeon and wild duck. Look for *civet de lièvre* (jugged hare), *civets de chevreuil* (venison casserole), *terrine de sanglier* (terrine of wild boar), *suprêmes de pigeon* (pigeon breasts) and *pâté de canard* (wild duck pâté, a speciality of the Amiens region).

The North is the principal fish-supplying area for the whole of France. The Channel fishing fleet brings into Boulogne, Étaples and Dunkerque sole, plaice, bass, turbot and herring for commendably swift distribution country-wide. Cockles and scallops are the speciality of Le Crotoy at the mouth of the Somme, mussels, shrimps and prawns abound and are sold direct from the boats or the fishermen's homes. That appalling combination of mussels and chips spills over from Belgium. Both *moules* and *frîies* are excellent but one at a time please. *Caudiers de pichons* is the local equivalent of the southern *bouillabaisse*, and all the better for being composed of cold water fish.

The rivers of the area teem with trout, which is to be found on every valley menu along the Authie, the Canche, the Course and the Somme. It has been the speciality of the Auberge d'Inxent for several generations of owners. The lakes - *étangs* - of the Upper Somme are a fisherman's paradise; he can be sure of a supper of carp, tench or eel. *Pâté d'anguilles* is a favourite way of serving the eel in restaurants and smoked eel, to my mind, is superior to smoked salmon.

The salt marshes around the river estuaries are prime grazing grounds for the lamb that end up on the tables as *gigôts de pré salé*. Unbeatable flavour. The dark rich soil of the market gardens - the *hortillonages* - of the area around St. Omer and Amiens produces superb vegetables. Thick soups make warming winter fare and *la soupe des maraîchers* or la soupe des hortillons is composed of whatever veg are available - cabbage, leeks, potatoes are staples, but peas and lettuce get used too in summer, along with plenty of herbs. *La soupe de potiron* features in autumn, made from pumpkin, flavoured with onion and leeks, enriched with cream.

Perhaps the regional dish most likely to be encountered is the *flamiche*, nowadays most likely to come in the form of an open flan or pie, filled with vegetables. And very good too it can be. Its origins were the leftovers from the bread-making, which used to be baked in the oven at the precise moment when the wood started catching fire. *Flamiche > flamme > flame*. It is not hard to see the resemblance to the Mediterranean staple, pizza, where the dough base is topped with tomatoes and olives instead of these more homely Northern vegetables.

Ficelles you are certain to encounter. Basically they are pancakes, stacked with fillings between the layers. Cheese and ham are the most common ingredients, lubricated with a cheesy sauce. Cut like a cake, eaten with a salad, they make a very satisfactory lunch dish.

Picardy produces 25% of France's potatoes. That's a lot when you think of the *frites* alone. The cultivation of the potato was introduced into France by a native of the eastern Somme area, Parmentier, and ever since 1785 many classic potato dishes bear his name, as in potage *Parmentier*. Dishes peculiar to this region include *pommes en coquettes*, indicating the use of plenty of cloves of garlic, or *en magomiaux* which is not as you might think courtesy of the Magimix but fried in lard, with onions, basted in cider. *Bigalan* is a traditional recipe used by every baker in St. Valéry; sliced potatoes flavoured with onion are baked in shortcrust pastry.

Ploughman's lunches have plenty of local cheeses to choose from. *Maroilles* is probably the most famous and probably the strongest. A little goes a long way, especially if you bring it home in a hot car. If you have never tried it before, make sure you buy a good specimen from a reliable *maître fromager* like Philippe Olivier in Boulogne. You will also find it used in dishes like *flamiche au maroilles* or *poulet au maroilles*. The name Maroilles comes from the Abbey which used to make it 1,000 years ago, but you may find it under other names like *Craquignon* or *Marolles* - and its by-products, with other flavours added, become *Sorbais, Mignons, Quarts* or *Baguette Laonnaise* according to the area in which they are produced.

Most of the cheeses of the North have robust flavours, to say the least. *Trappiste, Dauphin, Roller* and *Gris de Lille* are other varieties to look out for in the markets. The latter is also known as *Vieux Ponant* (Old Stinker), which says it all.

The Somme is an important centre for the production of sugar from locally grown beet. Sugar keeps out the cold, and Northerners have sweet teeth. In every Grand'Rue *pâtissiers* and *chocolatiers* will have pride of place. Specialities include *le crotelloy* (from Le Crotoy), *biscuit de Doullens*, and *tuile Amienoise*, an almond enriched biscuit curled like a roof tile (*tuile*) from Amiens. Amiens is famous too for another almond-based delicacy, the *macaron*, whose original (and best) recipe is fiercely contested between fifteen *pâtissiers*. The one thing they agree upon is the town in which it originated.

For important occasions, like weddings, funerals and communion there has to be a gâteau *battu*. It's a bit boring really - just butter, eggs, flour and sugar, well-beaten (battu).

Crêpes are found all over France, but *landimolles* only in Picardy. They add a little fresh cream to lighten the batter, and more than a drop of *genièvre*. Lard takes the place of butter, so the whole confection is cholesterol-ridden.

No wine is grown in the area, but the excellent beer helps to compensate. The nearer you get to the Belgian border, the higher the consumption. It can be more expensive than wine and - watch out drivers - far more alcoholic, but not to be missed. Rich Flemish *carbonades* (stews) and *potées* (thick soups) utilise the beer for cooking where wine-growing regions would slurp in the wine. Beer is also used in the preparation of *Maroilles* which is washed in beer every ten days throughout its four-month maturing.

Juniper berries make the clean-tasting *genièvre*, gulped down as a *digestif*, for which the little town of Houlle in the Pas de Calais is renowned. They crop up again to flavour cabbage and pork combinations.

And to round off this substantial fare? Try a *bistouille*. Coffee is laced with whatever alcohol comes to hand. Keeps out the cold anyway.

The Good Beach Guide

Among the many reasons for visiting this area - to shop, to eat, to stock up on wine, to embark on a journey elsewhere - rarely does one consider the beaches. Perhaps that is because they share our hostile weather, but look at any beach in southern England on a fine day and you will see a far higher people-to-space ratio than would ever occur in northern France. The fine sand stretches for the entire area covered by this book, from the Belgian border all the way to the mouth of the Somme, 200 km of coastline as well-endowed with dunes, rocks, bays and resorts as any in Europe.

From north to south, here is the range:

Bray-Dunes

Just inside the border, 10 km N of Dunkerque, lies **Bray-Dunes**. As its name implies, sand is its *raison d'être*. There are literally hundreds of kms of the stuff, spilling over into villages. There was once a great port here but in 1777 it was engulfed in a sandstorm that left only the clocktower of its church protruding. Its final demise came in 1943 when the Germans blew it up.

A century or so ago a philanthropic M. Bray bought up the entire area and established a summer seaside refuge for the workers of Dunkerque. Subsequently its fortunes declined and shabbiness set in. There are some signs of smartening-up, with an accent on sporting activities and family amusements, and enticements to *'les jeunes'*, like a summer rock festival.

I can't say I find it appealing in August when the population jumps from a peaceful 4,700 to a frenetic 100,000, nor in winter, when the sand flies into the hair and eyes, but pick a fine day and enjoy a walk along the magnificent firm beach, or along the prom (plenty of beach cafés). There is also a marked 14 km walk which continues inland to Zuydcoote, where the original port became silted up.

Malo-les-Bains

Dunkerque's best beach, to the east of the town. It takes its name from an entrepreneur, one Gaspard Malo, who a century ago bought up 600 hectares of sand and built some of the characteristic villas in the Anglo-Normand style. overlooking the fine beach. They are sadly faded and jaded now and probably in danger of being pulled down to make room for yet more boring apartments. This is a family-orientated resort, and a top residential area, with plenty of shops and restaurants to choose from. Ideal bucket 'n' spade territory.

Petit Port-St.-Philippe and Grand Port-St.-Philippe

Both these twin towns at the mouth of the river Aa boast magnificent beaches, where the sand is so firm that they double up as football pitches. For a taste of the briny you can't beat a walk out along the breakwater at GPF. I recommend this duo, which few Brits seem to have discovered. Plenty of good fish restaurants near the fishing boats lend plenty of atmosphere. **Calais'** firm sands offer a rarely appreciated opportunity to walk off that prolonged lunch, or to snatch air and exercise after a long car drive. Backed by dunes, they extend to the rows of wooden beach huts at **Blériot-Plage**, named after the aviator who in 1909 made the first cross-Channel flight from here.

Next comes **Sangatte**, nearest beach to the tunnel exit, and then, between the sheltering arms of the two Caps, Blanc Nez and Gris Nez, the village of **Wissant**, a prosperous port long before Calais but swallowed up in 1738 by drifting sand. Now the 12 km beach is firm and good for walking, great for shrimpers and rock climbers, probably one of the best along the coast. There are plenty of hotels and restaurants set back in the town centre.

This is the most attractive stretch of the whole littoral, with the coast road winding up above dramatic chalk cliffs; there are fine prospects on one side across the 19 miles of water to the rival cliffs in Dover and on the other the rolling Boulonnais hills. Great for walkers. The cliff paths are well indicated, dipping down to the cleft in the rocks that is **Escalles**. The interesting and sheltered beach here is approached by a lane from the main road. Refreshment available in the village.

Audresselles and Ambleteuse come next, the former with the remains of an old fort to clamber over, the latter a picturesque fishing village with a somewhat bizarre beach, scattered with huge flat-topped boulders. You can buy mussels and shellfish from the houses of the fishermen here, or consume a platter in one of the cafés.

Wimereux is better known and deservedly so. It would certainly be one of my favourite places to stay, near to the ports, with some of the best restaurants, a splendid b. and b., a prom for promenading, and a beach for beachcombing. The sands are firm and extensive - just so long as the tide is not high, when they disappear altogether and the waves tend to splash over the *digue*.

Boulogne's eastern beaches are spoiled by the ugly profile of the docks, but on the other side of the port are the beaches used by the Boulonnais at weekends -

Le Portel and **Equihen-Plage**, each with bars and cafés. Deep pine woods and fabulous beaches run all the way to Étaples, the fishing port at the mouth of the Canche. This is prime camping territory - lots of space, lots of shade, lots of sand. **Hardelot-Plage** is the best-known resort along this stretch. It's a modern, custom-built community, well equipped with seasonal cafes and holiday shops, geared towards summer villas and apartments and consequently a bit dead out of season, apart from the golfers.

An even newer resort is **Sainte Cécile-Plage**; the beach, one of the best, is ideal for riding along (stables nearby) but again it's all a bit desolate when the sun doesn't shine.

Le Touquet on the other hand keeps going year-round, with an abundance of shops, markets, hotels, restaurants and entertainment. The beach is unbeatable - miles of firm sands in three directions, left, right and centre too when the tide recedes seemingly for ever. Fractious would be the child who was not happy here, with the options of paddling, castle-constructing, shellfish-capturing and even enlisting in the beach clubs for juvenile exercises, trampolining and gymnastics. Conscience-free parents can get in some sun-worshipping secure in the knowledge that their offspring are fully and contentedly occupied. Le Touquet believes in fun for all ages. The more adventurous might like to have a go at wind-sailing (*char-à-vent*), popular all along this coast. Instruction courses are available on the beach, along with windsurfing and dinghy sailing classes.

Situated on the wide promenade is the answer to unkind weather. **Aqualud** boasts an *ambiance tropicale* regardless of what the temperature is like outside. It's a huge fun-filled experience of getting wet at the seaside without involving the sea. Waves aplenty, along with slides, chutes and whirlpools. See p.181 for more details.

Next comes **Stella-Plage** and **Merlimont** - more dunes, more windsailing and inland, Bagatelle, the pioneer of all French 'attraction parks', featuring the biggest toboggan ride in Europe.

The air in next-door **Berck-Plage** was discovered to be particularly rich in iodine, and the winter particularly mild, so a hundred years ago it became established as a medical centre specialising in diseases of the bone. You can still see adult prams with leg extensions being pushed along the prom but nowadays it has become a family resort, big, brash and busy. If you like a lively holiday, amusement-arcaded, pin-machined, souvenir-shopped, ice-cream-licking, *frites* galore, this is for you. There are 15 km of fine blond sand, ideal for the sand-yachting competitions for which the resort is known.

If noise and bustle is not what you are looking for, try the reverse. You will have to share the lovely 13 km walk along the north bank of the estuary of the river Authie from the dunes of Bec-de-Perroquet to Pont-à-Cailloux only with the birds.

Between the estuaries of the Authie and the Somme is 25 km of sandy shoreline. **Fort Mahon Plage** is a recently developed resort, a bit characterless but excellent for windsailing because it is never short of wind, and well equipped with beach-gear shops and restaurants. The road swings away from the coast southwards, to make room for the nature reserve of Marquenterre (see p.146). A detour to admire the 300 species of birds that drop in here is highly recommended.

On the north bank of the magnificent estuary of the Somme is the resort claiming to have the only south-facing beach in the North of France - **Le Crotoy**. In fact only a section of it faces south because it curves round the mouth of the estuary, but it's a very fine beach whichever aspect you choose, if perhaps a bit more bracing than its Mediterranean competitors. The town has lots of character, with brightly coloured fishing boats pulled up on the beach and a medley of fish restaurants serving Sunday lunchers massive *plâteaux de fruits de mer*. A good choice for an excursion on many counts.

At the very end of the region covered by this book comes perhaps my favourite beach of all. **Saint Valéry-sur-Somme** has many charms - a peaceful mediaeval ramparted *haute ville*, great historic interest, lovely walks along the river, a funny little steam train that puffs around the bay, and, most distinctive of all, the vast sands of the Somme estuary. At low water, accompanied by a guide, you can walk across to Le Crotoy, if you have two hours to spare. When the tide takes over the sand disappears and you are left with sparkling water and swooping gulls. There is, however, still a tiny secret beach at the very end of the promenade, too insignificant to be rated as a big attraction, but a charming place for a paddle and a picnic.

Golf Courses

Plenty to choose from. Here are some of the best:

Le Touquet Golf Club, Ave du Golf, 62520 Le Touquet, tel: (0)3.21.06.28.00; fax: (0)3.21.06.28.01.
2 x 18 holes: Forest Course and Sea Course.
1 x 9 holes: Manor Course.

Hardelot Golf Club, Ave.du Golf, 62152 Hardelot.
tel: (0)3.21.83.73.10; fax: (0)3.21.83.24.33.
2 x 18 holes: Dunes Course and Pines Course.

AA St Omer Golf Club, Chemin des bois, Acquin-Westbecourt, 62380 Lumbres.
tel: (0)3.21.38.59.90; fax: (0)3.21.93.02.47.
1 x 18 holes.
1 x 9 holes.
Unusually good restaurant, open to non-players too.

Nampont Golf Club, Maison Forte, 80120 Nampont St Martin.
tel: (0)3.22.29.92.90; fax: (0)3.22.29.97.54.
2 x 18 holes: Les Cygnes and Le Belvedere.

Dunkerque Golf Club, Fort-Vallieres, 59380 Coudekerque-Branche.
tel: (0)3.28.61.07.43; fax: (0)3.28.60.05.93.
1 x 18 holes

Wimereux Golf Club, Rte. d'Ambleteuse, 62930 Wimereux.
tel: (0)3.21.32.43.20; fax.(0)3.21.33.62.21.
1 x 18 holes

Arras Golf Club, rue Briquet Taillandier, 62223 Anzin St. Aubin.
tel: (0)3.21.50.24.24; fax: (0)3.21.50.29.71.
1 x 18 holes.

Markets

Weekly markets are important days in Frenchmen's lives. Here is the chance not only to buy the best seasonal produce around, but also to catch up with friends and neighbours and enjoy a good gossip. Unlike so many of our markets (of which there are depressingly fewer every year), the produce has not fallen off a lorry or been rejected by reputable shops. The French housewife would never stand for that. Do not imagine that by buying market vegetables you will be getting the cheapest, but rest assured that you will be getting the freshest. Farmers wives have risen at dawn to pick whichever crops are likely to beat the other stallholders. Sometimes they have only a bunch of herbs or a kilo of wild mushrooms to offer, or one rabbit or two chickens. Their tomatoes will not be identical, their potatoes will still have dirt on them, their artichokes will be knobbly, but they will have travelled the shortest possible distance from earth to shopping basket. Above all else their produce will be seasonal and if there is a seasonal glut the customer will benefit. If you've ever pined to buy not one small bunch but armfuls of asparagus, go in May and do just that.

There is more to marketing than bringing home some trophies, however. Wander around and feast all the senses on the colour, noise, smells and yes indeed the feel of the harvest. Altogether different from a session in Sainsburys.

I am talking specifically about the edible produce. I am not at all happy about the recent additions to the market, like raucous videos, cheap plastic in whatever form, nasty nylon clothes. They are the exception to what I said above. They might well be cheaper than those from a shop and they might well have fallen off a camion.

Here is a list of some of the more important markets in the area. They all pack up at lunchtime:

Aire sur la Lys: Friday: Grand'Place and Place Notre Dame.
Amiens: Sat. and Wed. main market; Tues. and Sat. covered *halles*.
Ardres: Thursday on the fairground.
Arras: Sat. and Wed.: Place des Héros and Place de la Vacquerie; Thurs.: Place Marc Lanvin; Sun.: Place Verlaine.
Berck: Tue. Fri. and Sun.: Place de la Mairie in Berck Ville; Wed. and Sat. Place de l'Église in Berck Plage.
Béthune: Mon.: Grand'Place and Place Lamartine; Fri.: Place Lamartine.
Boulogne: Sat. and Wed.: Place Dalton.
Calais: Sat. and Wed.: Place d'Armes; Sat. Thurs. and Sun.: Z.U.P. du Beau Marais.
Camiers: Mon.: Place Communale.
Dèsvres: Tue.: Grand'Place.
Étaples: Tue. and Fri.: Place de la Mairie.
Fauquembergues: Thurs.: Grande Place.
Frévent: Tue.: Place du Marché
Fruges: Sat.: Place du G. de Gaulle.
Guines: Fr.: Place Foch.
Hesdin: Thurs.: Place d'Armes, bd. Richelieu.
Licques: Mon.: Place Christiane Collette Evrard.
Marquise: Thurs.: Grand'Place Louis le Senecha
Montreuil: Sat.: Grande Place.
St Omer: Sat.: Place Foch.
Samer: Mon.: Grand'Place Foch.
Sangatte: Fri.: Place de la Mairie, Blériot.
Le Touquet: Sat. and Thurs.: Marché Couvert year-round; from 19th May to September, Mon. Thurs. and Sat.
Wimereux: Tue. and Fri.: place Albert 1er.
Wissant: Wed.: Rue Gambetta.

Hypermarket and Supermarket Opening Hours

Cité Europe at Coquelles, near Calais. Shops open Mon.-Thurs.: 10 a.m.-8 p.m., Fri.: 10 a.m.-9 p.m., Sat.: 9 a.m.-10 p.m., (N.B closed: Sun.) *Carrefour hypermarket:* Mon. to Fri.: 9 a.m.-10 p.m., Sat.: 8.30 a.m.-10 p.m.
Auchan, also near Boulogne: Mon.-Sat.: 8.30 a.m.-10 p.m.

Sundays: PG supermarkets are open from 9 a.m.-1 p.m.; most food and wine shops open until around 12.30. Calais beer and wine cash-and-carrys are also open on Sunday.

A Calais advice line deals with enquiries 9.30 a.m.-4.30 p.m. from Mon. to Sat. on 020 8348 0503.

Your Feedback

I very much hope that you find the new design of our French Entrée series appealing – and easy to navigate. As always, I have personally visited every restaurant or hotel listed here, and, unlike almost every other guide-book, we take no payment from hoteliers and restaurants. The reviews are my personal opinions and recommendations rather than an entry written by the owner!

I very much appreciate the comments regarding your experiences with existing entries – or recommendations of new places for me to visit. These experiences help make each edition even better. If you have any comments, please send your report to:

Patricia Fenn,
Aspect Guides,
32-34 Great Peter Street,
London, SW1P 2DB
or by email: reports@aspectguides.com
or visit our website: www.aspectguides.com

We hope that our efforts will greatly add to your enjoyment of La Belle France.

Calais, Boulogne and the North

Aire-Sur-La-Lys 62120 Pas-de-Calais

19 km SE of St. Omer, 58 km SE of Calais
Market: *Fri.*

I don't believe that many visitors to that British favourite, Les Trois Mousquetaires, ever get round to exploring Aire. They just lap up the comfort, then set off down the RN23 again, back to Calais or on to pastures new and rather warmer. Big mistake. There's a lot more than they ever imagined about this sizeable town, built at the confluence of four rivers, the Lys, the Melde, the Laquette and the Mardyck. It also stands at the junction of four canals, so there's a lot of wetness around.

Its centre of course, especially on Fridays, is the vast market square. Here is the imposing Hotel de Ville, now cleverly converted in modern but sympathetic style, to house a library, boutiques and some children's play areas. Its majestic belfry carries a restored carillon; Corinthian pilasters and a carved double-headed eagle amid battle standards all add to its importance. At right angles, on the corner of the rue d'Arras, is a gem, the Renaissance Hotel du Bailliage, built in brick and stone very early in the 17th century. Two sides are arcaded with Doric columns; above them even more delicate Ionic columns divide the façade into bays. I enjoy the details, particularly the statuary - look for St. James, St. Anthony, the theological virtues of faith, hope and charity, the cardinal virtues of temperance - strength, prudence and fortitude - and the elements of earth - air, fire and water.

The Bailliage has been put to good use - it is now a very helpful tourist office. Pick up a variety of leaflets, including an interesting circuit of the valley of the Lys.

Wherever you choose to stroll in the town, if you use your eyes (look up as well as down and across) you cannot fail to discover buildings that are two, three and even four hundred years old. One stroll should lead along the rue St. Pierre to the vast collegiate church, with its Gothic tower, finished only in the 18th century. It houses a statue of the Virgin, with a delightful story attached.

In 1213 Ferrand of Portugal was besieging Aire and the starving citizens prayed to the Virgin's statue in this church for salvation and, more urgently, bread. Miraculously the bread appeared and the virgin earned her title Notre-Dame-de-Panetière. She has since had an adventurous life but triumphed over all adversities. Come the Revolution and she was a prime target for destruction as an object of superstition, but a baker's boy claimed he wanted to use her as firewood and kept her hidden till the danger was past. In 1944, when bombs set the sanctuary of the church alight, Notre-Dame-de-Panetière was smashed to matchwood and it looked as though her end had come at last; but the citizens were not prepared to lose their protectrice so readily; they collected every splinter and put them together again, so that she can still be seen today, standing on a gilded carving of the moon.

I particularly recommend Aire to anyone with Scottish connections. Legend has it that the town was founded by Lyderic, prompted by his Scottish wife, the princess Chrymild. See for yourself if they don't both look Scottish - their giant effigies are still on occasion paraded through the streets and Lyderic has a fine ginger beard.

Auberge de la Treille d'Or ☒ S.

67 rue d'Arras
tel: (0) 3.21.39.02.62
closed: Sun. p.m.; Mon.

One street back from the Grande Place in an old building that they say was a 19th century coaching inn. The façade has a trail of golden grapes painted on it, to justify the name.

Here is the kind of old-fashioned family-run business offering the old-fashioned value that it's getting harder and harder to find. M. and Mme Tourais are welcoming and cosy and a bit old-fashioned themselves - all to the good.

The dining room is net-curtained, cosy, and yes old-fashioned. Jacky Tourais specialises in meat, so if you fancy a *filet, tournedos* or *fauxfilet*, this is the place to head for because the prices are very reasonable. He also likes to show what he can do, so more ambitious items are on the speciality menu - braised ham with spinach and champagne sauce, *profiteroles* stuffed with kidneys in a cream and calvados sauce and served with green apples. Fish also features - poached turbot poached *aux deux sauces et aux deux couleurs*, simply cooked sea bass, or skate *en habit vert*. A hefty starter is his *soupe de poissons*, with all the trimmings, for 6.4€. Other starters are just as interesting as the entrées.

Every day there is a *suggestion du jour* at 7.2€ and, except at weekends, a menu at 11.2€, e.g. *tourte fermière* chaude aux herbes followed by fillets of red mullet, oven-roast and served with seafood sauce. Then cheese or dessert. Other menus at 17, 24 or 33€ are all astonishing value.

"*We had an excellent four-course meal. The total bill for two, including aperitifs and wine, was 41€. The quality and presentation of the food was excellent and we were made most welcome.*" Lynne and John Goode.

☆ **Les Trois Mousquetaires** 🛏 ☒ M-L
Château du Fort de la Rédoute
tel: (0)3.21.39.01.11
fax: (0)3.21.39.50.10
website: www.hostelleriedes3mousquetaires.com

It was with audible sighs of relief that we turned off the *nationale* into the imposing gates and saw before us journey's end, the well-manicured, turreted, balconied, pinnacled and beamed Château de la Rédoute. I noted in the last edition how smart it was looking, as though the red bricks had been reddened, the white stone blanco-ed, and the wood freshly creosoted, with the pond water weed-free, and the spotless swans lined up beside the decorative ducks. That is still the case. Les Trois Mousquetaires is prospering.

The car park revealed a solitary French car among the GB upmarket models. How strange it must be to be the solitary Frenchman in your own country.

In the reception area, little has changed; it's still lots of dark oak, a bit feudal-style, but there seemed to be more suitcases to fall over by the desk, where its nice receptionist was clearly overworked, answering the phone, welcoming new guests, dealing with bills and even carrying bags herself. No sign of the Venet family until I spotted Philippe (more of him every year), busy in his office. He looked all wrong without his chef's whites on and I have the feeling that he's happier when he's wearing them rather than a suit.

Les Trois Mousquetaires

Two bad hotel choices running and a dank and drizzling day made the prospects of the luxury of the Musketeers all the more appealing. We sank into a leather armchair and ordered two stiff ones. I must admit that even with them at hand the thought did occur to me that we could have relaxed better in a cosy bar or lounge rather than the frenetic reception area and all those suitcases.

However, there was nothing to spoil our enjoyment of the comfortable rooms and efficient bathroom. The rooms have been decorated elaborately, with complicated pelmets and coronas over the bed, a bit fussy but spacious and well equipped. No chance of re-visiting the other 30 rooms or two apartments, since, as is the norm, they were all full; ours cost 104€ as do the majority; there are smaller rooms at 88€ and two with shower for 50€. There is 1 suite at 152c. In the annexe there are two more rooms at 58€ or 74€.

Fresh from a restorative bath, we skipped the thought of an apéritif since no-one else had settled in the reception area and proceeded into the large dining room, past the glass-walled kitchen, where several chefs, but not Philippe, were hard at it.

The décor is nothing special - greyish and brownish - so that nothing detracts from the food. The 21€ menu, Mon-Fri, is still extraordinarily good. Other menus are at 29, 42 and 59€. Husband enjoyed his chicken liver and diced bacon salad with chicory, then Licques chicken, simply roasted with garlic and potatoes with bacon, but I was a bit disappointed in my stuffed courgette flowers. I had imagined them crisply deep-fat fried, but these were stodgy. My flambéed trout with pink peppercorns was perfect though and, chosen from the 17 desserts, my Agen cup with puréed prune sauce and Armagnac and Husband's warm blueberry tart were both top-notch.

Coffee came with to-die-for home-made chocolates; they and the *amuse gueules* that had preceded the meal had shown the skill of serious talent in the kitchen. Madame Venet Mark II, the bijou Caroline, was very much in evidence to serve and to smile.

The Mousquetaires and I go back a long way and perhaps that is the trouble. It is not very helpful to compare present with past but I have to say that I do feel a certain nostalgia for the time when there were just four bedrooms, the restaurant was clearly Philippe's be-all and end-all, Madame Venet presided benignly, and the serving wenches came in flowery cotton dresses and mop caps (I'm not kidding and not so long ago either). I am not alone. The piles of fan mail do seem to have tailed off recently - the higher prices lead to higher expectations. Here is one letter selected from the more recent tendency:

"This is the first time I have totally disagreed with your assessment. The rooms were nothing to write home about and dinner was overpriced, appallingly slow in the delivery and served with a complete lack of charm by a surly young waitress. The final straw was when they arrived in the middle of dinner requiring us (yes requiring!) to fill in our breakfast order. When we said we wouldn't require breakfast as we were leaving at 7 a.m., we were told that it was impossible as reception would not be open.

Hugely disappointed and suggest you need to revisit. *Apart from anything, it was more like being in Surrey on Sea than France.* (Name withheld in case he ever wants to go back!)

So... The ☆ stays, but only precariously. I still think that this is a rare example of luxury in this area and that the food is good. Perhaps the easy custom is spoiling the atmosphere; in which case, with more examples, the arrow will be diverted in the next update.

AMIENS 80000 Somme

100 km from Boulogne

The new autoroute, the A16, now connects both Calais and Boulogne directly to Amiens, making this ancient capital of Picardy all the more accessible and an even more desirable candidate for a short break. To be sitting in a café in the *parvis*, looking up at one of the world's greatest cathedrals, the largest in France, less than two hours from arrival at the channel ports, is an opportunity not to be ignored.

Amiens' list of assets is a long one: its setting in a unique watery landscape far removed from traffic fret, the charming new St. Leu development which, yes, really does hint of Venice, the good shops, the abundance of restaurants, the university animation and of course, No.1 star, Notre Dame.

First impressions are of the cathedral's sheer size. Two Parisien Notre Dames would fit inside comfortably. Built on a spur above the river, providing a sensational backcloth from St. Leu, it splendidly dominates the city. Anyone remotely interested should buy a good guidebook to discover some of its wonders but, just to whet the appetite:

Trade in cloth, particularly in velvets, which are still produced in Amiens, was at its peak in the 13th century and provided the funds to build this testimony of faith and refuge from suffering for an age beset with plague and war. It is barely credible that its elegant and intricate form should have been completed in less than fifty years, between 1220 and 1269, resulting in an unparalleled unity of style. The vaulted nave, supported by a score of delicate pillars, soars away into neck-cricking distance. You won't find finer craftsmanship anywhere in the world than in the choir, where the 110 stalls are carved with 4,000 figures illustrating familiar biblical scenes translated into the life-style of the 16th century Amienois. Unfortunately too many visitors have weakened the fabric and visiting hours have to be limited. It was open from 2.30 to 5p.m. when I was last there, but check.

The most popular statues, reproduced freely on postcards and posters, are the youthful gilded Virgin, smiling, slightly flirtatious, with the infant Jesus nonchalantly perched on her hip, and the cherub known as The Weeping Angel. He looks down on the tomb of an archbishop known for his love of children and certainly looks sad; however, I tested the legend that if a Christian looked at him steadily for five minutes, the tears would begin to flow down his chubby cheeks. Alas, no trace of moisture manifested itself from the statue - the only eyes that watered were mine.

In winter you will have plenty of space to appreciate such details and to soak up the peace and beauty of the cathedral; in summer arrange at least one visit outside coach hours, and allow more time than you think you might need to absorb her benefices. Walk round the whole building to understand the scale and cross the road to sit on the steps opposite to study the west porches, with their army of elongated figures. Look for St. Firmin, the Spanish evangelist who became Amiens' first bishop, on the left porch, and find him again above the stalls in the south aisle, pictured against a 15th-century Amiens, whose cathedral, belfry and ramparts are all recognisable.

To add authority to my own enthusiasm I would quote Ruskin: "This apse of Amiens is not only the best but the very first thing done perfectly in its manner by northern Christendom."

The cathedral has miraculously survived the devastation of two world wars, when 60% of the venerable city was lost. The ancient ramparts are now replaced by a busy ring road. But it is still an interesting and animated centre economically, intellectually and artistically and those important buildings, like the Hotel de Ville and the Law Courts that were spared in the destruction, have been recently cleaned and restored. The Musée de Picardie in the rue de la République (0)3.22.97.14.00, N.B. closed Mondays) is a fine neo-classic building, inaugurated by Napoleon III in 1868. It is one of France's outstanding museums, both for its paintings (El Greco, Ribera, Fragonard, Boucher, Tiepolo, Guardi etc.), murals (Puvis de Chavannes) and sculptures from the Middle Ages to the 19th century. It also has a fine archeological collection.

Markets:

Behind the Hotel de Ville are the market *halles*, in a modern building. If you're looking for an occupation for a cold wet day, head right here, because there is plenty of colour and variety to cheer the spirit. The fish stalls in particular are an education. Open for Tuesday to Saturday from 9 to 5 and on Sunday from 9 till noon. On Saturday and Wednesday mornings there are more stalls functioning in the square outside, representing one of the most important markets in the Somme. Saturday too is the day when the market gardeners from the hortillonages set up their stands along the Quai Parmentier and on a fine day it's a very agreeable stroll along the banks of the glittering river checking out what is freshest and best

Once a year, in June, the market is held as it was in the past; the market gardeners progress down the river, dressed in full mediaeval garb, in high-powered boats full of freshly collected vegetables.

Every second Sunday there is a flea market on the Quai Parmentier. Haggling expected.

Shopping

Easy - just one long street, partly pedestrianised, stretching from the station to the modern glass edifice, the Maison de Culture. The landmark at the station end is the unmissable (some may say unfortunately) Perret Tower, the sole survivor of a plan to rebuild the district around the station after WW2. Its main claim to distinction was that it was the highest building in Europe at the time.

Turn your back on it hastily and walk down the rue de Noyon to the green be-fountained square of the Place Réné Goblet. The street-name then changes to rue des Trois Cailloux, pleasantly pedestrianised and lined with shops, past the wide Place Gambetta, a good place to stop for a coffee.

St Leu

Threaded by canals, the quarter of St Leu was created in the Middle Ages, when water brought power to the various mills operated by weavers, dyers, tanners and flour millers. As the industries faded away, so did the the area, the canals became clogged, the warehouses crumbled, the houses deteriorated, until it became a disgraceful slum, peopled with drop-outs. Even twelve years ago it was unwise to walk alone here and certainly not after dark.

The restoration programme begun then and still continuing today has been thorough and imaginative and now this is the most attractive area of the whole city. The old cottages have been rescued and painted in bright colours, antique dealers and boutiques have moved into the charismatic buildings and restaurants and bars abound. An intelligent move was to site the new science faculty of the university here, bringing constant animation to the area and regular custom to its bars. The cobbled Quai Bélu is the busiest and perhaps the most attractive of the renovated streets, and is literally lined with restaurants to suit all tastes and pockets. The Passage Bélu leads to the antique dealers' gallery. In a maze of ancient streets, look for the rue de Metz l'Evêque for another successful restoration programme. Bordering the area, the Pont du Cange is the oldest bridge in Amiens, where vestiges of the ramparts may be seen and battlements still indicate the old tower. From May to September on the first Saturday of the month, you can join a tour of the quarter at night, starting at 10pm.

Les Hortillonages

No visit to Amiens during the summer months would be complete without experiencing the Hortillonages, a unique waterworld as strange as anything dreamt up by Walt Disney. From mid April to the end of September you can take a boat trip from the chemin de Halagé (marked off the bvd. de Beauville), a 50 minutes' meander in one of the typical low, high-powered punts that give you a duck's eye view of some of the 300 hectares of gardens that stretch into the very heart of the built-up area of the city. They are bisected by 55 kms of *rieux* (small canals), and the larger navigable canals, all irrigated by the rivers Somme and Avre, and can only be discovered from a boat or by walking along the towpath.

Hortillon was the name given by Caesar's soldiers to the men who tended these gardens then to feed the troops and there were vegetable plots here even in pre-Roman times. Today the *hortillons* still get about in the distinctive flat-bottomed tarred boats - *bâteaux à cornet*.

The black rich soil of the gardens is banked above the waterline. Most of them sport neat rows of bumper leeks, cabbages and caulis - three crops a year they can produce - but there are flowers too and on a September visit it was the colour that struck me most. I had been expecting a wishy-washy watercolour effect of gentle greys and greens - but no, there was a positive riot of not only autumn leaves and scarlet creepers but of gaudy dahlias, mammoth artificial-seeming sunflowers, marigolds, asters, golden rod, not to mention purple cabbages, crimson tomatoes; rosy apples on the trees were as shiny and profuse as those in a nurseryman's catalogue. On most plots stands some kind of shelter, from micro-hut to keep the fishing gear in to dolls-house bungalows, often with attendant gnomes.

I thoroughly recommend a relaxing interlude spent here, preferably on a sunny day, when the water sparkles as you drift stealthily in intense quietness amongst the water-lilies, poplars and willows, disturbing a variety of wildfowl.

Hotels

Here, I have to break my rule of not including chain hotels, since there are few alternatives however, there is a highly attractive scheme, in which the first three of my chosen hotels participate. That is two nights for the price of one, arriving any Friday or Saturday throughout the year. Book at least eight days ahead, mentioning the *"Bon Weekend en Ville"* scheme. Confirm in writing or fax. So you effectively halve the price, making these hotels look very cheap indeed.

Best Western 🛏 M
2 rue de Noyon.
tel: (0)3.22.91.52.51.
fax: (0)3.2292.81.66.

Described as a *grande maison bourgeoise* the erstwhile Univers stands, grey and solid, on the main street; some of the rooms overlook a small park and these are the ones to ask for. The owner/manager is now M. Marteau and since Best Western have become involved a considerable amount of redecoration and re-arrangement has gone on; mercifully they have retained the big central well, which allows light and airiness into the whole hotel. All 41 bedrooms are now bright and cheerful, with good bathrooms. 58-96€ is good value, especially for two nights.

Relais Mercure 🛏 M
17-19 place au Feurre.
tel: (0)3.22.22.00.20
fax: (0)3.22.91.86.57.

Le Prieuré, Amiens

This is the old Postillion, which used to be a readers' favourite, partly because of its picturesque old building and partly because of its favoured position just to the west of the cathedral. Much of the character of the old coaching inn has been lost in the modernisation and in the contemporary décor but old beams and rafters have been retained wherever feasible. A whole new wing has been arranged across the courtyard, making 47 rooms in all, and a lift has been installed. The bar at the entrance is much more comfortable and no longer attracts the ebullient *jeunes* which used to make life a misery for those of us who sleep lightly and are allergic to pop music. So some good, some not so good. Perhaps the prices of 78-90€ are a touch high. Until you stay two nights that is.

Alsace Lorraine. 🛏 S

18 rue de la Molière.
tel: (0)3.22.91.35.71.

The general instructions "near the station" are not very helpful, especially if you are arriving by car, because of the one-way system and narrow lanes. Listen to one who found out the hard way:

approaching from the north (via *autoroute* or *nationale*), cross over the bridge, proceed up the bld Alsace Lorraine following signs to the *gare* and take the second turning to the left, into the rue de la Vallée, then second left and second left again into the rue de la Molière, where the hotel is on the left and parking is wherever you can find a space.

The hotel is a tall and narrow white-painted building in an unappealing area. The smartly painted navy-blue door is the first clue of the inherent stylishness. The decoration has been achieved in impeccable taste - lots of white, via curtains, walls and paint, softened with antique furniture, mostly pine, large 19C gilt mirrors and plenty of pretty lamps. There is a refreshing glimpse of a green courtyard beyond the entrance hall and a little breakfast room to the right where a scantily clad lady frolics on a swing beside a villainous looking suitor, in an old stucco-framed engraving.

The 13 rooms are all light and elegant, with decorative fabric bedheads and - oh joy! - effective lights. Bathrooms are modern but only one has a bath. 48-64€ The owners are pleasant and helpful, though I can't forgive one disgraceful lapse. On a freezing windy afternoon, just as darkness was falling, I returned to the hotel to get some writing-up achieved, to find the front door firmly locked. I sat on the doorstep for two miserable hours before the owners returned. And no-one put any money in my hat.

This is a good example of getting what you pay for. Three-star upwards have 24-hour reception, lifts, bars and garages. Two stars like the Alsace Lorraine do not. In cheerless winter weather it is often worth paying for comforts like an armchair in a warm lounge and a stiff drink.

Hotel Victor Hugo ➤ S

2 rue de l'Oratoire.
tel: (0)3.22.91.57.91.
fax. (0)3.22.92.74.02.

For those whose dates do not include a weekend, or who want to stay only one night, and are looking for a bargain, this is it. Strategically placed in a quiet central street, with friendly owners, the rooms cost a mere 35€, with showers; family rooms are available at 42 or 47€. They are simply but adequately furnished and soothingly decorated in cool white.

Restaurants

Dozens to choose from, no Michelin stars.

Les Marissons ⊠ M
> Pont de la Dodane
> **tel:** (0)3.22.92.96.66.
> **closed:** Sat lunch; Sun; 2-Jan. to 9-Jan.

Amiens' superlative - the prettiest, the fullest, the smartest, the most expensive, the best-known-restaurant.

The setting qualifies for that 'i' word - idyllic it has to be - in the St. Leu area on an island separating a canal and a stream crossed by a bridge, with all the lights of the bars on the Quai Belu sparkling in the water, and with that superlative back-drop - the floodlit cathedral.

In the garden fairy lights twinkle in the trees and in summer this is the place to book a table - a superlative aspect. It's pretty nice inside too. In the 15th century this was a boatshed, believe it or not. The character remains, the wood shavings do not. M. Benoit has chosen the colours of Picardy to decorate his charming restaurant - yellow walls, blue chairs, yellow cloths and curtains which are wisely left undrawn to take in the view of the looming Notre Dame. Old rafters, fresh flowers (and some plastic ones too), soft lighting, all make for a soothing ambiance. A stuffed swan tucked in the eaves and puppets (known in Amiens as *cabotans*) make talking points.

We made a huge mistake by straying from the 30€ menu and eating *à la carte*, resulting in a ridiculously high bill. I should know better, but neither of the choices on the menu - chicken which we had eaten for lunch, nor the *rascasse*, not my favourite fish, appealed. There was even a 19€ version - soup, salmon and apple tart - which would have been adequate if not exciting, but I wanted to test out the chef's capabilities. My smoked eel with cider vinegar and honey was rich and tangy, the scallops with wild mushrooms were cooked to perfection, and husband's salt-marsh lamb came with some unusual vegetables - *crosnes de Marquenterre* - a kind of salsify - but, with one of the cheapest bottles of wine, they cost nearly £90, which spoiled the taste somewhat. There is also a menu at 50€.

It could have been worse. My passion for scallops could have led me to order *La Kermesse de le St Jacques*, involving six courses featuring the delectable bi-valve and costing a cool 47€ a head. Even I might find that a bit much; *scallops carpaccio, tarama, crostillant, avec chou vert à la flan de bière* and *aux fromages*.

Couronne ☒ M
64 rue St Leu
tel: (0)3.22.91.88.57.
closed: Sun. pm Sat. 2-Jan. to 10-Jan. and 14-Jul. to 14-Aug.

Strangely enough Amiens has few straightforward, traditional, un-quirky restaurants but this is one. Untrendy, solid, respectable, reliable, popular with the *hommes d'affaires* (which is always a recommendation) and excellent value. Michelin awards a red Repas for its 15€ menu, which is three substantial courses of dishes like *gigôt d'agneau* and *sole bonne femme*. They also have menus at 22€ and 30€.

The address is St Leu, but you will find La Couronne in the main traffic-way, not in the touristy tarted-up *quartier*. You don't come here for the décor but for the food.

Amiens has an amazing supply of themed restaurants, some of them very good, many of them along the Quai Bélu. At no. 45, *Le Porc St Leu*, tel: (0)3.22.80.00.73 you can sample more pork products than you would imagine possible. *Boudins, saucissons, pâtés, terrines*, liver, chops, steaks, *rillettes*, roasts, grills, even an omelette stuffed with pork. Menus start at 20€. It's a pretty little restaurant with red check cloths and a tiny rear garden and, like all these restaurant suggestions, it has covetable tables outside overlooking the river. A few doors along is **La Pataterie**, where, surprise surprise, the theme is potatoes. The baked spud is a newcomer to France and does not appear in classical French cuisine, but they seem to have taken it to their hearts. Here there is a choice of about fifteen fillings, from the simple cream and chives for 4.8€ to the ubiquitous St Jacques at 13.5€. **La Langouste** is at no. 33, tel: (0)3.22.91.37.62, supplying the fishy element. All sorts, and especially its namesake, on menus from 14€.; closed Sundays, pm.

At the end of the quay nearest Les Marissons there's a noisy 'British pub' and at the other there's that rare French species, a wine bar; it's called **La Queue de Vache**, which was the old name for the quay when cows were watered at the riverside here. Along with the glass of wine you can order cheese, quiches and light snacks - a very useful alternative to normal French tucker.

La Soupe à Cailloux ⊠ S

16 rue des Bondes
tel: (0)3.22.91.92.70
closed: Mon. o.o.s.

Still in St Leu but across the bridge is this little grey-painted bistro, with simple wooden tables and floor, popular with students. If it has a speciality it is in eclectic dishes - *soupe au pistou, travers de porc* and *tarte au rhubarbe*. Menus start at 12€.

Not all the themed restaurants are in St Leu. One of the best is:

Les Bouchées Doubles ⊠ M

11 bis rue Gresset
tel: (0)3.22.91.00.85
open: every day

Almost opposite the Hotel de Ville, a cheerful pink and red brasserie catering for Amiens' carnivores. Great hunks of red meat, like the *piece bouchées doubles*, are high quality and cooked just the way you like it. Plat du Jours for around 7.2€. Eat *à la carte* for less than 26€. Good atmosphere. Recommended.

Le Bouchon ⊠ M-S

10 rue Alexandre Fatton.
tel: (0)3.22.92.14.32.
closed: Sunday, pm.

Not to be confused with the above, this is a cosy bistro with a décor of old tin plaques, near the Tour Perron, where chef Laurent Lefèvre offers some of the best cooking in Amiens. His touch is half way between Parisian bistro and Lyons brasserie-classic, with subtle refinements. Menus cost between 14-20€.

Le T'Chiot Zinc ⊠ S

18 rue de Noyon
tel: (0)3.22.91.43.79
closed: Sunday and Monday, lunch.

Pronounced like a sneeze, this narrow bistro in the main street is one of Amiens' most popular eateries. Outside on the pavement is a whole sucking pig rotating on the spit. There are five rooms altogether, with customers packed in wherever a space occurs. The patron/chef steers round the tables, shaking all the regulars' hands. Waiters never dawdle, the pace is frenetic, so don't come here for an intimate quiet evening.

The value is great - the cheapest oysters in town are to be found here – 10.8€ for a dozen No.3 Claires. A gigantic *plateau de fruits de mer* features a whole lobster at 54€ for two people. The 14.7€ menu includes wine and substantial appetisers. Chunks of garlicky *tête de veau* were plonked down almost before we were seated. Plenty of Picard specialities on the menu like *ficelle, flamiche, caqhuse* (I asked the waiter to explain what the latter involved but he was in such a hurry I only gathered that it involved pork and didn't sound very nice).

My *carpaccio* of salmon overflowed the plate and was good and juicy and husband's egg mayonnaise was a perfectly unfussy specimen; we were all in favour until the next course - sucking pig for him, *moules* for me turned out to be dry and over-cooked. In retrospect I suspect that might have been because, finding the pace too hectic, we asked for a ten minute respite between courses, during which our meal was probably kept warm. I'm not going to damn Le Zinc on this one experience because the vibes were good, even if you do risk indigestion.

Otherwise:

Brasserie Jules ⊠ M
    Bld. Alsace Lorraine
    tel: (0)3.22.71.18.40
    closed: Sun.

A new brasserie near the station in the Centre Commerciale and the nearest eaterie if you are staying at the Hotel Alsace and Lorraine. The quality of the raw ingredients here - fish especially - is very high and service and settings are efficient and comfortable. Light and airy for a brasserie; a reliable choice. Menus from 18.4€.

ARDRES 62610 Pas-de-Calais

17 km SE of Calais
Market: *Thurs.*

Occupied by the English for seventeen years during the Hundred Years War, and the connection has endured. Generations of English travellers have used it for a first and last staging post, especially before the autoroute bypassed the little town. The Grand Hotel Clément, once a simple family-run auberge known for its fine cooking, was a favourite cross-Channel bolthole.

The triangle of the steeply sloping, cobbled Place d'Armes, surrounded with venerable houses, roofs awry, is as charming as ever, worn grey steps still lead up to the Carmelite chapel which dates from the 17th century, avenues of lime trees lend distinctive character.

La Chaumière 🛏 S

67 ave. Rouville
tel: (0)3.21.35.41.24
fax: (0)3.21.00.97.47

A safe bet if you are looking for a small hotel, with parking, garden, and English-speaking *patron*. The twelve bedrooms are all different, good-sized, pristine, all with bath or shower. They cost a very reasonable 32-48€. No restaurant but several within walking distance.

Here is a somewhat less enthusiastic view: *"Smaller room this time and I don't think I'd call it faultless - no savonette or bathmat. And the radio was on at breakfast time (but quite quiet and not dreadful music). But there are lots of nice things - very pleasant guv'nor, and a good breakfast with offers of more coffee, jam, bread etc."* Ron Salmon.

Le Relais 🛏 ⊠ S

tel: (0)3.21.35.42.00

A very pretty black-and-white building in a leafy square; as its name implies, once a staging post on the route from the Channel to the south. The entrance has tiled floor, cane furniture, fireplace and well-stocked bar, presided over by blonde Madame Rivelou. In summer there is sitting and drinking available in the rear garden and car parking is easy in the courtyard.

Simple smallish rooms cost 35-40€ with shower and 43€ with bath. This would make a cheap overnight base for a family in the two *familiale* rooms - 48€ for three people. Breakfast is 4.5€ per person.

It has always been the food rather than the rooms that have drawn customers to the Relais. Good straightforward cooking, generous helpings on menus that start at 10.8€ and go up to 28.8€.

"The big dining room was substantially full and there wasn't a French person there. Pretty good though poêle descargots, gigôt d'agneau à la Bretonne (superb quality lamb), good cheeses followed by sorbet". Ron Salmon.

La Bonne Auberge 🛏 ⊠ S

Route de Guines, Brêmes
tel: (0)3.21.35.41.09
closed: Sun. p.m.; Mon.
1 km W of Ardres on a sharp bend on the D231.

Madame Desmulle shouts laughter. She doesn't just giggle, she explodes, and that's most of the time.

One thing that makes her hoot is the fact that her regular guests don't want her to change a thing. Another is that she's going to. Her seven minuscule bedrooms up in the roof, all flowery, cosy, very rustic, very cheap, have pleased generations of British just as they are, but they lack one thing that a younger generation demands and that is a bathroom apiece. Hitherto guests have accepted the snag of padding down the corridor, when the cost of a double room is 24€. 24€! Madame Desmulle shrieks at the idea. So, there has been a huge programme of reconstruction, which has ended up with en suite rooms and a considerably higher rate. Now everything is New! New! New! says Madame Desmulle, including lights, decoration and en suite bathrooms in every room. The prices will be approx. 46-48€ per room. The restaurant is open as per usual.

The food has always been a good reason for patronising l'Auberge. The dining room is bigger than you'd think, and there's another huge room behind, catering for all manner of celebrations. Items are pink napery, lots of plants, red velvet, big clock, artificial flowers, old gramophone and a photo of Princess Diana. Outside is a big garden where breakfast is willingly (with lots of laffs) served in summer.

Menus start at 11.6€ (*flamiche*, trout, dessert) and go all the way up to 38€, which rather grandly aspires to *foie gras* and turbot. I'd go for the ones in between with more homely dishes like *gigot d'agneau*.

If things had been a bit more settled there would have been no reason to remove the ☆, but until the dust has settled I fear it will have to go. I look forward to revisiting the new-style Auberge and no doubt having a few more good laughs.

Otherwise:

Le Francois 1er ⊠ M
    pl. Armes.
    tel: *03.21.85.94.00*
    closed: *Mon.p.m., Wed p.m. and Mon., 26/8-10/10*

An imposing building in the main square, housing a smartish restaurant, which I have not yet sampled. Reports welcome. Menus from 16€ (lunch).

ARGOULES 80120 Pas-de-Calais

10 km W of Nempont-St. Firmin, 39 km SE of Boulogne

One of the prettiest villages along the valley of the Authie. A 300-year-old lime tree provides much of the character, shading the central green, and artists still find inspiration from the nearby abbey and Gothic church.

The gardens of the Abbey of Valloires are famous and are looking particularly good at the moment, after very necessary tidying and re-planting: hundreds of garden enthusiasts visit every week to feast their eyes on the colours.

Les Jardins de Valloires
tel: (0)3.22.23.53.55
closed: 5-Oct. to 5-Mar.

Seven hectares of botanical gardens, planted with 4,000 varieties. Open to the public. 6.2€.

You can stay here in the Abbey and wake up in the morning to this splendid prospect. Rooms are available in what were once Cistercian monks' cells, but very spacious cells they must have been. They are now furnished with antiques and have a bathroom apiece, so although life here may still be contemplative it is certainly not Spartan. The rest of the abbey is still very shabby and houses a school. See Chambres d'Hôtes for full details.

Otherwise

Le Coq en Pâte ☒ M
tel: (0)3.22.29.92.09

Unrecognisable as the potentially attractive but disgracefully dilapidated old café which, with similar *patronne*, the Coq en Pâte used to be. Now this is a smart restaurant, with designer black chintz fabric and rose-coloured walls. Service in the pretty rear garden is particularly agreeable. I thought the menus a touch pricey at 15.2€ for merely *terrine*, omelette and ice cream, or 20€ upwards, but there's no denying it's a very attractive set-up, with sophisticated service and superior cooking.

Le Gros Tilleul 🛏 ☒ M

Place du Château
tel: (0)3.22.29.91.00
fax: (0)3.22.23.91.64
closed: Monday o.o.s.

Named after the giant lime tree, le Gros Tilleul has a long history. It used to be a renowned restaurant with a popular 'character' *patron*, then went through a painful period of deterioration. Now the whole valley seems to be prospering again and Marie Christine and Patrick Beuge are making major investments in the old inn. They have installed a swimming pool behind the hotel and equipped all the bedrooms, several of them brand new, with bathrooms, mini-bars and colour televisions. I find the older rooms very dark, set as they are in the roof, with tiny windows, and I cannot claim that the modern furnishing is what I would have chosen for an old country inn, but downstairs retains the rustic feel, with a comforting log fire burning in the restaurant on chilly evenings. Room rates are 61€, 72€ and 88€.

Menus 11.2€ mid-week, 15.5€, 23c, 31€.

ARQUES 62510 Pas-de-Calais

2 km S of St. Omer by rue d'Arras

There is a distinctly villagey feel to Arques, making it quite separate in identity from its neighbour St. Omer, although the two run into one another. There's plenty to see and do around here, making it a good alternative to staying in St. Omer.

The Neufossé canal links up here with the rivers Aa and Lys and little streams flow at random in front of the 17th century château to the public gardens (good for picnics) and into the lakes there. The town is probably best-known for its glass-making and visitors can take a tour of the Verrerie Cristallerie d'Arques (see St. Omer, p.163) and pick up some bargains in the shop there. Another very different tour is to the amazing hydraulic lift, the *ascenseur des Fontinettes* (apply to the grandiose 19th century Town Hall for details). It's certainly another aspect for those who think they know the Pas-de-Calais inside out to see the huge barges pulled up by the locks here and to realise what a remarkable achievement this engineering triumph was in the 19th century. And still is for that matter. Another diversion, always worthwhile in my book, is to take in the Tuesday market.

☆ **La Grande Ste Cathérine** 🛏 ⊠ S-M
  51 rue Adrien d'Anvers
  tel: (0)3.21.38.03.73
  fax: (0)3.21.38.17.39.
  closed: Sat. lunch, Sun. p.m.; 26-Dec to 1-Jan.

I hoped last time that a ☆ would be feasible here and the mail has indicated that indeed it would. Readers have unanimously enjoyed this 17th century ex-coaching house in the main street. There is a distinctly English pub feel to the mahogany and brass bar area, popular with both guests and locals.

The twelve bedrooms are well equipped, with private bathroom apiece, and cost 40-46€. This would be a good family idea, since there are suitable rooms available and lots of space at the rear in a large garden, practical not only for summer barbecues and candle-lit dinners but also for letting off juvenile steam. Very soothing to find a sizeable 'parc' like this in the middle of the traffic fret.

The cooking, served in the panelled dining room, is surprisingly sophisticated, with a variety of house specialities, like a *feuillété de crabe, au coulis de crustacés*. The 17.6€ menu includes good wine, a complimentary Kir, *amuse-bouche* and coffee, and then for example, an onion tart spiced with smoked bacon, steak *au poivre* or *suggestion du marin* served with *sauce Dugléré* (tomato). Then a fresh fruit flan, or a dark chocolate *marquise*. Excellent all-inclusive value which it would be hard to beat. Other menus at 24 and 32€.

"Sunday lunch was at the Grande Ste Cathérine with Penny Hemery. Once again she treated us royally and was delighted when we presented her with a copy of your Entrée. Many of our members have since returned individually and it has become a firm favourite for us". Ian Skelton.

The ☆ is for all-round good value.

ARRAS 62000 Pas-de-Calais

112 km SE of Calais
Market: *Sat., Wed.: Place des Héros and Place de la Vacquerie; Thurs.: Place Marc Lanvin; Sun.: Place Verlaine*

No way could I leave out Arras from this book which is about the best of the north. Certainly if I had to choose an out of season weekend break away from the coast, it would be right here. So, although it just misses my 100 km limit, as with Amiens, the boundaries were bent a trifle to squeeze in this unique town. After all, access is easy and quick, with the autoroute so near and the other guideline of an hour's drive can just be met.

Park near the huge Abbaye St. Vaast - the largest abbey in France - and you can walk through three squares, each one opening out of the last like a layered Russian doll, except that in this case they get bigger, culminating in the explosion of the Grand'Place, which must be one of the largest in Europe and is certainly the most striking. Its surrounding arcaded Flemish houses, with their ornamented stepped gables, red brick, old stone, create an intensely satisfying total harmony. So perfect is their design that the suspicion that one has stumbled into a stage-setting might well occur, and indeed the apparatus of a film crew lay sprawling on the cobbles on my last visit.

In fact an artful deception has been practised, in that most of these houses are not the 17th and 18th century originals they would seem, but a reconstruction from the rubble that was all that was left of the great squares after the 80% destruction of the First World War. The extent of the damage of four years bombardment can be seen in the (badly-displayed) photographs in the foyer of the impressive Flemish-Gothic Town Hall in the Place des Héros.

This is the normal home of the monumental giants, Jacqueline and Colas, who come out for an airing whenever there is the slightest excuse, like fête days or sports triumphs, when they are paraded throughout the town, providing great photo-opportunities. Built originally in 1891, they were destroyed in WW1, reconstructed, destroyed again in WW2, then rebuilt in the 1980s, a commendable statement of municipal confidence in the overriding and continuing attraction of the best of things past.

The photos illustrate how only a very few of the old Flemish houses still stood, their gables sometimes lurching drunkenly towards the hole left by their neighbours. It would make sad viewing had the renaissance been less thorough and successful.

Don't miss a guided visit to the underground tunnels, from the Town Hall (every day except Christmas Day and New Years Day, weekdays 10-noon and 14.00-18.00, Sundays and fêtes 10-noon, 15.00-18.30 [to allow for extra lunch time of course!]) These tunnels, excavated from the chalk, have a fascinating and lengthy history. Dug originally in the 10th-12th centuries, they were abandoned until the prosperous 17th and 18th-century merchants needed somewhere to store the wine and cloth waiting to be shipped to England. There are twenty miles of tunnels altogether, some of them connected to private houses. (Don't worry - the tour, which lasts half an hour, covers only half a mile.)

The tunnels have been put to many good uses over the years. In the 18th century when the thriving town was over-populated, they were used for housing the surplus population, and often thereafter for refuge. Arras has the doubtful distinction of being the home of Robespierre, who was particularly hard on his fellow-citizens during the Terror, so the underground labyrinth was the obvious hiding place. In more recent times 2,400 soldiers were billeted here in WW1 and photographs of their living and sleeping quarters bring the extraordinary story vividly to life as no mere account can do.

From the ridiculous subterranean to the sublime heights. Take the lift up to the belfry, 40m above ground level (including 33 steep and winding steps, unsuitable for those short of agility or breath) for a not-to-be-missed-on-any-account eagle's eye view of the town. It's a good idea to make this excursion early in your visit to get an idea of the layout and interrelation of the squares. This vantage point is the give-away for the pseudo antiquity of the houses far below. Their weathered façades might look ancient enough but the new roofs are definitely 20th century.

So vast are Arras squares that even the extensive markets that take place on Saturdays and (to a lesser extent) Wednesdays fail to fill them. This is probably the best market in the North and a visit contrived on one of these days is well worthwhile. The stallholders, with their bright umbrellas, offer a huge range of goodies, from the heaps of seasonal vegetables to nasty plastic toys.

Among Arras' other claims to fame are the *bleu d'Arras* - blue and white porcelain, originally made in the 18th century, on sale in many shops in the town today and on display in the museum housed in the Abbaye St. Vaast. On show in the abbey's cloisters and refectory are the tapestries which gave the town its name - arras - the weaving of which brought the prosperity that caused houses on the squares to be built for their rich merchant owners. Walk round the places, looking for the heraldic signs of the local craft guilds and of the ruling families of the time.

Shopping

The market, of course, is the obvious place to stock up on local specialities from the farmers' wives, with their half-dozen eggs, two cheeses and a bunch of herbs. The place des Héros is lined with little shops, some dedicated to food, some to clothes, some to antiques, but there are two that are quite outstanding. At No. 39 is Le Goút du Vrai, where Jean-Claude Leclercq carries on his family's tradition as *Maître Fromager* and purveyor of irresistible *charcuterie*, prepared dishes (think picnic) and comestibles in jars, tins and boxes (bring home for popular presents). He puts the caves beneath his establishment to excellent use by using them to store his huge range of cheeses, both local and national. In his brochure he writes that the art of *'affiner'*, which two generations of his family have mastered, consists of numerous careful treatments to the cheeses. First they are washed in water, then in beer, then in alcohol, turned frequently and brushed, in order to give them even more flavour and perfume(!) "This perseverance in our work," he writes, "confers on the cheeses *Le Goút du Vrai* (the genuine taste)."

The other shop worthy of special mention is for the sweet-toothed. Yannick Déléstrez at No. 50 on the other side of the place des Héros, has a wickedly tempting selection of all things naughty but nice - hand-made chocolates and pastries both sweet and savoury.

For clothes shopping the main area to head for is the rues Gambetta, and St. Aubert, where the department stores are to be found.

Hotels

Univers 🛏 ☒ M

3 pl. Croix Rouge
tel: (0)3.21.71.34.01
fax: (0)3.21.71.41.42 R
closed: Sun. p.m.; Jan, Feb.

What a pleasure it is to see this old favourite alive and well again, after several years of decline. A restored 18th century Jesuit monastery in a quiet square in the centre of town, within walking distance of the great squares, is a good recipe for an unusually attractive hotel.

The new owners have spared little expense in bringing the shabby

Grand Hotel de L'Univers

old building back to life. I particularly like what they have done to the dining room - exposed and cleaned the old brick, which is now a lovely blond colour, and chosen a yellow and green colour scheme, so that all is light and bright. The bedrooms have all been redecorated too, but in fact apart from renewing the fabrics, there was little else necessary here because the building's character - big windows, high ceilings, more light - provides the décor. None of them is particularly spacious, and the first one that we were shown was so midget-sized that there we had to climb over suitcases to get out of bed. Up in the attics, it was very dark too and although the price was modest 70€ we could not face the claustrophobia and changed to a first-floor beauty, 126€ well spent.

Menus start at 19.2€ and increase to 35€, with the bonus of good carafe wine. 37 rooms from 88-120€.

Plus points are the beauty of the building, its convenient location and the certainty of a quiet night. Less commendable are the cheaper rooms and the lack of any owner-management presence. It was a touch impersonal.

☆ Les 3 Luppars 🛏 S

49 Grande Place
tel: (0)3.21.07.41.41
fax: (0)3.21.24.24.80

Even more central, slap bang on the Grande Place, and no complaints of lack of personal touch here. Viviane de Troy died three years ago. The new *patronne* is Anie Libouton, very friendly. De Troy is a famous local name, thanks to the exceptional wine cellar accumulated by Jean de Troy. Son Robert is said to be one of the best-informed *sommeliers* in France, and is only too happy to take any interested party down to his magnificent caves below the hotel (and with any luck, sell them some wine).

Les Trois Luppars is always pointed out by the tour guides as the oldest house in the square. It has that distinction because it was fortunate to survive the terrible bombardment that destroyed its neighbours, but for many years it looked as though systematic neglect and decay would finish off what the war had failed to do. In 1990 the de Troys bravely embarked on a lengthy and costly restoration of the derelict building. Ask to see the photographs of the state it was in, in order to appreciate the scale of the task they were taking on. With no state grant, the façade still had to be restored meticulously in keeping with its historical importance. The three luppars after which the hotel is named (luppar is the mediaeval word for leopard) are to be found on the original plaque.

Behind the little rear courtyard is another old building under the same ownership, with the original mediaeval shutters in one room. The two buildings muster 42 bedrooms between them, quite modern in character, and functional, with different attributes, sizes and prices - so be specific when you book. A sauna is a new attraction.

Breakfast was another big bonus, with yoghurt, fruit and cereals supplementing the usual French fare; the butter came in pots and the jams were Bonne Maman and not foil-wrapped smears.

Here is one reader's experience: *"There was a gigantic funfair in the square outside the hotel and the noise was shattering, but Madame showed us to a quiet room on the 1st floor - 32€ with toilet and shower, and we didn't hear a thing. We actually joined in the fun in the square later in the evening. The breakfast was wonderful"*. Patricia Thompson. 42 rooms with prices ranging from 53-72€.

An historic little hotel, with modest prices, in a prime site, with delightful owners, merits a star.

Restaurants

☆ **La Faisanderie** ⊠ **L-M**
45 Grande Place
tel: (0)3.21.48.20.76
fax: (0)3.21.50.89.18
closed: Sun. p.m.; Mon., school holidays and 3 first weeks of August

Last time I wrote glowingly about The Pheasantry, I had to add a stop-press margin note: "inexplicably lost Michelin star". Even more inexplicably that Michelin star has not to date been replaced, since Jean-Pierre is cooking better than ever. He is undoubtedly one of the best chefs in the North of France. Perhaps this is a good time to pay him a visit because he is obviously trying extra hard and the prices are extra keen.

Here are a few examples of what you can expect: For starters: le *Gratin de Poissons*. Now fish gratin can mean anything from some tinned tuna topped with packet cheese to Jean Pierre's version, which uses whatever fish is best and freshest in the market that morning, topped with a delicate creamy, cheese infused topping.

La Faisanderie.

Terrine Maison - sad to say I have eaten (or rather left on my plate) a wafer thin slice of something from the local delicatessen, via a spell in the fridge, on many a menu of this price. Here the punchy juicy terrine is served with a selection of *crudités* for good measure.

Main courses, on average 24€ include a melt-in-the-mouth *confit* of duck or a reliable opportunity to try *Potje fleisch*, a traditional Flemish casserole which can be positively disgusting in less skilled hands.

On my most recent visit we chose the 36€ Menu de Terroir. Stuffed crab and sea bass with thyme for me, snails with Ricard and best end of lamb for him. Then both cheese board (and an excellent one too) and skilful dessert. The Menu Dégustation clocks in at 57e€, and wine is included in all menus.

The setting is as delectable as the food. The cellars of one of the 17th century houses in the Grand'Place, all cool grey vaults and columns, great atmosphere. Service is smooth, smiling and highly professional and the wine list an education. Don't miss this one.

La Rapière ☒ S-M
44 Grand'Place
tel: (0)3.21.55.09.92
fax: (0)3.21.22.24.29
closed: Sun. p.m.

Across the other side of the square is a restaurant very popular with readers, which I dropped in the last edition after a disappointing report. After another look I think it should be reinstated.

The decor is perhaps a touch odd in this elegant 17th century building, with wonderful caves underneath (reserved, alas, for business diners) - it's all rustic and folksy - but that does make for a cosy atmosphere.

The cooking is determinedly traditional, with some regional touches like a *flan au maroilles*. Good value for quantity and quality on menus at 14€ (not fête days), 19.2€, 26€

Otherwise:

La Coupole d'Arras
26 bld. de Strasbourg
tel: (0)3.21.71.88.44

My favourite kind of brasserie where the waiters wear long white pinnies and black waistcoats and there are potted palms in jardinières, art deco mirrors, café curtains, and red plush banquettes. So far so good, but the food is only so-so. I include it because it is the only restaurant I could find that is willing to feed travellers on a Sunday night. Advice here is keep it simple.

Chez Annie
14 rue Paul Doumer
tel: (0)3.21.23.13.51
closed: Sun. and weekday evenings

Ideal for a lunchtime blow-out at minimum expense, with maximum entertainment. 200 metres behind the belfry, so ideally situated for recovery after climbing all those steps. There are a fair number of steps here too up to the mezzanine floor, which has the best view of all the activity downstairs in the bar. Very much an 'in' place with the locals. Cuisine can best be described as *'familiale'* and none the worse for that. Copious menu 9.6€. Looks highly promising, reports please.

ST NICOLAS 62223 Pas-de-Calais

2 km N of Arras

Almost a suburb of Arras. Useful to know if driving in town centres makes you nervous, since it is just off the autoroute.

Le Régent ⊨ ⊠ M
rue A. France
tel: (0)3.21.71.51.09
fax: (0)3.21.07.87.56
closed: Sat. lunch and Sun. p.m.

"We had an excellent Sunday lunch here, the only English-speakers in the restaurant. The foie gras had clearly been made in heaven. We are already planning to stay here next year." Robert and Margret Pope-Hennessy.

The 10 rooms still cost only 48-59€, and the food is as good as ever. Arras businessmen still find it worth their while to drive out here in their lunch time to stoke up. The dining room, elegant and light, opens out on to a pleasant terrace where drinks are served and thence slopes down to the river Avre. Menus, copious and mostly traditional dishes, start at 22€.

LES ATTAQUES 62730 Pas-de-Calais

9 km SE of Calais

A mere 9 km and it's goodbye Calais sprawl and hello Canal-land. The inherent flatness is enlivened by the occasional barge, locks, bridges and towpaths. You can drive all the way back into the heart of the port by using the minor road at the side of Les Attaques bridge; it's a touch bumpy and probably ten minutes slower, but free from traffic rage. It amuses me to see the three parallel routes, the frenzied autoroute, the old lorry-ridden *nationale*, and my favoured lane, by sparkling water all the way, light years away from the alternatives.

There's not much more to Les Attaques than a few houses, a *Mairie*, an old station and:

☆ **Restaurant de la Gare** ⊠ S
  rte d'Andres
  tel:(0)3.21.82.22.28
  closed: for dinner except on Fri. and Sat. Otherwise lunch only. Also closed Mondays, o.o.s.

As its name implies, near the station, an insignificant little building, unremarkable until you look at the size of its car park, which is often overflowing with cars (French ones of course). Nowadays there are a few GB plates too because this is probably the restaurant that has won more friends over the FE years than any other. Readers return for a special treat, or schedule a meal there in their journey elsewhere, and then write to me to say nothing has changed.

This includes the two large rooms (another for local festivities at the rear), with flowery wallpaper, tiled floor and an overall beige impression. Locals prop up the bar and chat to nice Madame Rambaut. On the shelves is a fine array of cups from the Les Attaques football team. It's the scene that used to be familiar in every French village, but is now giving way to fast-food caffs.

Francis Rambaut is a butcher by trade, so this is primarily the place to find home-made *terrines, foie gras, rillettes, saucissons* and of course steaks, chops and offal.

The locals were all tucking into the *menu conseillé* (which has to be different every day because so many of them eat nowhere else).

For 9.3€ they got *galantine de veau, saucisse et sa garniture* and *tarte maison*. On the more expensive menus - 14€ and 22€ and 28€ - the smoked salmon and the *foie gras* are both home-prepared and the steaks change from *entrecôte* to fillet. Husband had just a steak and I had my usual - a hunk of juicy *terrine* and an unexpectedly huge portion of *crudités*. Madame thinks it's a bit strange to want them served together, but humours me.

Francis is looking very prosperous these days - bearded and portly - and I am delighted if this is the case because here is one restaurant I would hate to lose. The Mayor feels the same way - he was eating there on our last visit and higher praise and stronger validation for a restaurant's worth it would be hard to find.

A ☆ for consistent good value.

"What a clever discovery. Despite hitting a local wedding we had a reasonably promptly served Sunday lunch. The one point we would make is that there didn't seem to be a menu on Sunday below 13.6€, fair value though it was. We think it must be the closest restaurant to England which leaves one in no doubt one is in France". J. E Clarke.

ATTIN 62170 Montreuil. Pas-de-Calais

3 km N of Montreuil

☆ Au Bon Accueil ⊠ M-S
52 rte Nationale 39
tel: (0)3.21.06.04.21
closed: Sun. p.m.; Mon.; Wed. p.m. o.o.s. Two weeks in Feb; 19-Aug. to 9-Sept.

The *accueil* is as *bon* as ever from Jacques Delvoye and the cooking as toothsome from his wife Denise. Nothing but praise from readers, all delighted with the value on offer here.

One look at the number of French cars parked imaginatively on the bend of the *nationale* outside the villa-like restaurant and you know you can't go far wrong. It's a big dining room, decorated in country garden mode, and always busy, so book if a Sunday lunch is what you have in mind.

The dishes on the menus look simple enough but there is always a touch of imagination to liven up the predictable, and the ingredients are always obviously fresh. *Menu Express* at 14€ offers two courses and wine, *Menu Opale* adds another course, *Menu Azur* is 21€, *Menu Emeraude* at 24€ gets more sophisticated, and Menu Mer at 21€ allows you three fish dishes, dessert but no wine. The prices jump to a minimum of 22€ on Sundays and fêtes and they have a special tourist menu including a complementary Kir for 22€.

"*I liked the welcome from M. Delvoye and the lovely pink and green bright dining room. We began with three different fish dishes shared between us: a fresh crab mayonnaise, smoked salmon (particularly good) and a gâteau of salmon with a sauce nantua. All three were excellent, as were the home made bread rolls which were replaced regularly. Then a most unusual scallop dish: the hard shell was surrounded by pastry which you cut away to take off the lid and there nestling inside were the fresh scallops on a julienne of fresh vegetables. The hollandaise was served separately and we poured it over the scallops in the shell. A pear and blackcurrant sorbet rounded off a very good value lunch. I liked several of the touches, including a suggestion of three wines by the glass, one with each course, for 12.5€.*" Roger Davies.

The ☆ remains intact.

AUCHY-LES-HESDIN 62770 Pas-de-Calais

4 km NE of Hesdin on the D94

Dominating this rather unattractive village (excepting the church) are the grey paper mills, on whose site once stood the monastery that gave its name to the hotel. The dead and wounded from Agincourt, only a few miles away, were brought here to be tended by the monks.

☆ Auberge de la Monastère 🛏 ☒ M-S
> **tel:** (0)3.21.04.83.54
> **fax:** (0)3.21.49.39.17
> **restaurant closed:** Mon.; hotel/restaurnt closed: Jan

This is supposed to be a completely re-written book, and so it is, with this exception: I made the mistake of reading what I had written in the previous edition, and after a recent follow-up visit found that little had changed about the character of the hotel and its ebullient owner, so I have little useful to add or change. Will faithful readers

LE MONASTÈRE, AUCHY - LÈS - HESDIN

please therefore forgive me if I reproduce almost exactly the original text.

Go and read the Livre d'Or. It says it all: "hospitality, conviviality, generosity". M. Marécaux loves his work and it shows. The book repeats itself: - "We shall return". His clients come back and back and tell their friends, who come back and back too, so that you should certainly book to make sure of a reservation. Featuring in Wish You Were Here of course did no harm at all.

In October M. Marécaux was worried that he had no rooms left for New Years Eve. 200 guests join in the revels then, some of them farmed out to neighbouring hotels. I wonder why he needed rooms - who goes to bed?

N.Y.E. apart, evenings chez Marécaux are likely to run and run. His proudest boast is that he has played with Acker Bilk, so a session at the piano or the clarinet is a very likely outcome on a Saturday or Sunday, given the slightest encouragement. Clients come as much for the atmosphere as for the bed and board.

The dining room is long and green and gold and red, with flagged floors, beams and a raised log fire at one end. It looks at it's best in the evenings, when the candles are lit and an air of expectancy hangs over the place as before a theatrical experience, as this often turns out to be.

In spite of all his gregariousness, *M. le patron* still finds time to take his cooking seriously. His 20€ *menu Terroir* features the dishes of his beloved region, which he promotes so tirelessly, and generously include plenty of expensive ingredients like monkfish and scallops, guinea fowl and duck. If you choose to stay demi-pension you get special treatment: "I don't show them the menu - I just ask them what they want".

The long-suffering Mme Marécaux, who is as nice as her husband, looks after as much of the front-of-house as he will allow her to do. No doubt she had a hand in choosing the furnishing for the new bedrooms, which are 56€, with a view over the big rear garden and the courtyard, complete with aviary. The older rooms, more simply equipped and furnished, cost 35-48€.

"We can only say that the addition of the new bedrooms has been extremely tastefully carried out and little expense has been spared on the furnishing of the rooms, which were absolutely spotless. We enjoyed an excellent meal."

The ☆ clearly deserves to stay for cheerful good value.

AUDENFORT 62890 Pas-de-Calais

20 km SE of Calais by N43 to Ardes then D224 towards Liques, then D217. The mill is signed to the right

Even shorter and much prettier, but perhaps not so easy to find is the D127 to Guines - a delightful route all along the canal, and then the D215 to Licques. This takes a mere 20 minutes from port to mill.

Moulin d'Audenfort.

> **tel:** (0)3.21.00.13.16
> **fax:** (0)3.21.00.14.79.
> **Closed:** 20 Oct. to 25 Oct.

I wrote in the last edition about this last-minute discovery, quoting my fears that by spilling the beans I was wrecking the very advantages - peacefulness, simplicity, cheapness - that I admired so much. I was half right, half wrong. Of course, the mill has become popular - too popular with the Brits some readers claim - but the qualities remain unchanged. New owners took over a year ago and have made some changes that were much-needed, so the prices have gone up, but everything they have effected has been for the good, and the intrinsic beauty of the place remains unspoiled. It is not on any main road, nor on the way to anywhere, nor in any village, so there is no passing trade, and the peace and quiet are remarkable.

The mill's origins date back to the 17C and the river Hem still actually runs through the building. In the lounge you can peer down to the basin housing the ancient mill machinery and see the trout swimming below. The cumbersome old workings make a unique focal point to the room, with sheaves of wheat on their platform emphasising the rusticity.

There is also a little bar here, an open fire in winter, lots of squashy armchairs and settees. All very cosy and familiale.

Next door is even nicer. Here a huge log fire burns continuously on a raised hearth, girded by a club fender and surrounded by deep chintzy sofas. The dining rooml/lounge has beams, yellow cloths, tiled floors, yellow striped curtains and a rough brick wall - all country-fresh.

As are the thirteen bedrooms, all with bathrooms, mostly overlooking the babbling river. Sorne are in the mill itself, some in the adjoining miller's house, where three have terraces on which to enjoy summer breakfasts, and some in a right-angle annexe that runs between garden and river, so that you can lie in bed and fish from your window! They are all simply but comfortably furnished and cost around 53€.

The young owners, Françoise and Dominique Gurselle have great plans for the future and there will undoubtedly be more changes. They are, however, keeping their chef, Walter, whose menus are said to be getting more and more creative. They start at 11.9€ for the regional version and run to 26.7€ for the gastronomic blow-out,

I think that, although I have not stayed here since the new management, the star should stay - the unique potential is being realised and all reports have been favourable.

AUDRESSELLES 62164 Pas-de-Calais

13 km N of Boulogne

A strange beach, with sand in between great flat-topped rocks. Ideal for picnic tables. There's lots of character in this relatively unspoiled fishing village, where crabs and mussels are for sale from many of the low, whitewashed, Flemish-style cottages and there seem to be more boats pulled up in the streets than on the beach.

Chez Mimi ☒ S
tel: (0)3.21.32.94.00

Just the kind of simple fish caff that one hopes to find in a fish-dedicated spot like Audresselles. Accept the plastic cloths and relish the freshness of the produce. Mary Arvot (see La Goëlette in Wimereux), an excellent source of the latest gastro-info, is responsible for my visit here. Chez Mimi used to feature in early FEs but was removed when there were signs of decline and fatigue. Now, I am pleased to report that under the able direction of M et Mme Becue Rigourd, it's back on form. If you fancy a plateful of moules or a local lobster without the frills, this is the place for you.

AZINCOURT Pas-de-Calais

15 km NE of Hesdin

No matter from which direction you approach the village which we know as Agincourt, you could hardly fail to gather that something momentous happened here once upon a time. Fluttering banners, coats of arms in red and gold and heraldic devices suspended at the roadside see to that. There is a museum too, with a video presentation of the battle when in 1415 Henry V and Charles VI met in the combat that was to lead to 10,000 of the French nobility being slain or captured. Not an event for the locals to celebrate you might think. No, but the tourist money's good.

You can follow one of the signed trails around the battlefield, but it takes a considerable stretch of imagination to picture the noise, the excitement, the colour, the action of that misty October day when our king covered himself in glory. 6,000 French soldiers are buried here in a grave pit beneath the roadside calvary near the site of battle, now a blank ploughed field. It was here at the crossroads that Henry delivered his rousing speech upon St. Crispin's Eve.

In 2001, the new Azincourt Mediaeval History Centre museum was opened, bringing the battle back to life by using the latest museum technology. The visit includes a guided walk over the actual battlefield.

Open: every day from 9-6 from 1/4-31/10, and 10-5 from 1/11-31/3
Entry: Adults 6.5€, children 4.8€, family 16€
Tel: (0) 03.21.47.27.53

Restaurant le Charles VI ⊠ S-M
12 rue Charles VI
tel: (0)3.21.41.53.00

The grandfather and grandmother of Armand Boulet owned a somewhat run-down café here. Purpose-built this year next door is their grandson's brand new restaurant, all peachified. Its glowing paint may seem a touch incongruous in such a setting, on a corner near the battlefield, but it's certainly a cheerful sight in this refreshment-free zone. There are some nice touches, like portraying the grandparents to the right of the entrance to the new restaurant and decorating the chairs with engravings of archers. French or English I wonder?

"Gersende Boulet was quite coincidentally baptised with a medieval first name which has its origins in Provence. Her husband Armand is the son of the mayor of Azincourt and a well-travelled and experienced chef. The quality of the food is excellent and very reasonably priced, with menus (including drinks) starting at 13€ during the week and go as high as 30€. at weekends. The carte is changed daily. Ambiance chic but very friendly and relaxed." D. H.

BERCK-PLAGE 62600 Pas-de-Calais

17 km S of Le Touquet, 29 km S of Boulogne
Market: *Wed., Sat.*

Otherwise:

The whole town of Berck is an otherwise in my book, because, frankly, I just can't take it. I hate the sprawl you have to drive through to get to the front, and once on the front I can't wait to get away again from all the nasty souvenir shops and burger bars. The one natural asset that it is impossible not to admire is the vast stretch of sand, but even this I find intimidating in its scale and busyness.

The resort originated as a centre for invalids, who benefited from the unusual deposits of ozone in the air. There are still a number of medical establishments operating in the town, and strange adult prams can be seen being pushed along the prom.

Just in case anyone disagrees with me in my distaste for the place - a windsurfer or sand-racer perhaps - there are two hotel possibilities, both personally inspected (never let it be said I shirk the cause of duty). **Hotel de la Banque**, 43 rue de la Division Léclerc, tel: (0)3.21.09.01.09, currently being re-furbished, 56€ with bath, and **l'Entonnoir**, 31 Ave Francis Tattegrain, tel: (0)3.21.09.12.13, 37€. Both are within easy toddler-reach of the beach, and both are good value.

BERGUES 59380 Nord

9 km S of Dunkerque

One of the most interesting little towns in Flanders, well worth exploring. Walk along the quiet quays beside the river Colme, across the iron bridges, through winding cobbled streets, admire the stepped gables, double-storied slender windows and carved stone heads on the weathered 18th and 19th century houses and you cannot fail to be reminded of Bruges. The bad news is that much of this historic town was destroyed in 1940; the good news is that it was so sympathetically restored that you would hardly know.

Bergues can be quite confusing to navigate because, as an aerial map clearly illustrates, it is built in the shape of a ring, with the inner circle formed by the rue Carnot, the rue Faidherbe and the rue Nationale enclosing the Eglise St. Martin, with several squares opening off one another. If you have time to spare - and it would be well spent - ask at the Tourist Office in the Place de la République for a list of suggested walks, in and outside the gates. I append one below.

The centrepiece, in the main square, is the famous 16th century belfry, set ablaze in 1940 and dynamited by the Germans in 1944. The reconstruction - a slightly simplified version - uses the same yellow sandstone; the Lion of Flanders looks down from the inverted onion dome and the carillon of fifty bells in the octagonal wooden campanile punctuates the day with some of the most tuneful and prolonged chimes in all Flanders. I timed the one that rang on the hour and it lasted all of ten minutes. Those prepared to climb 199 steps to the belfry's summit, 117ft high, will be rewarded with a fine view of the surrounding countryside, netted with rivers and canals.

No prizes for guessing that the military architect responsible for the town's fortification was the ubiquitous Vauban. Four gates pierce the ramparts. The Porte de Hondschoote was built after the treaty of Aix-la-Chapelle in 1667, which gave Bergues to France. Vauban utilised branches of the river Colme to build a crown-shaped complex of bastions - the Couronne d'Hondschoote, surrounded by deep moats full of fish. Its layout can only be appreciated by looking at a map. The Porte de Cassel to the south is from the same date, its triangular pediment decorated with the sun emblem of Louis XIV. The other gates, Bieur and Beckerstor, date from the Middle Ages.

Vauban might be gratified to know that his fortifications were used by the French troops in the defence of Dunkerque and only fell when the Germans used 20th-century methods - dive-bombing and flame-throwing - to breach them.

This many-faceted little town can add some important art treasures to its other attractions. The pride of the Musée Municipale's collection is Georges de la Tour's Hurdy-Gurdy Player, one of two versions. Pieter Breughel, Cuyp and Jordaens are also represented.

The one thing surprisingly lacking is that the huge place de la République, with important belfry, lacks a good central brasserie. It's one of the few Flemish towns that do not boast a Taverne Flamande. The cafés that surround the *place* are pretty dismal plastic and pop. But there are compensations.

Bergues - walk. Takes about an hour, but it is always possible to cut it short, and double back into the town centre. Notice all the wonderful names:

Start at the belfry, for the rampart walk behind the sports hall, between the Tour des Couleuvriniers and the Tour des Faux-

Monnayeurs. Climb the stairs of the latter, follow the ramp that runs along the rue Pierre Decroo, to the Bastion St. Pierre. Go down stairs and follow the vaulted path to the Place Charles de Croocq. Through the park up to the flight of steps and take the lane behind, the rue Neuve des Capucins. At the end go down the steps at the Porte d'Hondschoote. Pass by the Maison des Ingenieurs du Roy, cross over canal near the lock gate, turn right and follow the rampart up to the Porte du Quai. Through gate, along the quay up to the Porte du Port. Cross over the canal again and take footpath to the Caserne Leclaire. If you have the energy, climb to top of the Porte de Bierne for a good view. Walk on top of ramp up to the Poudrière du Moulin and back to the belfry via the Porte de Cassel. Drink beer in the place.

Unfortunately the hotel scene in Bergues is not good. One reader had a very unhappy experience at a former entry, le Tonnelier.

Otherwise:

Le Commerce 🛏 S
   tel: (0)3.28.68.60.37

A pretty little hotel near the church, spotlessly clean.   13 simple rooms, all but four with showers, cost from 29-59€.

The restaurant scene is another matter:

☆ Le Berguenard ⊠ M-S
   1 rue Faidherbe
   tel: (0)3.28.68.65.00
   closed: Sun. p.m.; Mon.

Emanuel de Langhe is a *traiteur* as well as a *restaurateur* and I always find this a good sign - it means that everything is home-made. The money has gone here where it does most good - in the cooking and not in the décor. Le Berguenard is a simple little restaurant in a side street, with nothing pretentious about its table settings, or, for that matter, about the food, which relies on good ingredients carefully prepared. Fish is Emanuel's speciality and his 30€ menu should be enough for fish-lovers to make a detour to Bergues especially to eat here. A *panaché* of sole and salmon was anointed with a sweet garlic sauce, and served with rice that had been cooked in flavoursome stock, and a fillet of brill came with a lime sauce. Passion-fruit mousse was a perfect finish to the meal. There is a 27€ version, again featuring fish for its first course - layers of sea trout in flaky pastry - followed by veal chop with chicory, on a bed of creamy mashed potatoes There are two further options, one at 32€ and the Menu Dégustation at 47€.

You should book - Le Berguenard is not only small, it is relatively new and everyone wants to try it. Once they do they go back.

Le Cornet d'Or ⊠ L

26 rue Espagnole
tel: (0)3.28.68.66.27
closed: Sun. p.m. and Mon.

Chalk and cheese from the previous entry. Le Cornet is a serious, rather grand restaurant serving serious, rather grand food. Jean-Claude Tasserit's talents have been widely recognised since I first wrote about him, and his Michelin star has brought him well-deserved prosperity. His clients from Dunkerque and *environs* keep tables occupied but nevertheless he manages to produce a 29€ mid-week menu, which is remarkable value. One other at 48€.

On an earlier visit I enjoyed asparagus and wild mushrooms cooked in cream and sole stuffed with *langoustines*, both superb and arrow-worthy. The fact that there is no arrow to this edition is not because I know that his cooking is any less praiseworthy but because the restaurant was closed when I tried to visit (and it wasn't Sunday or Monday). Nothing on the file to help me, so we must wait and see. Pity.

☆ Le Pont Tournant ⊠ S-M

Bierne-par-Bergues
tel: (0)3.28.68.61.66
Open: lunchtimes only and Saturday dinner; closed Saturday lunch

Outside the town walls, set back from the D916. More confusing to find now that there is a new roundabout. Hard to explain, but don't despair if you find yourself doing a U-turn to get there. Ask anyone, because everyone knows Le Pont Tournant.

It overlooks the canal, so would be particularly agreeable in fine weather. Not that most of its businessmen clients care - they are very happy munching away indoors in the fug. Technically the large dining room is divided into *fumeurs* and *non-fumeurs*, but, this

LE CORNET D'OR, BERGUES,

being France, check the habits of your neighbours before you sit down. Most of them will be regulars - Le Pont has celebrated its 30th anniversary and should know by now how to please them.

The décor will be recognisable as that of many such a French establishment where food comes first - mock beams, speckled tiled floor, *rustique* chairs, amber glass windows - but that's not important. You come here to please the tastebuds rather than the eye.

The menus at first sight look rather dull but in fact produce a good deal more than first impressions might reveal. Look no further than the cheapest one at 16€ if you want just a two-course lunch - the *plat du jour* and dessert. For more choice head for the 23€ version, for substantial portions of *terrine* (dish left on table) with crudités, then perhaps a Flemish speciality like *Potje fleisch* if you have a good appetite, then cheese and dessert. Highest price menu is 35€. There is also a generous buffet, from which you can help yourself to cold dishes and the famous fruit tarts.

Good honest cooking at good honest prices and starred accordingly.

"Excellent food, excellent service. An ideal place to have our last meal of the holiday before making for the Tunnel. 3 hours of undiluted pleasure." Lesley Bayliss.

BÉTHUNE 62400 Pas-de-Calais

34 km N of Arras, 40 km SW of Lille, 65 km SE of Calais
Market: *Mon., Fri.*

I asked two shopkeepers if the carillon in the belfry always struck so eccentrically - I noted it was always on the hour, usually on the half-hour, sometimes on the quarter hour and sometimes in between. They both said they were so used to it they never listened. That's a shame because it's a delightful little jingle that cheers up the large cobbled central square, and warms the hearts of the customers sitting outside the numerous cafés - I counted nine - that surround it. How praiseworthy that the citizens do not allow a little problem like the chill northern climate prevent them enjoying al fresco conviviality.

The belfry too is worth noticing - 14th century, the oldest in the Pas-de-Calais. And so are the eccentric buildings, particularly on the north side of the *place*, where they are so narrow that there cannot be more than one room on each floor. Their style is a mixture of Flemish and art deco, all spiky, gabled, balconied and carved, some wood, some stone. In fact none of them are the originals. After the devastation of WW1 the entire square was rebuilt. Béthune has had more than its fair share of destruction. The Germans, who occupied it during the last war, fired the entire kilometre between the *place* and the station as a parting gesture of hatred.

☆ **Marc Meurin** ⊨ ⊠ L
15 pl. de la République
tel: (0)3.21.68.88.88
fax: (0)3.21.56.37.15
closed: Sun. p.m., Mon. except fêtes, Tues. a.m.; first fortnight in August

Béthune might not be the most obvious place to find the top-rated chef in the whole of the North of France. Its proximity to Lille no doubt helps. But wherever Marc Meurin cooked, a meal in his restaurant would undoubtedly *mérite le détour*. I asked him what was the difference between one and two star (Michelin) cuisine, but I'd come to the wrong man. M. Meurin has never strained every fibre to join the exclusive club of just seventy chefs in the whole of this cuisine-obsessed country that can boast the second *macaron*. He just loves his job and happens to be very good at it. When he heard that he had been promoted in April 1998, it was a total surprise. He had neither striven nor hoped for the honour. So his reply was that nothing had changed. He cooked as he had always done (superbly). I realised, after eating chez Meurin recently, that I didn't really need to ask the question. My tastebuds told me all I needed to know. Here was an intensity of flavour, an attention to detail, a passion for fresh ingredients, a flair for combining subtle taste affinities that I had never found in the best one-star establishments.

His restaurant is tucked away in a quiet leafy square not far from the town centre in an elegant turn-of-the-century house. The reception area, presided over by blonde Madame Meurin, is charming, with red and white *toile de jouy* wallpaper. The colour scheme is repeated all over the house; in the three small dining rooms (tables well apart, atmosphere intimate); fresh white paint relieves the dramatic red walls. Red and white curtains, red and white striped high-backed chairs, red and white porcelain table settings, red and white fresh flowers and ruby candles may sound over the top, but believe me the impression is far from that, so clever has been the balance. The only touches of downright grandeur are the glittering chandelier and the sweeping staircase.

Marc Meurin is a hands-on chef and Mme. Meurin the maître d'h. He is to be found in the kitchen, not toadying up to his clients or appearing on television. He did find time, after all his customers had been served, to come and chat with me but otherwise his is the hand that stirs the sauce.

I dined on the cheapest menu, *Le Menu Curiosité*, at 48€ (at lunchtime there is a bargain Menu du Marché version at 35€). The meal started as it meant to go on - deliciously. When I tasted the preamble - three tiny *amuse-bouches* - I already knew I was in for an unforgettable experience.

A mousse of pumpkin with tomato jelly, a tender baby *langoustine* wrapped in a courgette shaving with a shellfish sauce, and a cauliflower soup, creamy beyond imagination, with chopped *cêpes* a surprise in the bottom, came in three little white porcelain dishes, one oblong, one square and one round, each holding a mere mouthful of ambrosia.

Marc is known not only for his imaginative use of unusual ingredients but also for his enthusiasm for local ones. Eel from the Somme came next - *anguille de la Somme* au vert sur toast. Three thin slices of fish, crisp on the outside, meltingly tender within. The *au vert* meant a creamy winey sauce, reduced to transparency and liberally sprinkled with herbs, served on a thin slice of unsweetened brioche.

More local produce next - the quails in his *suprème de caille fermière aux girolles, légumes étuvés à la fleur de sel* came from the little village of Licques, famous for its poultry. He used just the breasts (the extravagance totally justified by the result). They came in a sticky red wine sauce enlivened by punchy wild mushrooms. Perfect though they were, they were eclipsed by the vegetables. 'Étuvé' has no direct translation in English. 'stewed' certainly won't do. Here it meant cooked very gently in butter, covered, resulting in the most amazingly flavoursome potatoes ever, alongside melting baby onions, and juvenile carrots.

The dessert choice proved a real tug. True investigative spirit should have led me to *le flan de réglisse chocolat à l'infusion de thé vert*. Liquorice (*réglisse*), rarely seen on English menus, is the flavour of the month in France for both savoury and sweet dishes and the infusion of green tea would have been a first. I chickened out, however, at the potential richness and settled for the alternative - *la galette crèmeuse à la pêche de vigne*. I knew that *pêches de vigne* were quite different from ordinary peaches, but this was my first sampling. Their flavour is much more intense and I shall certainly look out for them again. The Meurin treatment involved topping a mini-pancake, enriched with cream, with half a peach that had been poached in champagne. How could I regret missing the liquorice after that?

Petits fours were a chocoholic's fantasy - truffles to die for. And the two squares of glistening home-made toffee, one chocolate, one caramel, meant that a bag of the usual varieties will never be the same again.

Yes, I can tell the difference between one and two stars.

Remember you read it here first - hot from the press is the news that the Meurins have just completed six lavishly comfortable rooms above the restaurant. They show off the versatility of the red and white theme by being all different. The bathrooms stick with white - marble. Each room - more of a suite really, with sitting space - has a well-equipped kitchenette. Ingredients for breakfast - cereal, bread, fruit, eggs, etc - are supplied, then it's up to you to do the cooking. They cost 88€, 104€ or 136€ which is good value considering the luxury on offer, the fact that you can stock up the fridge with your own booze and thus avoid bar bills, and the delight of only having to stagger up the stairs after the Meurin feast.

☆ for the best cooking in the book.

Otherwise:

Vieux Beffroi 🛏 ☒ M

48 Grand'Place
tel: (0)3.21.68.15.00
fax: (0)3.21.56.66.12

This old hotel centre-stage on the square is now part of a complex of three hotels, virtually taking over the town's accommodation. The 65 rooms range from 45-61€. Menus from 24€.

BEUSSENT 62212 Pas-de-Calais

31 km SE of Boulogne, 10 km N of Montreuil

The river Course flows wide and free here, past a picturesque and still functioning mill. On the D127 is an example of interesting local industry - Les Chocolats de Beussent. I had tasted the end result in various top restaurants in the vicinity, now I had the chance to find out how they were produced. I recommend the experience. The chocolate shop is open for purchases (preceded by complimentary tasting) from Mon. to Sat. from 9.00-12.00 and from 14.00-19.00. Group visits to the factory behind the shop are arranged by appointment in the afternoons and if you're lucky you can tag on and see the ingredients assembled and packed. The enterprise is run by two brothers, who have another shop in Paris, and one of them is likely to be your guide. Only the finest chocolate, rich in cacao, is used. If you want to be sure of seeing the workings of the factory on an English-speaking tour, telephone ahead to check on possible times, tel: (0)3.21.92.44.00. Les Chocolats de Beussent, 66 rte de Dèsvres.

Le Restaurant Lignier ⊠ S
4 pl. de la Mairie
tel: (0)3.21.86.50.55
closed: Wed.; Sun. p.m.

I had been put off previously by Madame Lignier's indication that she specialised in groups, but repeated praise from readers persuaded me to put prejudice aside and I'm glad I did.

The building is in the heart of downtown Beussent - that is on a corner opposite the mill. True the big rear room is designed for groups but there is another more atmospheric one with just six tables, which I liked much better. The tables double up for use by bar customers. Lignier is very much the nerve-centre of the village.

During the week the 10.8€ menu looks good value - *bouchées à la reine, omelette aux champignons*, dessert, wine or beer included - but look at the 16€ version for something altogether fancier. *Terrine de légumes au Noilly Prat, Effiloché de saumon à la crème d'algue, millefeuille aux Maroilles, marinés à la bière*. Somewhere out there is a chef who enjoys cooking. Nothing amateurishly rustic about those dishes. Other menus at 22€, 30€ and 39€.

☆ Josiane et Daniel Barsby (Ch d'H)L
124 rte d'Hucqueliers, Hameau le Ménage
tel: (0)3.21.90.91.92
fax: (0)3.21.86.38.24

The rule for including *chambres d'hôtes* in this book is that they must be special. The Barsbys' 19th century home, part manor, part farmhouse, set deep in peaceful lanes, amply fulfils this requirement. To find it drive past the Restaurant Lignier and climb a narrow leafy hill, with picnic tables thoughtfully set out to make the most of the surprisingly good view. After 2 kms look for the house on the left - no sign, deliberately, but it's the only substantial property on the road.

They have hardly any need for signs - open just a year when I visited and already well-booked by word-of-mouth.

Daniel is a sculptor in wood, as will be very evident immediately inside the front door. Examples of his talent, bold and distinctive, some of them begging to be bought (but not for sale) are all over the house. His studio is a stunning room, rising up to lofty rafters, with a gallery from which to look down on him working either at his sculpture or at the lace patterns which he designs for *Calaisien* lace manufacturers. He will happily show you the delicate painstaking designs of which he is a master.

The five bedrooms are all generous, in size, fittings and views. Bathrooms are definitely in the luxury class, with power showers and deep tubs. Colours, in keeping with the scale of the house, are bold - lots of crimsons and forest greens, not pretty pretty pastels, No skimping of the extras - bowls of fruit are provided in the rooms, bon-bons too, and bathroom perks, along with thick new towels.

Their windows all look out onto unblemished countryside via extensive grounds. Outbuildings (more rooms in the future perhaps?) are as immaculately preserved as the house. The new owners have obviously invested untold time as well as money in the restoration.

Breakfast, included in the price of 72€, is special again. Not only the usual French standard bread and croissants but fresh farm eggs and of course freshly squeezed o.j. Or, I imagine, anything else that you fancied - Josiane is an extremely accommodating hostess.

An undoubted arrow for unusually comfortable rooms and a good breakfast at a very reasonable price, charming hosts and the guarantee of a peaceful night's sleep, far away from the crowds but only 20 minutes from Boulogne.

Reports welcome

BLENDECQUES 62575 Pas-de-Calais

4 km S of St. Omer by D77

A surprisingly compact 'village' community feel, complete with church and market place, quite distinct from St. Omer's other amorphous suburbs.

Le Saint Sébastien ⇔ ☒ S-M
2 Grand'Place
tel: (0)3.21.38.13.05
fax: (0)3.21.39.77.85
restaurant closed: Sun. p.m., Mon.

A real village pub. This is the kind of simple family-run hotel/restaurant that used to be so common in France and is now giving way to plastic and pop. There is a cosy wooden bar, and a *restaurant gastronomic*, and each one is a star in its category.

In the more formal restaurant you need pay only 23€ for melon and Parma ham, guinea fowl stuffed with mushrooms and apple tart with caramel sauce. There is more choice on the 30€ - oysters, *filet de boeuf* - and less on the 13.4€ - *ficelle Picarde, poisson du jour* or the *plat du jour*, and then *dessert du jour*. Nothing wrong with that.

Double glazing takes care of possible traffic noise. All except two rooms (which overlook the parking lot) look out onto the main road, so those who like to sleep with their windows open should maybe consider alternative accommodation. They cost 42€.

It's usually good news when the chef is a woman (my theory is that she has to try harder to get accepted, particularly in France) and that is the case here. Jeannette and Pierre Duhamel have reversed roles so that she cooks and he is front of house. And a friendly and helpful couple they are.

BOLLEZÉELLE 59470 Nord

47 km SE of Calais, 22 km NE of St. Omer

One of the prettiest drives in this area is to take the D928 out of St. Omer, following the river Aa and then turn right at Watten on to the D226, which leads through some relatively (for this interminably flat territory) hilly countryside.

Bollezéelle itself is a village of neat little Flemish-style houses, a few shops, the church of St. Wandrille, built in 1606 with even earlier foundations, and a rash of new buildings spreading further every year.

☆ Hostellerie St. Louis ⊨ ⊠ M
   tel: (0)3.28.68.81.83
   fax: (0)3.28.68.01.17
   closed: Sun. p.m., Mon.

Built as a private house in 1760, it was bequeathed to the village at the end of the last century by its old, blind and unmarried owner for use as a home for the elderly. Now it has become a very popular middle-priced hotel, conveniently sited near both autoroute and ports.

As you approach the tall, narrow building, with grey slate roof and steeple topped by a flagpole, an encouraging sight is people sitting on wooden chairs on the terrace overlooking the extensive garden and watercourse, all socialising over their drinks. A hotel where no-one talks to anyone else is usually a sign of discontent.

Inside it's all very cheerful and very peachy. The cheerfulness extends to the ever-smiling *patronne* - "Just call me Bea" - who is bound to be at the reception. Flemish-born, multi-lingual, she soothes away any problems and helps with new ideas for local appreciation.

"An excellent hotel with superb food and nice rooms", Colin Pugh. "The bed was the most comfortable I have had in France", C. A. Finch.

The bedrooms are named after regions of France - Artois, Flandres, Touraine. They cost 51€ with shower, 58€ with bath. Jura and Dauphiné are suites - 72€- and Brouilly is suitable for wheelchairs.

The food has been greatly enjoyed by most readers; there was one grumble about the cost but if you take the *menu du marché*, three courses *selon le marché*, it need cost no more than 22€,. Next one up is 29€, and Côté Mer is 40€.

Starred for safe convenience and a pleasant welcome.

BOUBERS-SUR-CANCHE 62700 Frévent Pas-de-Calais

4 km N of Frévent , 76 km SE of Boulogne

Another flowery little village in the pleasant valley of the Canche, dominated by the gates of a secretive château, next to the church; an agreeable place to stop for a picnic under the espaliered lime trees. There are lovely walks nearby.

Otherwise:

La Cremaillière ☒ S
   Place de l'Eglise
   tel: (0)3.21.03.60.03
   closed: Tues.

Just a village café, where an omelette and glass of wine, preferably taken at a table outside, would make a restful lunch break. During the week there is a different *menu du jour* every day, 14.4€, and one more at 19.2€.

BOULOGNE-SUR-MER 62200 Pas-de-Calais

32 km S of Calais
Market: *Sat., Wed.*

A tale of two towns. To know Boulogne you must acquaint yourself with an industrialised, post-war, concrete-functional port and a 13th-century ramparted citadel. The former is noisy, traffic-beset, equipped with average shops, some better-than-average restaurants, and the buzz of a working fishing harbour; the latter is a community insulated by thick stone walls from the rest of the world. Footsteps echo in cobbled streets; on grey winter days ghosts outnumber tourists.

Shopping

The lower town, from which many quick-hoppers never venture, is not a thing of beauty in its post-bombing reincarnation. A grid of streets is lined with boutiques, a couple of chain stores and plenty of *charcuteries, pâtisseries and chocolatiers*. Here are the best:

Outstanding is Philippe Olivier, *maître fromager*, in the rue Thiers. Supplier of prime cheeses to most of the renowned restaurants in the North of France, not to mention a good few in England, he usually has around 300 varieties in stock. Beneath the narrow shop are his caves, kept at different temperatures to suit different varieties at different stages of their *affinage*. Show any interest in his great passion, and Philippe will no doubt escort you on a guided tour. Ask specialised advice on what to take home or consume on a picnic, the crucial question being: "When do you intend to eat your purchase?"

For charcuterie head for Bourgeois, 1 Grande Rue, the ideal pre-picnic stop. Choose from a confusingly extensive range of *saucissons, terrines, pâtés*, cooked meats and specialities like *petit salé aux lentilles* (salt pork with lentils). If you're self-catering consider the roast chicken sold in a bag in which it can be re-heated.

Irresistible pâtisseries come from Fred, on the Place Dalton, a decidedly upmarket but unintimidating establishment, where you can pick up a sandwich as well as a celebratory *gâteau*. But for the best bread in town Demarchez on the corner of the rues Faidherbe and Thiers has the edge. Two elegant pillars of gastronomy are the Comtesse du Barry in the Grande Rue and, even better if you want a truly impressive present, Hediard's, an outpost of Paris' famous foodies' paradise. This one is just outside the old town walls at 7 rue Porte Neuve. A one-off is Idris in the Grande Rue, whose window is ablaze with colour from dried and glacé fruits and nuts. Nouvelles Galeries sometimes comes up with interesting items a touch different from British chain store stock and is worth a look at Christmas time for toys and Christmas decorations.

In the Haute Ville there are several quirky specialist shops. I particularly like Des Mystères de Fanny (owned by Fanny Willemart), on a corner of the Place Godefroy de Bouillon, a needlework and crafts shop, which will sometimes sell you the stuffed toys expertly made up from kits. or decorative tapestries. Chantal and Pierre Vanheeckhoet's shop in the rue de Lille is crammed with present ideas.

Boulogne is not so hypermarketed as Calais. If you don't feel you've been to France unless you've pushed a trolley, there is Auchan, 6 km on the RN 42 at St. Martin-lès-Boulogne; or the Centre Commerciale de la Diane, with a PG supermarket. The latter is useful to know because of its 2 hour free parking, within easy walking distance from the town centre.

Best shopping of all is to be found in the Saturday morning market (smaller one on Wednesday). It's the biggest and best in the region, spilling out of the sloping cobbled Place Dalton into the adjoining streets. Farmers' wives come from miles around to set out their treasures - half a dozen creamy goats' cheeses, bunches of herbs, seasonal booty like wild mushrooms, and patently fresh eggs spattered with farmyard. One-stop shopping it is not but much more fun.

The Place Dalton, is the only part of the Basse Ville to have retained its pre-war character. It is presided over by the church of St. Nicolas, mostly 18C, transept vaulting a century earlier. This is the heart and belly of the town, the scene of ceremonies secular and religious. At Christmas-time the cobbled surrounds are charmingly decorated with white-painted birch trees sparkling with simulated frost and tiny lights, and the venerable patron saint, St. Nicolas himself, distributes sweets to the children. The stalls in the market sell cheap milk chocolate images of the saint; the smarter *chocolatiers* don't miss a commercial trick and offer dark and white chocolate versions.

There are plenty of bars around the place whose tables offer both sustenance and the opportunity to observe the action before climbing up the Grande Rue to the Haute Ville. You could take the car but somehow it will seem an anachronistic intrusion into the centuries-old calm. It's a ten-minute puff up to one of the four gates let into the massive ramparts. Built in the 13th century by the Count of Boulogne, on the site of a Gallo-Roman foundation, the ensemble is an impressive 400 metres square, decorated by 17 turrets. Try and find time for a pleasant stroll around the sentry walk, accessible from each gateway, for inspiring views of town and port.

From this fortress 3,000 Boulonnais put up a fierce resistance

Boulogne

against 30,000 English troops ordered by Henry VIII to capture the town. It was only after the betrayal by the Governor of Boulogne, Sire de Coucy de Vervins, that the English triumphed. The population fled from Boulogne to Étaples and Abbeville and the town remained an English possession until 1550 when Henri II paid a ransom for its return. In 1680 Louis XIV's ubiquitous architect, Vauban, advised the king that the outer walls of the citadel were in such bad repair that they would have to be demolished and re-built under his jurisdiction. These are the walls we see today.

The heart of the old town is named after Sir Godefroy de Bouillon, leader of the First Crusade and a member of the House of Boulogne. Here is the imposing 18th-century Hotel de Ville. From the interior you can scale the 12th-century belfry, the oldest monument in Boulogne, for more stupendous views over port and surrounding countryside. Adjacent is the place de la République, with 19th-century neo-classical law courts. Napoleon and Charlemagne are the occupants of the two niches.

Dominating the Boulonnais countryside for miles around is the dome of the basilica, and from the countryside is the best way to see it. Close up it somehow seems diminished and less impressive. It was built between 1827 and 1866 on the site of a previous cathedral destroyed during the Revolution, but retains the original Romanesque crypt. The cathedral was named after an apparition of the virgin in the 7th century. Her wooden statue, crowned with gems, stands in the central chapel, except on the last Sunday in August, when a procession in mediaeval costume, perpetuating the centuries-old pilgrimage in her honour, still takes place in the town.

It seems to me that fresh air is being pumped into the old town; it used to be a somewhat gloomy, lonely place, neglected by all but the most assiduous history-connoisseurs. Now there are new and interesting boutiques and restaurants lining the main street, the rue de Lille, and the tourists are outnumbering the locals. Well, you can't have it both ways. If only there were a recommendable hotel up here in the tranquillity.

Just Outside

Boulogne was heavily involved in Napoleon's project of invading England. The port, bristling with ships, was bombarded several times by Nelson's fleet. The first Légion d'Honneur was awarded by Napoleon himself in 1804 at Terlincthun, just outside the town. A small pyramid marks the spot where the Emperor's throne stood.

3 km north, by the N.l., is the Colonne de la Grande Armée. Napoleon assembled 132,000 men and 2,000 ships, ready to launch his attack on England, and the marble column was intended to commemorate his achievement. When the invasion fizzled out in 1805, because Napoleon had to concentrate his Grande Armée against the Austrians, he understandably lost interest. The column was completed eventually by Louis-Philippe. 263 steps lead to a platform, 623 feet above sea level. Here is the view on which Napoleon must have planned to train his telescope - the white cliffs of you-know-where.

The entire coastline was heavily fortified with gunsites and forts; one of them is Heurt Fort, 3 km to the south-west of Boulogne on the small island facing the resort of Le Portel. Here there is a sandy beach dotted with rocks and bordered by a promenade; in summer there are several good fish restaurants, but it is all very dead out of season.

Boulogne's history of fortification, bombardment and destruction continued; in the First World War it was a front line British base with a heavy flow of maritime traffic and surrounded by military camps, hospitals and munitions dumps - an obvious target for the heavy bombardment that followed from the Germans only sixty miles away. In WW2 the Germans invaded the town on the 25th May 1940 and occupied it for four years. It was transformed into a veritable fortress and an important submarine base, and this time the bombardment - 487 times - came from the Allies, with many civilian casualties. Liberation came on the 19th September 1944 by the Canadian army.

Nausicaa

Bvd Ste Beuve
tel: (0)3.21.30.99.99
Open: 9.30-6.30 from 1/9-30/6;.9.30-8 from 1/7-3-1/8. Closed from 7/1-25/1. Entry to permanent exhibition: adults 11.2€ low season, 12.8€ high season; children 8€ low season, 8.8€ high season. Special exhibitions: 3.2€ adults 1.8€ children.

Not an aquarium. A Centre National de la Mer, aiming to educate as well as amuse, this gleaming glass edifice on the front is a must for any visitor, of whatever age, to the town. Graphically aided by state-of-the-art techniques it tells the ecological story of the submarine world. Fishing, farming, pollution, conservation are all dealt with imaginatively and forcefully.

Younger customers will find plenty to amuse and question. Like how does it feel to be caught up in a net with a shoal of tuna? What happens if I stroke the fish? Why does the starfish curl up in the palm of my hand? They will relish having a good shudder at the gruesome conger eels and toothy shark, and will probably suffer less from *mal de mer* than their elders when they stand on the bridge of the trawler simulation and are battered by noise and spray in a howling audio-visual gale.

For a more soothing experience make for the Caribbean. No need to travel, no need to learn to scuba, here is the sunshine dazzle, the humidity, and nose-to-nose contact with fish as vivid and bizarre as any diver ever witnessed.

The Centre includes a well-stocked library, gift shop, cinema, bar and smart restaurant. If possible avoid school holidays, when there are queues and chaos.

To celebrate it's 10th anniversary in 2001, yet more innovative marvels were added. If you think you've been there, done that, you don't know the half of it. A simulated three-dimensional deep sea dive in a submarine introduces you to even more marvels of the deep and the grand finale to the guided tour is a new vast circular aquarium stretching from floor to ceiling, with a Son et Lumiere performance, while whales and dolphins cavort around the spectators.

The latest project, to be completed in 2002, is the new building at the end of the exhibition dedicated to fishing and the manufacturing processes of sea produce. All very right and proper since Boulogne is France's foremost seafood processing centre.

Visitors will be invited into Le Bistrot du Port, a sea pub, where they can sample fishy snacks with a glass of wine. They will be shown the origins of what is on their plate and learn how to conserve seafood.

Hotels

The dearth of interesting hotels in Boulogne continues to amaze me. Here is the best of a very dull bunch but personally I would forget staying here and head for either Hesdin-le-Abbé (p.129), or Wimereux (p.191).

Le Métropole 🛏 M

51 rue Thiers
tel: (0)3.21.31.54.30
fax: (0)3.21.30.45.72
closed: 20 Dec. to 4 Jan.

Central, well-run by the pleasant Lejeune family, with agreeable breakfast room and a small garden. There is now parking for 12 cars at 8€ per night. Bedrooms are small but reasonably well-equipped with mod cons and adequate bathrooms. 25 rooms 72-78€.

Restaurants

☆ Chez Jules ⊠ M

Place Dalton
tel: (0)3.21.31.54.12
fax: (0)3.21.33.85.47
closed: 6 Sept. to 4 Oct.

Several changes here in my favourite restaurant, and all for the better. Whenever I am asked where to eat in Boulogne I unhesitatingly indicate Chez Jules. There are lots of restaurants, bars and cafés taking advantage of their central position around the Place Dalton, but only one Jules. It is now bigger (not always a good thing) and better (if that were possible) in that with the option of eating upstairs in the first-floor light and pretty dining room, there is more likely to be a free table downstairs, where all the action is. Here is the huge wood-fired oven, where they cook the best pizzas in town, and all the pzazz of a busy popular brasserie that could only be French.

But Jules is not just a pretty pizzeria. You can eat as well here at a more sophisticated level as anywhere else in town. The fish is irreproachable, whether you choose a simple bowl of *moules*, a selection of oysters, a *brochette* of seafood or a classic sole *meunière*. There are three menus from 19-36€, pizzas and 'le welsh' from 6€; on the cheapest is a touch I particularly applaud - the bowls of *rillettes* or *terrine* are left on the table for you to help yourself.

Wherever you eat in Boulogne it is inevitable that you will share the restaurant with fellow-Brits. At Chez Jules the ratio of locals to tourists is testimony to the value on offer.

A ☆ for honest value.

☆ La Coquillette ⌧ S
10 rue de l'Enseignement-Mutuel
tel: (0)3.21.83.37.51
Closed: Sun., Mon.

I asked for endorsement for a ☆ for La Coquillette in the previous edition, and in came the confirmations that this was indeed a find. It's tucked away in a residential area, off the Place Navarin, a brown-shuttered, colourfully window-boxed old house, where the specialities are Italian-based. Fresh pasta, like *tagliatelles au pistou et lardons*, or a more sophisticated version with fresh salmon, are the dishes to go for, but the *gratins* are excellent too and for those with healthy appetites, the menu at 12.5€ is a sell.

With a modestly-priced wine list and friendly service from the *patronne*, this is the place to head for on a budget outing, secure in the knowledge that quality and quantity have not been sacrificed to keep the bill down.

"The best place has to be La Coquillette, which we would never have found without your guide. A delightful little restaurant, with simple, impeccably served food - we loved the andouillettes - and a very pleasant welcome." Jennifer Storey.

☆ for good value and the best Italian cooking in the area.

Sucré Salé ⌧ S
13 rue Monsigny
tel: (0)3.21.33.81.82

Look in the pedestrianised precinct by the theatre to find this pretty little *salon de thé*. Readers have agreed that it's a pleasant haven to sip an elegant cuppa and enjoy French *pâtisserie* at its best, or a home-made ice cream. It's popular at lunchtime too, for light dishes, salads and savoury tarts.

La Cave du Fromager ⌧ S
23 and 30 rue de Lille
tel: (0)3.21.80.49.69
open: 09–19 hrs except Sun. (10–15).

Only someone as passionate about cheese as Marie-Renée Frémont could possibly conceive devising a double-spread menu in which every item featured that heavenly cholesterol-laden ingredient - cheese. Her restaurant, unique in the region, is on one side of the main street of the Vieille Ville and the shop where you can buy take-homes is opposite.

'Le Welsh', for some reason I have yet to fathom, is almost a Boulogne speciality, with every brasserie in town serving a version, but none so good as here - just the thing for a chilly day warm-up. Cheese *feuillétés, fondues, raclettes, gratins, quiches,* salads, all around 4.5-8€, or just... cheese, tout simple. Or not, as the case may be. Some of the dishes are not simple at all, like *mousseline de bisque de homard au Brillat Savarin* which comes with any entrée and a dégustation of as many cheeses as you can tackle for 20€ (makes even me feel queasy), or *noix de St. Jacques au Roquefort* 9.6€.

Three course menus are good-value at 8.9-13.1€.

Even the desserts veer cheesewards. *Fromage frais* with a blackcurrant syrup or tarts filled with fruit on a *mousse de fromage,* or even prunes stuffed with *Roquefort*. Hope the Channel's not too choppy on the way home.

Estaminet du Château ☒ S

2 rue du Château
tel/fax: (0)3.21.31.92.96
closed: Wed. p.m. and Thurs.

I used to rack my brains to conjure up any eating suggestion, however doubtful, in the Haute Ville, but there are signs that restaurateurs are realising the potential up there, away from traffic fumes, where tables can be set with safety on the pavement and there is even room for a garden or two. The Estaminet is the name that regularly crops up as the best of the bunch. Because its prices are so reasonable - 16€ for a good menu - and because there are still not many competitors, you will find the clientele is mostly Brits, but give it a try - the owners, M. and Mme Davenet, are trying hard.

Brasserie Le Châtillon ☒ S

6 rue Charles Tellier
tel: (0)3.21.31.43.95
Open: Lunchtime only
closed: Sat. and Sun.

The opening times say it all - this is a restaurant for the workers. The workers in this case being the fishermen and those engaged in the fish canning business in the port. Perversely I am always more excited about finding a restaurant hidden in an unlikely setting, especially if it's away from the tourist track, than one obvious to all. When the Grape Shop personnel told me that the best place to eat fish in Boulogne was, surprise surprise, in the port, I couldn't rest until I had tracked down Le Châtillon.

I found it near the Bassin Napoleon. (Drive into the port and ask). It is a large, totally unfussy brasserie, a bit smoky and still full of customers at 3 p.m. You eat fish and nothing but the fish, fried, baked, poached, or raw, and it couldn't be fresher. Prices vary according to the catch of the day, chalked up on the blackboard.

An experience. I look forward to the reports on this one.

Incidentally, the owner of Le Châtillon also runs a good fish shop, l'Ecailler in the rue de la Lampe.

Otherwise:

Recommended but not yet sampled by me: **Gourmandière**, 6 rue des Religieuses (off the rue Faidherbe). For interesting salads, quiches, omelettes, Philippe Olivier's cheeses and traditional dishes like boeuf Bourguignon.

And from a trusty local correspondent: *"The* **Cyrano** *almost opposite the France Telecom office at the end of the rue Victor Hugo (9 rue Cooquelin) is where my French chums eat when they're in town, with old fashioned chef and equally rotund wife.*

Across the river is La Braserade (Chez Bruno, 9, rue Alma). Managers from the fishing port eat here each lunchtime, enjoying the smart surroundings and a copious menu at 13.6€ which includes the largest hors d'oeuvre board imaginable. It's difficult to find, being reached through an archway under the modern block of flats facing the Ibis on the far bank, closed: Sun. Mon. p.m." Bob Smyth

BOURNEONVILLE 62240 Pas-de-Calais

6 km N of Désvres, 19 km E of Boulogne

Lovely countryside around here, due east of Boulogne, in the forests of Boulogne and Dèsvres, along the river Liane, past sleepy undiscovered villages. Bournonville is the hub of five mini-roads, so check the map carefully unless you want to get lost, which is a most agreeable prospect in these parts. Whatever you do make sure you work up an appetite for:

☆ Auberge du Moulin ☒ S
tel: (0)3.21.83.87.61

I have to admire the stamina of French Entrée faithfuls. When I rashly offered many years ago to pay the bill if anyone could produce proof that they had waded through the full menu here, I never expected to be still receiving applications all these years later! (Sorry, this offer's now off!). Nothing much has changed in this unpretentious café/restaurant/bar, least of all the menu, which costs 14.5€. In these days of weight/cholesterol/calories consciousness it does you good just to read it:

1. Cream soup - tureen left on table for seconds and thirds (strictly inadvisable).
2. Smoked salmon - steaks of it. Or trout *meunière*, or fresh salmon or *terrine* of chicken.
3. Braised ham or tongue, with carrots and lots of gravy.
4. *Gigôt* of lamb - three steaks this time, with enough haricot beans and potato to feed a family for a week. Or guinea fowl, or quail.
5. Salad
6. Cheese
7. Apple tart, with cream naturally.

Starred for sheer political incorrectness and the amount of pleasure it has given happy guzzlers.

N.B. Don't think of going on a Sunday without a reservation.
   "We spent three hours there, having struggled our way through their now famous six course lunch, aperitif, coffee and wine, for 17.6€. The place was teeming, both dining rooms in use, with a huge log fire in ours. We kept walking outside to cool off. I am attaching a couple of menus, signed on behalf of two of the couples who managed to finish every course, though we did leave some of the wine." Ian Skelton.

BRAY DUNES Nord

11 km N of Dunkerque

Otherwise:

It's a strange coast road to Bray, the northernmost limit to this book, through housing estates where the omnipresent sand dunes make fine playgrounds for local kids, skirting hamlets with unpronounceable Flemish names, and past factory blocks and secretive high concrete walls. The railway line is one side and the autoroute on the other, but here in between is a kind of no-man's land. Access to the beach, which is the real *raison d'être* for development here in the first place, is amazingly difficult. When you do find a turning to the left in Bray it leads down to a windswept promenade and mile upon mile of beach up to and beyond the Belgian border. It's good for a breath of the briny, but not recommendable for much else. The restaurants and cafés are strictly for the tourists and snap shut out of season. I don't think many of those tourists can be Brits. Sheltering from the gale, we asked for tea in a café and were told they didn't have any. *"Les Anglais!"* they said with a despising gallic shrug.

BROUCKERQUE 59630 Nord

*4 km E of Bourbourg on the D2, 35 km E of Calais,
with easy autoroute access*

A nothing-special village, mostly modern, set in the flat Flemish countryside.

Middel-Houck ⌧ S-M

> pl. du Village
> **tel:** (0)3.28.27.13.46
> **fax:** (0)3.28.27.15.10
> **website:** www.mh-receptions.com
> **closed:** Sun-Wed. p.m.

This spic-and-span brick restaurant in the village centre, heavily be-geraniummed, has been thoroughly approved of by numerous readers. I say 'restaurant' rather than 'hotel' because it is in the dining room that its priorities lie. The four bedrooms are clean and adequate but no more (35.2€); nevertheless I am sure they are a very welcome retreat after a substantial dinner here, with absolutely no driving. they no longer offer hotel services.

The mid-week menus range from 17-44€, and this is the one that most of the businessmen, from Dunkerque I surmised, were tucking into when I re-visited. Lots of hearty Flemish dishes but salads too. Nice Madame Morez told me that at weekends the atmosphere is more *familiale*. Recognised as being the best cooking for a long way around, so you should book.

"*We had two pleasantly furnished and very comfortable neighbouring rooms. There was plenty of choice on the 14€ menu. Two of us started with a kind of Welsh rarebit on salad and the other had chicken liver salad. We all chose tender pork medallions surrounded with nouvelle cuisine-fashion new potatoes, leeks and cauliflower. Sweets were a large plate of profiteroles for one, cherries and chocolate for no 2 and I chose a tarte aux pommes, beautifully flambéed at the table.*

The village was just the right size for a short walk to the charcuterie where we shopped for our return journey and the boulangerie where sweets to take home were gift-wrapped by Madame while the locals waited for their bread quite cheerfully."

CALAIS 62100 Pas-de-Calais

37 km N of Boulogne
Market: *Sat., Wed.: Place d'Armes; Sat., Thurs., Sun.: Z.U.P. du Beau Marais*

No wonder English visitors feel at home in Calais. For more than two centuries, from 1347 to 1558, it was indeed an English town. After his victory at Crécy in 1346 King Edward III laid a vicious and determined siege to Calais, which its courageous citizens resisted for almost a year before, starving, they capitulated. In retaliation for their unwillingness to co-operate earlier, the king proposed to exact revenge on its burghers. The famous group depicted so vividly by Rodin volunteered their lives in exchange for a promise that the rest of the town should be spared. It took the compassionate pleading of his wife, Queen Phillippa, to persuade the king to pardon the brave hostages.

Rodin's statue, simple and dignified, stands outside the bizarre Town Hall, grey, sombre, and intensely moving amongst the strident begonias. Walk round the group and see that each man is a masterpiece of character-drawing, from the patriarchal St. Eustache to the agonised youthful Pierre de Wissant. Maquettes and studies for this masterpiece are in the Musée de Calais, well worth a visit. Don't miss the watercolours of the English artist Bonington, and look at the views of early Calais, like the 19th-century William Callows of the Place d'Armes, to realise the extent of our loss.

In the museum too are more examples of English influences - the lace for which Calais is famous, once an important industry, for which the machinery, designs and artists were brought over from Nottingham in the 19th century.

Under English rule, protected by great walls and moats, garrisoned by a force of 2,000, Calais flourished for two centuries under the royal flags of Plantagent, Lancaster, York and Tudor until it fell to the Duc de Guise in 1558. When the town was signed away to the French forever in the 1564 Treaty of Troyes, the English queen, Mary Tudor, was so shocked at its loss that she declared that on her heart after death would for ever be engraved the word Calais.

Yet the links continued. After Napoleon's defeat British entrepreneurs flocked into Calais eager for new commercial pickings, and when Dunkirk was being evacuated in 1940 it was the troops in Calais who stood firm to the bitter end. Churchill recognised their bravery by calling the town the little bit of grit that saved us.

The English invasion of Calais still happens every day when thousands of shoppers pour off the ferries - more passengers than in any other port in the world. A peaceful, mutually beneficial invasion nowadays. We get the cheap booze and a (diluted) taste of le Continent, and the shopkeepers get busy tills. Equally profitable has been the intrusion of British supermarkets, irritated at the profits drifting towards the wine trade in France and staking their claim to a share of this highly lucrative market while the duty-free going is good.

Booze-buying

No-one knows for sure how much longer before this wine bubble is burst, but pro tem it would be foolish not to take advantage of the savings to be made and Calais is well-equipped to help you do so. Here are some suggestions:

Calais Wine and Beer, rue de Judée, Zone d'Activités Marcel-Doret. Near exit 3 off the A26. Open daily from 6 a.m. to midnight. Wide range of international wines in cheaper bracket. British staffed.

Pérardel Wine Market, 365 ave. Antoine-de-St. Exupéry. Just beyond above. Turn left at bottom of rue de Judée. Open daily 9.30 a.m. - 7 p.m. 500 varieties, from plonk to exclusive vintages.

Champagne Charlies, 14 rue de Cronstadt (off rue de Moscou). Foot passengers should follow signs to Centre Ville. Wide selection of wines and beers.

Beer Lovers, ave. de Verdun. Take exit 14 before Chunnel on the road to Calais beach. Open daily. Wide range of wines and beers. Tastings.

Just outside Calais, at the entrance to the tunnel, is the Cité Europe. This is where most Brit booze-fanciers with cars will head for, playing safe with familiar names like Sainsbury and Tesco. Like it says, it's a cité. Vast. So allow plenty of time to find it (appallingly badly signed, and all in French) and navigate within it. You either love huge shopping centres or you hate em; I belong to the latter camp, but can just see how, if it's wet outside and you have hours to kill, this might be the answer. I wish it had the cheerful atmosphere of American malls, rather than that generated by cross, tired, bored customers. In true investigative spirit, I tackled the mammoth, in order to be able to report first-hand:

No signs to guide me to my target, Tescos. Which car park to head for? Toss a coin. Parking outside the sign which read Tescos seemed a good idea, but no. I had to walk the full length of the parade back to the main door. No sign of Tescos inside. Subsequently found it one floor down. Dying for a loo. Back to starting point. Four loos for how many cross-legged ladies?

After several more visits, I think I have got it taped, and have to admit that if you stick to the rules, bulk wine-buying here can be a relatively painless experience. Tescos have become more user-friendly and now you can telephone your order ahead and have it waiting for you to collect. Buy a sample bottle at your home branch to sample before you leave and if you like it, find the same variety here at a considerable saving. If, however, you decide to pay for your ferry fare by saving on booze, this is the place to do it. Park at the rear, following the livraisons signs and you can pick up a trolly at the same time. The checkout girls will even give you a mock coin to release the chariot

Calais

Make straight for the dégustation station and buttonhole a sommelier. Nowadays they all speak English and are extremely knowledgeable and helpful. Tell him what you like and he will advise and offer tastings. When you have loaded up, ask for someone to help you push your booty to your car and unload. A small tip is an appropriate gesture.

Other Shopping

The main shopping streets are: the rue Royale, best for chocolates, *pâtisserie, charcuterie*, fashions and presents; then past the Tourist Office, where it all gets a bit seedy around the railway station and becomes the bvd Jacquard. Here is the French Woolies - Monoprix - and the slightly more upmarket Le Printemps. At the busy Place Albert 1er (with its opulent baroque theatre, and a statue of Joseph-

Marie Jacquard, who invented the loom for unskilled workers to produce lace) turn left into the bvd Lafayette. There's a much more gallic atmosphere than the streets nearer the port. This is where the Calaisiens do their daily shopping and the market is in one of the side streets in the pl. Crêvecoeur.

Natural Assets

If all this shopping has included picnic ingredients, where to consume them? There are two park possibilities: one is by the rue Richelieu, off the rue Royale, and the other, the parc St. Pierre, with plenty of shade and benches, is opposite the town hall. Here is the *Musée de la Guerre*, the war museum, housed in an old German bunker, used for telephone communications during WW2. Posters, tracts, memorabilia and letters are a poignant reminder of the Resistance, the occupation and the bombing. Open 20-Feb. to 20-Dec., daily from 10a.m. to 5p.m.

Calais has another asset that, surprisingly, is rarely mentioned - a magnificent beach. Infinitely superior to any across the water, with literally miles of fine sand when the tide is out. With time to spare before the ferry or on a day trip with the kids, head in this direction. If you are not picnic-equipped there are plenty of cafés that will fill the gap.

Hotels

The hotel scene is not bright. The old Meurice used to have a certain faded grandeur, but nowadays there is more fade than grand and nowhere else that offers anything more enticing than a modicum of comfort and a useful first or last night bed. At least I can suggest two options that won't break the bank and are good representatives of the two-star bracket:

Richelieu 🛏 S

17 rue Richelieu
tel: (0)3.21.34.61.60
fax: (0)3.21.85.89.28
closed: Christmas and New Year

In a quiet side street, overlooking the park, run by the same management for many years. All 15 rooms, whether with bath or shower, are 46€; they're all differently furnished, some with tiny balconies looking out onto greenery, so it's worth asking to see more than one if possible.

Pacific 🛏 S
40 rue du Duc-de-Guise
tel: (0)3.21.34.50.24
fax: (0)3.21.97.58.02
closed: New Year (27-Dec. to approx 8-Jan.)

Madame Duhamel has taken over here and has been re-decorating the 19 rooms one by one. They cost 42€ with bath, 36-40€ with shower and loo The garage is an extra 4€. There's a particularly spacious lounge and p.d. room, which used once to be the restaurant. Madame Duhamel is happy to offer special prices out of season, so try negotiating.

Otherwise:

For those who are happier with three-star accommodation (though in this case I think the more modest hotels offer better value), there is the **Metropol'Hotel**, which looks more interesting, situated on the quayside, than proves to be the case. 40 rooms starting at 58€ including a suite for 144€. 45 quay du Rhin, tel: (0)3.21.97.54.00; fax: (0)3.21.96.69.00; www.metropolhotel.com . Or the **George V**, 36 rue Royale, tel: (0)3.21.97.68.00 fax: (0)3.21.97.34.73. The 40 rooms are often engulfed by groups or seminars. 61-80€. The only option if you insist on dining in your hotel.

Restaurants

☆ Le Channel ☒ M
3 bvd de la Résistance
tel: (0)3.21.34.42.30
fax: (0)3.21.97.42.43
closed: Sun. p.m. and Tues. 23-Jul. to 7-Aug.

If I say there is nothing new to write about Le Channel, that is high praise indeed. As long as there have been French Entrées, and a good time before that, Le Channel has been no. 1 restaurant in Calais, and never once let that go to its head. It may be old hat to recommend a restaurant that everyone knows and is in every guidebook, but that is exactly what I do when asked Where shall we eat in Calais? Playing safe was never my style, but here it would be folly not to do so. Reliability is Le Channel's middle name.

From time to time the decor changes - currently raspberry velvet high backed chairs, matching carpet, oil paintings on panelled walls - and a few new dishes join the menu. Perhaps we can expect more experiments now that the two Crespo sons have joined forces, one as *sommelier*, one after a stage at Robuchon, but I don't think that the *hommes d'affaires* that are the mainstay of the clientele (always a good sign) would like to see their favourite menus messed about too much.

Madame Crespo's welcome has not wavered. However busy the service, she miraculously contrives to be near the door when new customers arrive, to show them to their table and make them feel at ease. Likewise Joseph Crespo, installed behind the glass of the open plan kitchen, supervising his team of chefs and *commis*, manipulating his pans, still finds time to lean over the counter to shake hands with old friends. I stood there for a while, watching the dexterity and speed, and every single dish that emerged looked totally admirable.

The staff, in their formal black and white, seem to have assimilated their bosses' spirit - they know that the right orders have to appear on the right tables in double-quick time if the recipients are to catch their ferry (and in order to re-use the table) and manage to combine efficient briskness with a smile.

The 16€ weekday menu is a snip - well worth crossing from one Channel to another expressly - and never skimps with expensive choices like Dover sole or *langoustines*. Fish is always good but so are the *terrines* and local dishes like *coq à la bière*. Tarts are home-made of course and so are the ice creams. You really can't go wrong.

The ☆ is for consistently high standards, excellent ingredients, well-cooked, and delightful owners.

☆ Aquar Aile ⊠ M

Plage de Calais. 255 rue Jean-Moulin
tel: (0)3.21.34.00.00
fax: (0)3.21.34.15.00
closed: Sun. p.m.

I had been put off by the situation - outside the town heading west, and the building, an ugly modern block of flats - but I'd been missing a treat. Take the lift up to the first floor for a view that merits the word fabulous. The décor is the sea. Vast curving windows enclose the prospect of waves, yachts, ferries, beach huts, sand, giving a whole new meaning to panoramic. Do not fail to book a window table to get your money's worth.

The marine theme continues with a blue/green/grey colour-scheme, glossy ceiling painted to match. For those who missed out on the view, the other seating is still pretty good news - comfortable tapestry banquettes, ideal for intimate dining. The tone is decidedly upmarket, with pristine starched napkins, expensive china and smooth service from professional black-and-white-garbed staff.

Smooth service does not always come with smiles; at Aquar Aile the waiters have forgotten they're French and actually seem to be pleased to see you, even when, as I did, you order just nine oysters and a glass of Muscadet for lunch. For just under 14.4€ we could have spent the afternoon tackling a palette de pêcheur, a generous assortment of fish, wet and shell. Complimentary appetisers of a fishy persuasion and *petits fours* even if you don't order coffee. It's all excellent value for the quality on offer.

Menus from 21€, including wine during weekdays; 26€ or 37€ for the serious lobster-fanciers.

A ☆ for Calais, No.1 fish restaurant, with good value and pleasant service thrown in.

Côte d'Argent ⊠ M.

1 Digue Gaston-Berthe.
tel: (0)3.21.34.68.07
fax: (0)3.21.96.42.10
closed: Sun p.m. Mon.

The third of Calais' fish restaurants. On the 'digue' but lacking the wonderful view of Aquar' Aile, because there is a large car park between restaurant and sea. Inside, only the draped and flounced yellow curtains are not in keeping with the resolutely nautical theme. Portholes, ropes, sextants, compasses, oil lamps, wheels, charts, lifebelts, propellers, pulleys make the message clear. You are going to come into close contact with the sea, i.e. you eat fish.

There are menus, like the 16€ version, that offers soupe de poisson, fillet of place and desserts from the laden trolley, but in fish restaurants, especially at lunchtime, I always counsel spending your money on one superb piece of fish. Like a Dover sole, which here costs 18€.

L'Histoire Ancienne ⊠ M
20 rue Royale
tel: (0)3.21.34.11.20
fax: (0)3.21.96.19.58
closed: Sun., Mon. p.m.

Décor 1930ish, with art déco lamps, leather banquettes and Toulouse-Lautrec approximates decorating the bar walls; bistro-style, but with cooking that combines bistro simplicity with a touch of sophistication. The Comtes, Patrick, and Claire, used to run La Diligence, next door to the Meurice, which had less of the bistro, more of the plush about it. I like this version far better.

The bistro bit that pleases me is that there were no tut-tuts when I ordered only a starter at lunchtime and husband fancied just a good steak. The sophisticated part came with the quality and the presentation. My stuffed mushrooms came beautifully arranged on a classy black plate, sprinkled with chopped chives and scattered with designer leaves. The dressing was spot on, the stuffing generous with the garlic, the herbs and whatever the delicious toothsome filling was. An excellent 6.2€ worth, especially as there was no quibbling about entitlement to their special offer - a takeaway bottle of wine for every table on production of a ferry or tunnel ticket - "We like our English friends." (Just as well, because there's a lot of 'em about.)

Husband's *entrecôte* proved large and juicy with lavish garnish of chanterelles and melting baked potatoes (not many French know about them) 13€. Next door ordered the 21€ menu and oohed and ahed over the *soupe de poisson*, again presented with style and an array of white side dishes for the *rouille, croutons* and cheese. Their children ate well for 8.8€ - egg mayo, escalope of chicken and ice cream, but you have to be under 12 to qualify. There is another excellent menu at 26€. There are two other menus at 10€ and 16€.

It is not difficult to guess that Patrick sometimes likes to cook special dishes, a touch more interesting than the menu basics - *Les Petits Plats de Patrick*. These involve some of his favourite sauces, like saffron cream sauce and a deep dark mushroom version. Fish is another speciality and, as it says on his brochure, "Good tasty roasts at a price you can afford."

La Pléiade ⊠ M

32 rue Jean Quehen
tel: (0)3.21.34.03.70
closed: Sat. lunch, Mon.

In one of the turnings west of the rue Royale at the sea end, a pleasant little restaurant, green façade, nondescript décor, paintings of boats indicating a fishy emphasis. Daily specialities written on the blackboard are always a good sign. In this case they include dishes like *l'épaule d'agneau, confits de rognons, timbale de poissons à l'aneth, filet de cabillaud à genièvre* - all interesting stuff. The 17€ menu offered plenty of choice (other more sophisticated versions with an extra course at 22-29€).

My choice was a light flaky *feuilleté de moules*, with flavoursome sauce featuring plenty of garlic, and mussels cooked *à point*, then crispy halibut filled with mustard seeds and white wine sauce, roast local cheeses and local ice cream. All excellent value, even if you can only manage half a dozen oysters at 10.4€.

☆ Grand Bleu ⊠ M-S

8 rue J-P Avron
tel: (0)3.21.97.97.98
closed: Sat. lunch; Sun.

A little nautically-themed restaurant just where it ought to be - on the quay. It's good to have a fishy meal where freshness of the produce takes precedence over flashy presentation and expensive décor, and the cost is kept proportionately low. That said, fresh fish nowadays costs plenty, wherever you buy or eat it, and if it doesn't it probably doesn't answer the job description.

Here the dining room is modern and unfussy, with navy blue cloths and napkins and grey chairs. The cooking can be unfussy too - nothing beats a perfect *sole meunière*, which here costs 19.2€, but you could ask for a professional version of *aumonière aux deux saumons* or *le saint-pierre à la fleur de thym* if that is your wish.

Menus start at 21-26€ but as in most fish restaurants, my view is that it is preferable to eat *à la carte*, from a bowl of mussels to a lobster, according to appetite and budget.

☆ for excellent fishy value.

Otherwise:

Le George V ⊠ M
36 rue Royale
tel: (0)3.21.97.68.00
fax: (0)3.21.97.34.73
closed: Sun.; 23-Dec. to 4-Jan.

Long-established Calais restaurateur Bernard Beauvalot successfully combines two restaurants under the same roof: 'Le George' is the gastronomic leg and 'Le Petit George' the bistro. The former is surprisingly elegant, with a welcoming fire for inclement weather, and serves hefty portions of traditional food. Fish and pastry are its declared specialities, but I think of it more in terms of *choucroute* and casseroles.

The livelier bistro 'accepte les jeans' and feeds their owners on menus from 15.5€. À la carte express meals for those with a ferry to catch.

CAMIERS 62176 Pas-de-Calais

19 km S of Boulogne, 10 km N of Le Touquet
Market: *Mon.*

The sand dunes and pines around here remind me of the Mediterranean, but the windswept appearance of the Plage St. Gabriel gives the game away.

Turn off the main road just opposite the sign to the *plage* to find the by-passed village of Camiers.

Les Cèdres ⇔ ⊠ S
64 Rue du leux et Moulin
tel: (0)3.21.84.94.54
fax: (0)3.21.09.23.29 R

Drive round the back of this seemingly typical French bourgeois villa to find the new guest wing built around a courtyard. There are 27 simple rooms at 48-72€, which I call good value in this popular holiday area, and so near Le Touquet. It would certainly make a good family base, with the sands so near. You can be assured of a peaceful night's sleep, away from the main road, and there is safe parking.

Menus from 14-27€. *"The Vandroy family, including young Master*

Edouard and his dog Lola - made us feel most welcome and were happy to accomodate reasonable whims vis-a-vis timing of eating. We found an interesting array of dishes well cooked, presented by an equipe of great professionalism." Mike Cooper-Cocks.

CAP BLANC NEZ 62179 Escalles

10 km SW of Calais

This is the part of the Côte d'Opale that irrefutably confounds those still labouring under the misapprehension that the North of France is (a) flat and (b) dull. The coast road leaves behind the sand dunes and weekend chalets after Sangatte and sweeps up and up to reveal a stunning panorama of rolling farmland to the left and white cliffs dipping into the sea to the right. Do not fail to turn off at the sign to Cap Blanc Nez, park the car by the memorial to the WW1 victims and walk to the cliff edge to enjoy the spectacular view. Better still carry on walking down the well-maintained cliff path to Escalles, far below. This is just part of the network of cliff walks, all taking advantage of the truly glorious countryside around here.

Le Thome de Gamond ⊠ M

Mont d'Hubert, Cap Blanc Nez
tel: (0)3.21.82.32.03
fax: (0)3.21.82.32.61
Open: lunch and dinner during July and Aug; rest of year, lunch only
website: www.capblancnez.com

On the opposite side of the road, signed to the *Musée Transmanche*, is an example of what the French do so well - a restaurant that takes advantage of an unusually attractive feature (in this case the view) and does not take advantage of the built-in custom.

The Frechou family have designed their sizeable modern restaurant to make the most of the view over the Boulonnais countryside, with huge windows to take in the panorama. Fresh from the ferry on a Sunday afternoon, we found the place still full of happy eaters demolishing *plâteaux de fruits de mer* (22€). There is a three-course menu at 15.5€ for the fainthearted, going up to 35€ for 7 courses, and my yardstick for prices - *moules* and sole - cost (5.6€ for a starter) 9.3€ for a main course and 15.5€ respectively.

CAP GRIS NEZ 62179 Pas-de-Calais

30 km N of Boulogne, 32 km S of Calais

Not the best beach along this privileged stretch, but then the standards are high - there's sand enough to satisfy most. To the cross-channel swimmers it must look like heaven. Just across the water are those cliffs, and yes they are very white.

Les Mauves 🛏 ⊠ M-S

Cap Gris Nez
tel: (0)3.21.32.96.06
closed: 15 Nov. to 1 Apr.

Can't understand why I get so little feedback to this pleasant old-fashioned hotel, quietly situated at the approach to the Cap, 500 metres from the sea. It has a peaceful flowery garden ideal for relaxing after a long day, a nice rustic dining room, with carved chairs, polished floor, copper whatnots, and there is that rare amenity for little French hotels - a bar in which guests can mingle when it's too cold to sit in the garden. Pristine bedrooms have all mod cons and *patronne* Madame Cugny is friendly and helpful. Perhaps it's a touch expensive? But then the season is so short.

    Menus from 20€, 16 rooms 42-88€, breakfast 7.5€.

Otherwise:

There's the famous (the modest claim is 'renowned as far as Brussels, London and even beyond') **La Sirene**, perched on the cliff edge, with unbeatable views through its panoramic windows. Continues with its menus centering on seafood, with lobster still the speciality. Menus from 19.2€ **tel:** (0)3.21.32.95.97 **closed:** Mon; mid Dec - end of Jan.

CASSEL 59670 Nord

50 km SE of Calais, 32 km NE of St. Omer

High on the list of must-sees in the whole region, Cassel is unique. The approach, slowed down because of the cobbles, past prosperous villas, through avenues of chestnut trees bent in combat with the habitual wind, gives little hint of what to expect until you drive through the 17C porte de Bergues, which makes a fine proscenium arch for centre stage - the Grand'Place. The scene is more stage setting than reality, with the huge Place - one of the largest in Flanders and steeply sloping - surrounded by aristocratic buildings. There are coats of arms of noble families over doorways that lead into secluded courtyards and weathered rooftops that might have existed since mediaeval times. Might have, but probably didn't, thanks to the fire that roared through the town in 1940, destroying everything in its course.

The slopes of Mont Cassel, 176m high, have been fortified since time immemorial - understandably so since they are the highest for many a league. Normans, Flemish, French, Spanish and English all fought here; Romans camped here and engineered seven roads from the town towards the coast or to connect with their other strongholds.

Marechal Foch, Commander-in-Chief of the Armies of the North, made this his headquarters and spent "the most distressing hours of his life" here, between 23rd October 1914 and 21st June 1915. With the English General Rumer, he directed the Battle of Flanders from the town. His statue is still in command, high above the town in the Place du Château (no château now) by the old windmill (or copy of the 16th original that was burnt down in 1911). From here, abetted by a *table d'orientation*, you can see five kingdoms, they say - those of France, Belgium, Holland, England, and heaven. So pick a clear day.

It is a town that inspires stories and legends. It was the local giants, Reuze Papa and Reuze Maman (still paraded through northern towns on feastdays) who dropped the huge mound of earth on which it stands.

There is a peaceful 'English garden' up here, with shady benches and walks marked out through the trees. Those disinclined to climb can drive all the way up and stop for refreshment at an establishment as unusual as Cassel itself:

☆ Estaminet T'Kasteel Hof
    8 rue St. Nicolas
    tel: (0)3.28.40.59.29
    closed: Mon - Wed all year round.

Clinging to the side of the very steep hill, with fabulous views from its terraces, this little wooden restaurant has bags of character, totally uncontrived. The ground floor looks like a shop - perhaps it was once - with the counter still in position and an eclectic assortment of objects hanging from the ceiling, on mantelpiece, floor, niches, every available surface. Baskets are suspended from on high, with a rocking horse, a collection of hats, enamel pans, flat-irons, enamel jugs, dried flowers and hops. An antique stove takes care of the heating; floor is bare wood, tables ditto, chairs wicker. Upstairs is more of the same, with an amazing panorama from the veranda. Must be lovely in summer.

The flavour of the month is determinedly Flemish. No wine, because it does not come from this region. But beer... the menu lists pages of varieties, *blanches, blondes, ambres, brunes* and *fruitées*. You can even buy it by the kilo (4.8€). There are bottles of home-made fruit juice made from local produce - the friendly barman (owner?) encouraged me to taste. I sampled rhubarb, strawberry, blackcurrant, apple, raspberry and several more. All very fruity. With the addition of local gin, a range of tempting cocktails is on offer. I liked the sound of *'Gen'pom'* - gin with apple - and *'Cherche Mourette'* gin and blackcurrant.

Food follows suit: all farm produce is used to conjure up the *carbonades, flamiches* and of course the ubiquitous *Potje vleish*. You don't have to order a heavy main course though - there are *pâtés, saucissons* and *rillettes*. *Crêpes* and sweet tarts take care of the desserts. I had to try *paaptart* which I had not come across before - brown sugar and raisins. There are sorbets too, flavoured with *chicorée, bière,* and *genièvre*. Definitely different.

To the right of the entrance there is a little shop, selling some of the chef's produce, along with a great variety of beers. You could at least buy a postcard of the extraordinary décor.

Do go - great fun. ☆ for delightful eccentricity.

Otherwise:

Back in the town all round the square are eating/drinking possibilities cafés, restaurants, pizzerias, *crêperies* and a *cave à bières*. Remember these are for the tourists and don't expect too much.

La Taverne Flamande ⊠ M
34 Grand'Place
tel: (0)3.28.42.42.59
closed: Tues. p.m. and Wed.

Every Flemish place has to have its Taverne Flamande and this is Cassel's. It's quite smart inside, with astonishing views of the Flanders plain far below from the *terrasse panoramique* at the rear.

Authentic Flanders cooking appears on the 14.2€ *menu flamand*. This is the chance to try *waterzoi de volaille à la gantoise* - chicken in a kind of béchamel sauce - and *tarte flamande aux pommes et à la cassonade* - apple and blackcurrant tart - or even *crêpes flambées au Houlle* - pancakes doused with gin. Other menus at 10.8€ and 15.5€.

Readers have approved, so don't let my impression, which was coloured by indifferent reception, put you off. The rival Hotel Foch across the square was even cooler, so perhaps they don't need to try too hard.

The river Course and its valley

Heading south from the ports you have several route choices. Stick to the *nationales* or *the autoroute* if you are in a hurry, consider the yellow and white roads on the Michelin map if leisurely delight is more important than speed. The D127, which follows the valley of the Course, is the pick of the bunch. Follow it from Dèsvres to Montreuil and any preconception that the Pas-de-Calais is all built up/boring/flat/same-as-home will vanish. Drive through the flowery unspoilt villages like Courset, Parenty, Recques, Beussent, Inxent, lining the rushing, sparkling little river that plays hide and seek, vanishing on one side to re-appear on the other; sometimes, as at Doudeauville, it disappears altogether, only to spout anew in the next village. Extend exploration to the lanes and valleys on either side of the river to find a succession of time-warped sleepy crossroads, cottage gardens, churches, ponds, bars, fruity-smelling farms and streams that run into the Course, with names more imposing than the reality - the Baillonne, the Bésinghem, the Brimoise are little more than trickles - but very attractive picnic-worthy trickles.

I cannot claim that the Course is a secret any more - there is even the *Circuit Boulonnais* marked out along it for first-time tourists to follow - and every time I drive down it I find more modern bungalows to regret, but the picturesque crumbling whitewashed barns still predominate and the way of life of the farming residents remains much as it has been for generations.

Accommodation and eating options are limited. **The Auberge d'Inxent** (page 135) is one possibility and there is now an excellent upmarket **B&B at Beussent** (page 74) as well as the long-established

Le Relais Equestre at **Inxent** (buy the Chambres d'Hôtes book!). The **Restaurant Lignier** at **Beussent** has a loyal following (page 75) and for those who are looking for something definitely basic - perhaps an omelette or grilled chicken - there is **Grémont-Cocatrix** down by the trout farms in **Zérables** and the **Bon Accueil** at **Engoudsent**.

Crécy

The scenery changes abruptly as you approach Crécy, from green valleys and hills to open plain. Good battle country.

At first glance there is nothing to distinguish this little town, wide market street, a timbered house or two, from any other. But stop the car and look at that war memorial. As in many another mourning Picard town, it takes pride of place in the centre of town. What is unique about this one is the date of the inscription: "à la memoire des Français morts en defendant leur patrie, 26 Août, 1346". The other side of the cross commemorates the bravery of Jean of Luxembourg, the blind King of Bohemia, brother of King Philippe, who opposed Edward III. Determined to 'strike a blow for France', he ordered his men to tie him to his horse during the battle, where he was slain along with 1,300 French knights, the cream of the French nobility, and 30,000 men-at-arms. In recognition of his gallantry, our Prince of Wales wears his badge of black shield and plumes to this day.

On the battle site itself, a lonely hilltop above the plains of wheat, there is little else to mark the battle, except the tattered flags of four countries - Bohemia, Luxembourg, France - and Britain.

It's a shame that there is no special restaurant or hotel in the town centre to revive pilgrims and to encourage more visitors to this historic site.

Otherwise:

There is the **Hotel La Maye** just outside, a modern building with nice garden and terrace. 11 rooms 42.4-56e; meals from 10.4e. Rue de St. **Ricquier, tel:** (0)3.22.23.54.35, **closed:** Sun. p.m. Mon.

LE CROTOY 80550 Somme

65 km S of Boulogne

There are encouraging signs that things in this little port on the north bank of the estuary of the Somme are looking up. Its history has been: fishing village/popular Sunday lunch treat/steady decay/new interest. Paint has been applied to shaky balconies, flowers embellish civic borders, new hotels emerge, old ones get spruced up, the customers return. All good news in fact.

I have always found it very agreeable to work up an appetite by promenading round the curve of the bay, photographing the fishing boats pulled up on the beach to be painted in vivid colours, past the nice old stone house built on the remains of the Château de Crotoy where Joan of Arc was imprisoned before crossing the bay on foot to St. Valéry, and on to Rouen. From here I continue the walk along the beach, which must be one of the finest of all the fine beaches of the North. Le Crotoy claims that it has the only south-facing beach along this coast. Well... true, for part of the way at least, but the bracing wind ensures that it never feels southern. More Skegness than St. Tropez.

Appetite assured, the next step is to scan the menus of the restaurants lined up by the port. There are plenty to choose from, and it is indeed very pleasant to commandeer a table on the pavement and order a plateful of steaming *moules* and a *demi* of Muscadet. But my advice is not to expect too much, These are strictly tourist restaurants and neither their prices nor their talents are geared for gourmets. If you spend 7.2€ on *moules marinière* you will be well-satisfied; if you order a *sole meunière* you will not, even if the price (which says it all) appears to be a bargain at 12€. Fresh fish *never* comes cheap, even in a fishing port. For those looking for something different I have found a couple of alternatives, described below.

☆ **Les Tourelles** 🛏 ☒ M
rue Pierre Guerlain 2-4
tel: (0)3.22.27.16.33
fax: (0)3.21.22.27.11.45
closed: 3 weeks in Jan.

The old home of the Guerlain perfume family has been transformed into a stylish new hotel. The red bricks have been restored, the witches' hats atop the towers and pinnacles painted blue, the balconies' paint newly whitened, the shutters renewed and, lo, we have an idea of how the mansion must have looked in its Edwardian heyday. Inside it's another story. The style here is more Scandinavian or New England seaside, with bare blond floorboards, unfussy white drapes, blue easy chairs, wicker, canvas, light filtering to every corner. Very Anouska Hempel, very chic, very nice indeed.

Outside is a well-furnished terrace overlooking that amazing estuary view, which must be the most attractive place in le Crotoy to have lunch or an aperitif, and at the rear a pleasant shady garden. A lounge bar with live piano music in the evenings takes care of the problem of where to gather in wet weather.

I loved it all and would have liked to see a room, some of which have magnificent views, but of course they were all occupied, and the guests saw no reason to leave such an agreeable location so that I could have even a glimpse. So reports will be eagerly awaited.

Lunch I can report on. Another world from the town eating scene. The food was as light and modern as the hotel, well-cooked and presented. Unusually for France I was able to order a delicious starter (*terrine* of roast vegetables) and not feel inadequate. The dinner menu looked equally desirable, featuring a very un-Gallic range of dishes, abjuring anything ponderous. Menus from 20€.

17 double rooms, 2 singles, 46-61€. Readers' reports favourable, so a ☆.

Otherwise:

Aux Trois Jean ⊨ ⊠ M-S
Digue Jules-Noiret
tel: (0)3.22.27.16.17
fax: (0)3.22.27.21.28
closed: 20 Sept. to 4 Oct.

Right opposite the best part of the beach, separated by a large terrace, where tables are set for refreshment throughout the day. Eating continues inside, with sensibly priced menus for families. The rooms are not particularly spacious but all are bright and light, with good bathrooms.

8 rooms at 56€.

Mado ⊠ M
Hotel de la Baie (H)M-S
tel: (0)3.22.27.81.22
fax: (0)3.22.27.85.43

This used to be the reason for coming to Le Crotoy - to eat at the legendary Mado's, presided over by the eponymous *patronne* and her parrot. Mado and parrot, alas, are no longer with us but the name and the restaurant continues. Everything has been smartened up, with fresh green and red paint and a dispersal of most of the atmospheric clutter of the glassed-in terrace (full of tourists) and the dark interior (full of French). The theme is still fishy, and the end product more reliable than those along the prom. The weekday menu costs 14.4€ and at the weekend, Menus start at 21€. Be prepared to linger.

Upstairs are three rooms which have beaten me every time, both under the old regime and the new. They are always taken, often a year ahead. I believe that they must have superb views, but cannot speculate beyond that, except to confirm that readers, who have been cleverer than I, have been happy with their stay here.

Three rooms at 48€.

CUCQ 62780 Pas-de-Calais

3 km S of Le Touquet

Virtually a suburb of Le Touquet, pleasant, well-groomed. Look out for a sharp bend in the D940 Berck road, and on the right is:

La Petite Auberge ⊠ M
933 ave. de la Libération
tel: (0)3.21.94.33.03
closed: Sun. p.m. and Mon. o.o.s.

A ravishingly pretty, low, whitewashed old Picard farmhouse, with brown shutters and lace curtains, tables and chairs outside and loads of geraniums. Inside is pretty too in a beamy cottagey way. Menus are 14.2, 19.2, 25€, with my price guide ruler, the sole *meunière*, clocking in at an average 17.6€.

Popular, so be sure to book.

DÉSVRES 62440 Pas-de-Calais

19 km SE of Boulogne
Market: *Tue.*

Dèsvres is devilishly difficult to drive out of. Getting in is easy - sometimes I've done it by mistake, finding myself in that huge sloping main square without even trying. But once trapped, they do not want to let you go, so they have contrived a hub of eight roads, with minor roads forking out of them, and obscure signs to ensure you end up back in the square. Last time, as we sat in the car poring over the map, determined not to be beaten, the kind driver parked alongside offered help. When we told him where we were heading, he tried to explain the route and then gave up - "just follow me" he said and set off corkscrewing round the town till he was satisfied that we could not go wrong.

It's worth taking this risk, however, because Dèsvres is a pleasant little town, with bags of character. It's best known for two assets, the Maison de la Faïence and the Café de l'Agriculture.

The town has been famous for its faïence since 1764, and celebrates the fact by establishing a museum showing in an audio-visual salon the history and in the *salle eau-terre-feu* the technique of the pottery. You can buy examples there or in one of several shops in the town. Open from 1-Apr. to 31-Oct. every day except Mon. from 10-13h and from 14-18.30h. In July and August it is open on Monday too. 4€ admission fee.

That's dealt with a feast for the eye. Now how about the tastebuds?

Look no further than in the main square, the place Léon Blum, which is most animated on a Tuesday when the market takes over. Then you should certainly book your lunch table.

☆ Café de l'Agriculture ☒ S

22 pl. Léon Blum.
tel: (0)3.21.83.07.72
Lunch only during the week. Open Sun for lunch and dinner.

As *rustique* as they come. Run by a team of jolly, beaming ladies. *Patronne* Madame Telliez does the welcoming, others are at the stove or peeling vast buckets of potatoes - you have to go past them to get to the lavs, which now have gained in hygiene what they have lost in character (no longer squatters).

The restaurant is surprisingly big, with cabbage roses flourishing on beige wallpaper, furnished with grandfather clocks, family *armoires*, a vintage gramophone, a corner fireplace and a photomontage of an autumn glade, but in early December it was hard to see the décor for the tinsel. It's a flexible dining room, at it's cosiest when confined by the first set of curtains to just eight tables. One set on and the size doubles, one set further and you're talking Sunday lunch and parties.

Main courses - rabbit, chicken, *fricassées*, stews - cost 6.4€ and starters - *terrines*, crudités, soup – 3.2€. Dessert costs 2.2€. There is a three course menu, which changes daily, for 9.6€, a *plat du jour* for 6.4€ and pichet wine at 1.9€.

Husband chose roast chicken - half a bird that had undoubtedly spent a gutsy life strutting round a courtyard, now charred and sizzling, rich brown juice accompanying and little lardons of bacon lending extra flavour.

Expecting fresh veg in an authentic French restaurant like this would be asking *trop*. Chips will have to do. But we did have the evidence of our own eyes en route loo-wise, that these were not out of the freezer.

I met my match in the *terrines de la maison*, served in hunks rather than slices. The rabbit was so good that it slipped down easily, the *fromage de tête* was only half consumed, the liver *pâté* less so, and as for the *rillettes* - a mere *dégustation* was all I could handle. All four perfect specimens, which, with a green salad, good bread, pickled samphire, gherkins and shallots, made a robust if not particularly elegant lunch for 3.2€.

I love the lack of affectation, the home cooking and the honest welcome of the good ladies and wish there were more of the same breed. ☆ for good country value.

Otherwise:

Café Jules ⌧ S
11 pl. Léon Blum
tel: (0)3.21.91.69.72
open: every day

On the opposite side of the square and until recently a similar establishment to the Agriculture. Now there has been a change of management and it has gone all upmarket. The 15.5€ menu lists dishes as esoteric as *gratin d'asperges* and *pavé de saumon frais à l'oseille*, but to be fair the *terrines* for which Café Jules was famous are still there and simple country dishes like pork chop with mustard sauce and jellied rabbit. Other menus between 12.5€ and 22€. On Sunday the price jumps to 24€ and you get soup, then perhaps scallops in cream sauce, then a house speciality, *coq à la bière* or perhaps *civet de sanglier aux pruneaux*, and pud.

I liked Jules the way it was, but it is not fair to judge the new version by comparisons with the old. I'm pleased they've kept all that wonderful faience.

More reports please.

DUNKERQUE 59140 Nord

46 km NE of Calais

The port that will forever be associated with the heroism and tragedy of the evacuation of May 1940, when 350,000 men were rescued, under heavy fire, from the now fun-loving beaches of Mâlo and Bray-Dunes. Its growth since then has been phenomenal - it is now France's third largest port, divided into several basins. From the Bassin de Commerce you can take a boat tour around the waterways.

Dunkerque boasts two art museums, the *musée d'art contemporain*, surrounded by a sculpture park, and the *musée des beaux arts*, built in 1973, with collections of paintings from 16th-20th centuries.

I always get lost in Dunkerque. Can't even find the sea if I don't pay attention. Every time I dither between the conflicting directions - *port, plage, bassin, centre* - and end up totally confused and lost in the endless suburbs. I cannot claim that this is an easy-to-love town. It's just too big and sprawly and the flavour of the port does not spread far. I suppose it's not Dunkerque's fault that there is nothing antique to admire - 80% of the town was destroyed.

So, I would really counsel staying and eating outside the town. (See Tétéghem, Coudekerque and Cappelle la Grand.)

L'Hirondelle ☒ M-S

46 ave. Faidherbe
tel: (0)3.28.63.17.65
fax: (0)3.28.66.15.43
restaurant closed: Sun. p.m.; Mon. lunch

Head eastwards down the main drag, the ave. Faidherbe, to Mâlo-les-Bains, which is Dunkerque's residential area, with a fine sandy beach, and look on the right for this ultra modern (and garish) hotel. 42 rooms cost 49-62€. Their forfait soirée buys two people dinner, bed and breakfast for 87€.

Otherwise:

Borel 🛏 S
6 rue l'Hermite
tel: (0)3.28.66.51.80
fax: (0)3.28.59.33.32

If you have to stay in the town, at least you have a view of the port from this modern hotel between two bridges. 48 rooms cost one price of 69€.

Au Bon Coin ⊠ S-M
ave. Kleber, Malo les Bains
tel: (0)3.28.69.12.63

Decorated with yellowing photos of celebrities who have visited this long-established bistro in an insalubrious corner of the main road. Good for freshest fish and unpretentious atmosphere. 14.4€ mid-week menu.

DUNKERQUE-TÉTÉGHEM

59229 6 km SE of Dunkerque.
2 km from Calghouck by D4

A nondescript residential suburb, unremarkable except for:

☆ La Meunerie 🛏 ⊠ L
174 rue des Pierres
tel: (0)3.28.26.01.80
fax: (0)3.28.26.17.32
website: www.fishroute.net/meunerie
restaurant closed: Sun. p.m.; 2 Jan.

It's hard to imagine that this elegant complex was, as it name implies, a flour-mill. But indeed it was, transformed by it's previous owner, Jean Pierre Delbé.

In addition to the elegant restaurant there are now nine luxurious bedrooms, approached by a glass walkway. They are all different in size and style, but all come with a spacious marble bathroom, Louis XV decor and English telly, looking out onto an interesting interior garden. They vary from 88-120€, and there is also a highly luxurious suite with jacuzzi, which clocks in at 1.56€. Breakfast costs an additional 12.8€, but is one of the most desirable ever, on which you could certainly last out until dinnertime.

The restaurant is the big draw. They have three menus at 29€, 40€ and 63€ (crab tart with oysters, flavoured with dill, noisette of salmon with hazelnut cream, roast chicken with seasonal veg and a magnificent pastry table, offering fresh fruit and home-made sorbets) all topped up with irresistible *petits fours*. It appears they still do all of that. They have a further menu, which is probably the best value, if you have the confidence to leave it to them who know best, it is the *La formule Meunerie* menu at 58€. This one changes every day according to what is best in the market, and includes everything from kir to coffee, with carefully chosen wines accompanying four courses. An excellent deal, when you consider the high standards. They also serve Philippe Olivier cheeses.

There are special *forfaits* available out of season which are worth enquiring about.

DUNKERQUE-COUDEKERQUE-BRANCHÉ 59210 Nord

4 km S by D916

☆ Soubise ⊠ M

49bis rte de Berques
tel: (0)3.28.64.66.00
closed: Sat. lunch, Sun. p.m. Three weeks in Aug.; New Year

This pleasant 18C building did escape the wartime destruction and is charmingly decorated with old Limoges porcelain. Chef Michel Hazebroucq has won one of Michelins red *'repas'* symbols for a menu whose price is not nearly as exalted as his reputation (20€). Go for it. The menu changes every day, as all good menus should, according to the whims of market and season, but there is always plenty of good fish. Other menus up to 39€. Traditional ingredients, traditionally cooked. Readers love it, so a ☆.

DUNKERQUE-CAPELLE-LA-GRANDE 59180 Nord

5 km S by D916

Le Bois de Chêne ⌧ M
48 rte de Bergues
tel: (0)3.28.64.21.80
closed: Sat all day, Sun. p.m., Mon. p.m.

Mostly fish, well cooked by Flemish Christian Vandeneeckhoutte (phew) in this popular restaurant at the side of the road opposite the canal. Cooking is substantial northern fare. The cheapest menu at 18.4€ includes three courses, three wines and coffee. The next one up at 34€ had some more interesting offerings, like a gratin de bouchots, which I just can't imagine (bouchots are whelks - how do you tenderise them?).

ÉSCALLES 62179 Pas-de-Calais

14 km SW of Calais

The best of the lovely coast road, the D940, between the two ports lies between the headlands, an area promoted as *Site de Deux Caps*. The views are spectacular, there is rarely much traffic and you can bowl along high above the Channel feeling that this is what a holiday is all about. The village of Éscalles lies below Cap Blanc Nez. Take the turning marked *Plage* for a pleasant stroll (or short drive) through fields of corn and beet down to the beach, with its variety of sand, stones and rocks. For lengthier walks, the coastal path is highly recommended.

Otherwise:

There are two family restaurants in the village, the **Restaurant du Cap** and l'Escale, tel: (0)3.21.85.25.00 which also has simple rooms from 33-51€. A good base for an unsophisticated family holiday.

ÉTAPLES 62630 Pas-de-Calais

27 km S of Boulogne
Market: *Tue., Fri.*

If you need a contrast from Le Touquet's somewhat artificial atmosphere, cross the river Canche to the workaday port that WW1 troops knew as Eatapples. No gloss, no sophistication, no hotels to speak of here. The residents just get on with their everyday lives, often centred round the fishing boats that unload their catches on the quays. Tuesday and Fridays are the big days, when the central market takes over the main square.

There ought to be plenty of simple fish restaurants right alongside the boats and indeed there are, with predictable names like Au Marin Joyeux, La Marine, Les Trois Lanternes - but nothing special to recommend, and not one that inspires reader-enthusiasm. (I hope I'm wrong - let me know.)

Otherwise:

Les Pecheurs d'Étaples ⊠ M
quai de la Canche
tel: (0)3.21.05.04.29
Open: every day

I had high hopes when the local fishermen set up a co-operative to market their fish and built a smart modern fish market topped by a restaurant with good river views. They have two other restaurants, one in Boulogne. All a bit so-so. The bill tends to be more than you'd expected and the fish less inspiring. But if you keep it simple, choosing perhaps the fish of the day, or just a bowl of moules you may not be disappointed. And the view is good.

FAVIÉRES 80120 Somme

5 km NE of Le Crotoy, 61 km S of Boulogne

Turn off the main coast road, the D940, on to the little D140, and drive through a maze of country lanes to find this village, amidst marshes, willows and not much else.

☆ Clé des Champs ⊠ M
tel: (0)3.22.27.88.00
closed: Sun. p.m.; Mon.; 31 Aug. to 11 Sept.; 4 Jan. to 24 Jan.; Feb. school holidays

A pretty rustic low white building set alongside a patch of grass that serves as the village *place*. Surprising out here in the middle of nowhere to come across a bevy of cars, parked French-style, higgledy-piggledy, as near the entrance as they can squeeze. That's because the French are prepared to drive some distance to the best value in the area. He who ventures thus far at the weekend without a reservation will not only be unable to park nearby - he won't find a free table.

The main dining room is as pretty as the exterior promises in a cosy, flowery *rustique* way. The overflow gets the much less attractive secondary room - another incentive to book early.

Four kinds of home-baked rolls are the kind of attention to detail that singles out la Clé as something special. Then, even on the cheapest menu, complimentary *amuse-bouches*, again indicating the generosity of the value here. The menus are sensibly short (another good sign), so even before we taste a morsel, we know the omens are good.

Seasonal ingredients, even to the extent of using blackberries picked nearby, are another plus point. Fish is particularly good, with not very far to travel, and vegetables are unusually lavish, but although the chef is wise enough to know when to treat perfect materials simply, that is not to say that he is not well able to produce more sophisticated fare, like a *terrine* of peppers topped with aspic flavoured with artichokes.

In order to qualify for the Michelin red *repas* rating, indicating good value, the price of the menu has to be kept below 16€. La Clé qualifies - 14.5€. There are other menus up to 40€, but there is hardly any need to stray from the bargain cheapo.

The ☆ remains for good value, unusually good cooking.

FRUGES 62310 Pas-de-Calais

51 km from Boulogne, 19 km NE of Hesdin on the D928.
Market: *Sat.*

By local standards Fruges is a big town. All the action centres on the market square, around a couple of bars and restaurants.

Otherwise:

Café du Centre ⊠ S

2 rue du Maréchal Leclerc
tel: (0)3.21.41.46.50
closed: Tues. pm.

A kind reader first alerted me to the joys of the Café du Centre, and on first glance I was not impressed - shabby dun-coloured façade on a busy street. Closer inspection then revealed that there was more to the café than originally met the eye and it went in the last book. This time again, I was on the brink of excluding it until I paid another visit and re-discovered the honest good value on offer here. Just like modest French restaurants used to be before the deep freeze and micro. Once past the vociferous bar and it all looks up. The back dining room has been redecorated in cheerfully bright colours and, as before, all is spotlessly clean and wholesome. There is even a small garden.

The clue to the worthiness of the restaurant is the fact that M. Logez-Mallet, the *patron*, is also a *traiteur*, so you can rely on the *terrines, saucissons* and made-up dishes being first-class. Midweek there are three choices from dishes like steak, lasagne, rabbit or couscous for 10.4€, including wine. On Sunday, for 17.6€ you get *coquilles St. Jacques, ris de veau* and two other courses.

Go on - give it a try.

GRAVELINES 59820 Nord

20 km E of Calais

Gravelines owes its existence to the fact that six hundred years ago Philippe d'Alsace, Count of Flanders, deflected the course of the river Aa through the town. Today the town lies on the right bank of the Aa, still surrounded by the ramparts which have been necessary over the intervening centuries to defend the town from all manner of invaders. It was finally recaptured for the French monarchy, whose rights were confirmed by the Treaty of the Pyrenees in 1659. The ramparts you see today were built by the peripatetic Vauban, judiciously commissioned by Louis XIV. In 1706 Vauban became Governor of Gravelines, and from that post later rose to become Marshal of France. The very stones of the place are steeped in history. Spanish troops assembled here to invade

England when the Armada arrived (the plan went awry); during the Napoleonic wars Bonaparte thought it would be a good idea to set up 'La Ville des Smogglers', welcoming English smugglers to carry away brandy, in an attempt to evade the British blockade. The fortifications continued to serve their purpose well as recently as 1940 when they were an important factor in the defence of Dunkerque.

Nowadays the citadel, known as the arsenal, still intact, is set behind grassy banks and moat, and houses temporary exhibitions. Do take a walk inside the fortifications to discover a beautifully kept garden, with clipped yew pyramids and plenty of restful benches. Walk round above the moat - the view is a bit on the flat side but it's all remarkably peaceful nowadays.

The little town itself is agreeable, too, boasting a late flamboyant Gothic church with a Renaissance doorway carved in 1598. Superb 17C woodwork inside the church and some splendid tombs. The town's centre is a market square, and a fine belfry.

Hostellerie du Beffroi ⇔ ☒ M

Place Charles Valentine
tel: (0)3.28.23.24.25
fax: (0)3.28.65.59.71
restaurant closed: Sat. lunch; Sun.

An old building, tactfully restored ten years ago, in the main square. It boasts an Irish bar, which makes a good meeting place, a smart restaurant, La Tour, and a brasserie for casual foraging. Menus start at 16€ in the restaurant and 8€ for a plat du jour (there is no separate brasserie) with good carafe wine. The 40 modern rooms are well-equipped, cheerful and bright. 58€ or 68€, both rates with bath.

Otherwise:

I am told that the best fish restaurant hereabouts is Le Turbot in the rue de Dunkerque.

HALLINES 62570 Pas-de-Calais

6 km W of St. Omer

This is another of the three villages - Arques, Blendecques are the other two - which almost run into the south of St. Omer, but somehow manage to retain their individuality. To find it take the D928 and then the D211 to the prominent church and gaudy graveyard, with all the charm of the river Aa flowing through under a bridge in the village centre.

☆ **Hostellerie St. Hubert** 🛏 ⊠ M
1 rue au Moulin
tel: (0)3.21.39.77.77
fax: (0)3.21.93.00.86
closed: Sun. p.m.; Mon.

I predicted when I first found the Hostellerie for FE12 that it would be the next in the long line of château hotels near the Channel ports that have been swallowed up by the tour operators and subsequently over-run by our compatriots. Wrong. Don't ask me why but that just hasn't happened and even my file isn't overflowing with readers' comments. Don't understand it.

It is one of the many idiosyncratic 19C mansions that proliferate in the North of France. The interior is much more elegant than most, with many of the original decorative features retained and restored. An important white marble staircase leads to the truly lovely pine-panelled dining room. On a bleak winter's night, with a big fire crackling away in the marble fireplace, the crimson walls echoing the warmth and the chandelier glittering, it looks at its best. In summer though it must be very pleasant to look down through those tall windows to the lush grounds, with the river rushing through.

The place settings are Limoges and there is discreet piped classical music; the service is friendly but efficient and there is a pleasant family feel about the place, generated by Mme Delva, who welcomes. The young *maître d'* is helpful and knowledgeable. The cooking is sophisticated without being chichi - lots of good fish and perfect local cheeses. Menus start at a very reasonable 34€.

The nine rooms are all different, as the price range, from 72-128€, reveals. In summer I would certainly think it worth while to pay for one overlooking the lovely garden, but they are all spacious, with high ceilings and good mod cons. In winter we took the cheapest, with a fine view of the cemetery.

☆ for style, peacefulness, good cooking.

HARDELOT 62152 Pas-de-Calais

20 km S of Boulogne

Possibly the best beach along this whole stretch of best beaches. Along with top-notch golfing, expensive villas set in extensive pine woods, well-manicured lawns and flowerbeds, this would seem to be the resort with everything going for it. Everything that is, except a heart. Hardelot tries hard to mirror Le Touquet, but it doesn't have Le Touquet's pedigree. In season it looks raw, out of season it's a shut-down ghost. But I don't suppose the kids will complain when they see the sands and the ice cream bars and the shops selling beach essentials, nor the golfers who often prefer the greens here to the busier Le Touquet scene. While I failed to find the ideal hotel for the former, the latter are well catered for at:

☆ Hotel du Parc, Restaurant l'Orangerie 🛏 ☒ L

tel: (0)3.21.33.22.11
fax: (0)3.21.83.29.71
closed: 17 Dec. to 13 Jan.

Probably the most agreeable combination of comfortable hotel and fine restaurant along the Côte. The hotel gets it just right - no glitz but rather an airy modernity, featuring white paint, cane furniture, big windows. The 81 bedrooms, mostly with a terrace overlooking the forest, follow the same style - lots of room, lots of light, bright and cheerful. Good bathrooms and all mod cons make the price 90-127€ (depending on season) reasonable in this luxurious setting.

A good place too for shoulder-season breaks, since the huge swimming pool surrounded by lavishly dotted recliners is well heated and, of the five tennis courts free to hotel guests, two are indoors. Golfers get special rates on the local course.

The chef is now Frederic Baret (replacing Bruno Andrieux).

☆ for casual luxury and excellent cooking.

HAZEBROUCK 59190 Nord

62 km SE of Calais, 22 km E of St. Omer by N42

There is an air of bustle and purposefulness about Hazebrouck that I enjoy. The wide and wonderful main square is always full of cars (parking difficult but lots of animation), the restaurants and bars abuzz. If you are unlucky enough to hit a cold or wet day in the north, head here for a dose of cheerfulness.

The Germans launched one of the most damaging attacks (in terms of human life) on the town in WW1, aiming at its important railway network, and it suffered again in 1940 when the spire of one of the wonders of the north, the 15th-century church dedicated to St. Eloi, was bombed. The church is still worth a visit; walk behind it to discover a surprising peacefulness emanating from the béguinage. These little villages-within-a-town have been built in the Flemish region ever since the 12th century to shelter pious widows and to allow them to spend the rest of their lives in perfect harmony. There is a famous example in Bruges, which is on all the tourist routes, but not many people discover this other example.

Back to the liveliness of the Grand'Place, dominated by the vast 19C Town Hall, with a most impressive façade. A row of chunky Doric pillars supports the arches of the colonnade, in which students socialise.

Hotel Gambrinus 🛏 S

2 rue Nationale
tel: (0)3.28.41.98.79
fax: (0)3.28.43.11.06
closed: second and third week of Aug.

Look through the pillars and a large 19C building painted bright pink fits the frame. This is the Gambrinus, Hazebrouck's only hotel, conveniently situated between station and market square. Each floor is decorated in a different colour, peach for the first floor, green for the second, blue for the third. The 15 rooms are small but cheerful and spotless, with an en suite shower, and cost 50€. Breakfast is served in the raspberry red room downstairs.

☆ La Taverne Flamande ⊠ M-S

61 Grand'Place
tel: (0)3.28.41.63.09
closed: Sun. p.m.; Mon.

In almost every market square in the north you will find a Taverne Flamande, but this is my favourite. It's an archetypal brasserie, with all the bustle of black-trousered, white-aproned waiters weaving through the tables, bearing aloft plates piled high. Piled particularly high in this case, especially with the indispensable northern **frites**, and very good they were. There are leather seats inside, occupied by well-fed perspiring local businessmen, and plastic ones outside occupied by hopeful tourists.

Maybe the latter, like me, had only wimpish appetites at lunchtime and settled for one of the famous quiches - Maroilles, Lorraine, *au poireaux, au saumon* and *aux oignons* (the best), served with green salad, but the *hommes d'affaires* obviously had no problem about getting stuck into the 14€ *menu du jour* - *terrines, campagne* or *poisson*, then venison liver with onions, then cheese, then a *gratin de pommes*. The *plat de jour* was also going down well, a *sauté* of veal with mushrooms in a cream sauce for 7.5€.

I love the atmosphere, I love the warmth, I love the food, I love the prices, I love the friendliness of the nice patron, Bernard, so a ☆ of course.

Le Centre ⊠ S

48 Grand'Place
tel: (0)3.28.48.03.62
closed: Tues. p.m., Wed.

If you get caught in Hazebrouck on a Sunday or Monday, or if the Taverne is full, do not despair. Le Centre, on the same side of the Place as its rival, is another praiseworthy *brasserie/ creperie/pizzeria/saladerie/restaurant-traditionnel*. Christian Van Inghelandt is patron here. Walk past the hectic flowered wallpaper of the bar to a long narrow room beyond (or sit outside on the terrace of course). Here 10.4€ buys the local speciality the *tourte aux poireaux*, followed by a *rôti de boeuf* and dessert or coffee (10.4€ buys any entrée, plat principal and dessert or coffee) - good value. You can take the lighter option, the *formule fraicheur* for 11€, which entitles you to raid the *buffet froid* and top that up with dessert. The regional menu costs 17.6€ and there is another at 28€.

Auberge St. Eloi ⊠ M
60 rue Eglise
tel: (0)3.28.40.70.23
closed: Mon.

As its name implies, near the church, on the main road. A little modern restaurant, unremarkable from the outside, comfortable within.

The 15.5€ menu (not Suns) offers good value, particularly as it includes wine. Home-made *rillettes* are of tunny fish and shrimp, followed by either the *poisson du jour* or the *viande du jour* - a formula of which I greatly approve - followed by desserts. There is a *menu affaire* at 24€ which, together with the opening times, indicates who are the main customers, and two others at 30€ and 39€. More reports please.

HESDIN 62140 Pas-de-Calais

61 km SE of Boulogne
Market: *Thurs.*

If only Hesdin had a hotel worthy of the delightful little town, I could wholeheartedly recommend it as the perfect choice for a short stay. Quite different from anywhere else in the region, with its cobbled streets, threaded by rivulets of the river Canche, crossed by hump-backed bridges, and spectacular market square.

Dominating the town from its vantage point in the square is the imposing Hôtel de Ville, originally the home of Charles V of Austria's sister, Mary of Hungary. The sumptuously decorated balcony was added in 1629 and the belfry in 1875. Inside are some rare 17th-century Flemish tapestries. It's an incredibly rich and majestic building to find in what is now such an insignificant little town, as indeed is another treasure just off the square - the church of Notre Dame. Built in brick in the second half of the 16C, it was further embellished with a wonderful stone Renaissance doorway, an ensemble of Corinthian columns, swags, coats of arms, angels and towers. The interior is richly furnished - look for the 18C misericords in the choir stalls.

I like the size of the town too - big enough to support some interesting shops, small enough to wander round comfortably before settling down in the square preferably outside one of the several bars and brasseries. *The Globe* is the one I recommend but you'll have to be there early if you want to claim a table from the locals, especially on market days.

Thursday is the day when the square and surrounding streets fill up with the stalls of farmers and their wives from neighbouring villages. It's worthwhile arranging your tour around it.

Another bonus is the surrounding countryside. The most attractive approach is from the north via the D108, through the pretty villages of Embry, with a stream flowing by and a white folly church on a hill, and Lebiez on the river Crécquoise is just as charming. Wamin, centred round its château, is another pleasing hamlet if you're in detouring mood. This will lead through the deep forest of Hesdin, amongst whose oak and beech trees wild boar are still hunted. A good place to consume the goodies bought in the market, on picnic tables set out in the glades.

Absolutely no joy with hotel accommodation in the town itself.

Restaurants

Just outside is the Trois Fontaines HR(M) at 16 rte Abbeville à Marconne, tel: (0)3.21.86.81.65, which has 10 quiet rooms at 56-67€ and serves meals from 15.5€.

"Very comfortable, all in a line overlooking the garden, with chairs to sit outside", Georgina Miller.

La Brêteche ⊠ M
19 rue du General Daulle
tel: (0)3.21.86.80.87

Very good news to see this old restaurant revitalised in new hands. Young and friendly Christine and Fabien Oudart have been installed here for just a year and have already made many improvements and innovations. There are three dining rooms: upstairs, with big windows overlooking the town and a big fireplace, is the pink version; the two alternatives are yellow and blue or red and white, all three now fresh and cheerful.

Fabien is gratifyingly obsessed with using only fresh ingredients and it shows. His specialities include home-smoked salmon, rabbit used in a *carbonade* and local farm chicken, cooked until it becomes **fondant**. The menu is 15.5€, with a special *terroir* version at 22€.

Otherwise:

L'Ecurie ⊠ M

17 rue Jacquemont
tel: (0)3.21.86.86.86
closed: Sun. p.m.; Mon.

An enchanted setting, through a courtyard, in an old stable. It was always an attractive building but now that it has been completely renovated it is understandably the most popular restaurant in town, involving a booking if you want to be sure of a table. When they are full, as on Thursday mid-day, service tends to get a bit fraught and the reception is not all one could wish for. Even at other times, it is distinctly on the languid side, so don't go in a hurry.

The décor does not rely entirely on the historic building for character, nor does it tend to the dark and gloomy norm of antiquity; the owners have boldly decided to go for fresh pastels and a contemporary feel, with lots of light. Similarly, chef Jean Luc Lecoutre combines traditional dishes with modern interpretation. Fresh produce, everything home-made. During the week his *'menu affaires'* (14€) appeals as much to the shoppers as to the businessmen, including as it does three courses and a drink. Other menus are 19€ and 24€, the latter chosen entirely from the carte.

Mixed reports.

Flandres ⇔ S ⊠ M

22 rue Arras
tel: (0)3.21.86.80.21 **fax:** (0)3.21.86.28.01
closed: last week of June-first week of July; end of Dec-first week Jan.

Sadly the hotel Flandres does not live up to the restaurant. I have a list of grumbles about several aspects of the former, but only plaudits for the latter.

"The welcome was as dire as usual and our room just as drab but nevertheless it is good value if it is simply used as an overnight stop. There certainly should not be an arrow as far as the hotel is concerned but the food was up to its usual high standard with excellent fresh crudités on the hors d'oeuvre table and superb rare spit-roast beef". Jonathan Paul Diamond.

"Extremely good value for money. The first course was a mountain of white fish and boiled potatoes with delicious home-made mayonnaise -

HÔTEL CLÉRY HESDIN - L'ABBÉ

simple, yet so effective. Next came a salmon steak in light sorrel sauce and some really toothsome chips and finally a good selection of sorbets. As you say, the dining room was full of local businessmen - as well as all the local gendarmerie who were clearly enjoying themselves."

All of which doesn't leave me much to add, except to say that a slight falling off of standards detected since these letters were written means the arrow has to go. I would probably choose either of the other recommendations in the town nowadays because the atmosphere there is less serious. That said, if you are looking for straightforward French cooking, approved of by local businessmen (sure sign of reliable high standards), in substantial quantities, you could do far worse than try the Flandres.

Menus start at 13.6€ with good carafe wine. The 14 rooms cost from A double room with bath costs 50€, and a buffet breakfast is an additional 8€.

HESDIN L'ABBE 62360 Pas-de-Calais

8 km SE of Boulogne on the N1

☆ **Hotel Cléry** 🛏 ☒ **M**
tel: (0)3.21.83.19.83
fax: (0)3.21.87.52.59
hotel closed: 2 Jan. to 25 Jan.
restaurant closed: Sat. lunch

The hotel takes its name from Baron de Cléry who built this architectural gem in the late 18th century. It's not grand or large enough to be termed a château, - just an elegant gentleman's country home. It's a very thin building, which means that light pours in from the floor-to-ceiling windows from both sides. Straight ahead from the front door is a small salon, and there are two more to the right, perfect for aperitifs and teatime cuppas, smart but not intimidating, cosy fire in winter.

To the left are two pleasant dining rooms. Given the rooms' perfect proportions and the amount of light, it would be almost impossible to furnish them badly. The present young owners have opted for contemporary patterned curtains on pine poles, primrose walls, defining the panels in the ceiling by painting them golden yellow and white.

Elsewhere in the main building the decoration is more traditional. Up the elegant Louis XV staircase are the best rooms, spacious, furnished with antiques, some with stunning views over the extensive grounds.

In the rooms contrived from the old stable block Laura Ashley reigns supreme. Variations of her familiar flowery fabrics and paper are in every room, and very attractive too. The French think so - L.A. is the height of decorator-chic. I certainly felt very much at home in ours - the same sweet-peas. The bed was king-sized, there was a good bathroom and, unusually, plenty of putting-down space for sponge bags and paraphernalia.

The 5 hectares of gardens are now a major attraction. Quite extensive walks have been marked out in the woodland, and it is all very peaceful and pleasant to stretch car-weary legs in the shady tracks. There is a tennis court too, but the idea of a swimming pool was scotched as being too noisy. The whole concept of the hotel is rest and relaxation (Relais de Silence). Certainly the occupants of the numerous recliners on the lawns looked peaceful enough.

Breakfast costs an additional 9.6€ but is worth it. Apart from the usual croissants and bread there are cereals, fresh fruit, yoghurt, three kinds of jam in pots not foil, and ultimate test - freshly squeezed o.j. Service both at breakfast and at dinner is suave, the china is fine, and the ambience refined. Unfortunately the cooking did not live up to the rest of the experience (menus starting at 14.4€ for lunch, and starting at 23€ for dinner)

The rates vary according to season. The six cheapest rooms, with shower, cost on average 60€ (68€ at the weekend) and the most expensive cost, again on average, 132€ (142€ at the weekend).

The hotel is starred for charm, comfort and pleasant owners, but I counsel eating elsewhere until the cooking is sorted out.

HESDRES 62720 Wierre Effroy. Pas-de-Calais

3 km SW of Wierre Effroy, 20 km SE of Boulogne

Just a hamlet perched up a hill. Road numbers are not a lot of help in this maze of white minor roads and it will be a case of 'I wouldn't start from here' on whichever direction I suggest. So look for it in the pretty unspoiled countryside due east of Wimereux, threaded by the river of the same name.

La Rencontre ☒ S

tel: (0)3.21.33.20.72
closed: weekdays. Last orders by 8.30 p.m.

A tiny cottage on the corner of two very minor roads; Madame Roland is the cook . Inside is everyone's idea of a cottage interior, charmingly rustic, simply furnished.

The food is totally in keeping, prepared from fresh local ingredients and organically grown vegetables. I learned a new term - *'légumes bio'*. 16€ for a four course menu.

This one is a unique country treat. Let me know if it deserves an arrow. Many wily locals think it does, so make sure you book.

In the rear garden are some attractive gîtes, if anyone should be interested.

HOULLE 62910 Pas-de-Calais

6 km NW of St. Omer

It really is a surprising area to be found east of the N43. Water is the dominant theme and canals, streams and rivulets criss-cross the flat Flemish farmlands and dictate the setting of villages. Houlle is particularly watery, with shimmering lakes providing homes for waterfowl. There are several alternative eating possibilities in or near the village and all you have to do is to back your fancy, hopefully follow the signs from the main road and get lost in the watery wilderness a couple of times.

L'Auberge de l'Étang
12 Impasse des Étangs
tel: (0)3.21.93.05.26
closed: Sun. and Tues. evening from 15 Apr. to 15 Sept.; evenings from Sun. to Thurs o.o.s.

This ridiculously pretty little whitewashed old farmhouse used to be called after its previous owner, Mère Poupart, and then it was really rustic, both in food and character. The new owner, Jérome Delplace, has realised the potential of the place - all low beams, gleaming copper, flagged floor - and worked out his own formula for capitalising on his property and packing most of his trade into lunchtime. Here is one reader's view:

"Set menu at lunch is amazing value at 17€ for four courses of really good well-presented food. Total bill for three including aperitif, bottle wine and coffee 72€. Still can't believe what good value it was for such an excellent meal." Mr. and Mrs. M. Shaw.

The Shaws are quite right - it is good food, it is good value and the auberge is strikingly attractive. That's the good news.

The bad is that M. Delplace is totally inflexible. The Shaws had his set menu and it suited them fine. If there had been one item on it that did not suit them - say an allergy to fish or offal - there would have been absolutely no alternative. Nor can you request a slighter meal. We took two friends there for lunch and none of us wanted all three courses. We ended up paying the 17.6€ per person for *terrine* for one (request for green salad to go with it refused), and chicken for the other two. At no stage when we booked the table or arrived at the auberge had we been warned

131

of the house rules and they certainly are not mentioned in the brochure.

The other caveat is that there are two rooms and the larger of the two is usually occupied by groups. This was the case for us - one large table taken over by vociferous Germans, which left us very much in the minority, alone next door. The large coach outside would normally have warned us off but we had arranged to meet our friends at the table and anyway I wanted first hand experience. M. Delplace, quite unabashed, told me that it was groups he was trying to attract.

So the answer is certainly try the auberge if you can manage a full lunch and are prepared to risk an obdurate no-choice menu. If these conditions apply you will enjoy the excursion.

HUBY-ST-LEU 62140 Hesdin. Pas-de-Calais

1 km NE of Hesdin

The local forest is nicknamed The Cathedral of Old Oaks, because its lofty oak trees are so dense that you can hardly see the sky above, and the result is awe-inspiring. This is the valley of the Ternoise, a good base for exploring that river and the other six that thread through the green countryside.

Take the St. Omer road and on the steep hill climbing out of the town look on the right for:

La Garenne ⌧ M
> 54, Rue de 8 mai 1945
> **tel:** (0)3.21.86.95.09
> **closed:** Mon.; one week in Jan.

An ancient posting inn, dating back to the 16th century, where Didier, front of house, and Bernard, chef, hold court. If the atmosphere strikes you as theatrical it is hardly surprising - Didier was well known on the Paris stage, and has brought with him to Huby his love of colour and originality, so that a meal here is going to be a performance in more ways than one.

Depending on the number of customers, there are two optional dining rooms, each with a huge eye-level log fire. Even in chilly July there was a cheerful blaze. The smaller room has cherry painted walls stencilled with green ivy leaves, flimsy white muslin is draped artistically if confusingly over ancient beams, a cartwheel hangs from the ceiling, and on every available surface is an assortment of objets, not necessarily d'art, but certainly eclectic - saddles, mirrors, fossils, paintings....Flowers, not necessarily in their first flush of youth, are lavishly scattered in anything that will hold water, tablecloths are rosy pink, and the general effect is of warmth and generosity.

At weekends the larger room next door is used too, also with a log fire, also cosily unconventional. On my last summer visit, Didier was lamenting that the weather had been so gloomy that they had not been able to eat in the garden as he had planned. It's a pleasing prospect - not at all like the rabbit warren that the house name suggests, but well-tended and organised, with tables and chairs shaded beneath white parasols, good lighting, gravel paths, lots of shade - all one could wish for in fact for summer carousing, if only the sun would co-operate.

The menu changes each week. The 27€ version offered, for example, *ficelle de Picardie, jambon grillé,* cheese or fruit tart. You get an extra course on the 33€ menu, which has some interesting

LA GARENNE, HUBY-ST-LEU

translations like 'scallop marine mollusc'. *Delice de sainte Feriole* does not appeal when it becomes 'duck fatted liver rolled in ham' and I never did get to work out what a medaillon du grand large approximates, but my scallops were perfectly cooked and the tunny steak with white wine shallots and 'slip of bacon sauce' was irreproachable. There is another menu for 41€.

La Garenne's hospitality never stops. The place is open all day for crêpes, drinks, tea and coffee. A comfortable lounge and bar is a rare asset.

There has been no feedback this year, so the star goes. Please tell me if it should be reinstated.

HUCQUELIERS Pas-de-Calais

29 km SE of Boulogne by D341 and D343

Hucqueliers is easy to navigate – just two main roads, crossing neatly in the middle, which is the heart of all the action, centring on a couple of bars and restaurants.

Otherwise:

Auberge d'Hucqueliers 🛏 ⊠ S

1, Place de la Republique
tel: (0)3.21.90.51.61
closed: Sun. p.m., Mon. p.m.

As we were peering doubtfully at the hectic décor of the auberge - bright green and brighter green - one of those battered old Peugeots that spell instant France pulled up and a rubicund face leaned out of the window to inform us, with many an illustrative gesture, that *"On mange très très bien ici"*.

Well we couldn't ignore a tip like that; unfortunately the infuriating *journée de fermeture* beat us once again; it was Monday, and we never got the chance even to peer inside. All I could do was to check out the menus. An omelette and chips costing 5.6€ would have done us fine. Other menus, starting at 7.2€, looked just what one would wish for in a simple country inn - *poulet aux fines herbes,* or *plat du jour.*

Rooms, uninspected, cost 45€, including breakfast.

INXENT 62170 Montreuil. Pas-de-Calais

32 km S of Boulogne

Probably the best-known village along the D 127, following the river Course. Take the path beside the church to walk along the river without a road intervening. It flows fast and wide here - hang over the bridge and you may see one of the trout for which the region is famous. The main reason for the village's popularity is that it is the site for a restaurant well-loved by several generations:

Auberge d'Inxent ⌂ ☒ M

318 rue de la Vallée
tel: (0)3.21.90.71.19
fax: (0)3.21.86.31.67
restaurant closed: Tues. and Wed.

Having been in the same family for many years, the auberge then had several new owners in the past few years and there have been changes. The great and the good Elizabeth David, who wrote about the simple inn serving simple country food - trout and chicken were about the limit of the menu - would not recognise the place now, nor its menu. Mercifully the exterior remains the same - wisteria tumbling from the wall of the old Picard farmhouse - nor has the entrance hall, with its flagged stone floor and wonderful old white tiled stove. Walls have been knocked down, however, to enlarge the dining room, and there is a new reception area so a certain intimacy has been lost in the process. We were the only diners, which made the musak even more obtrusive.

Fate took a hand in deciding that Jean-Marc Six should be the owner of the Auberge. Working in a restaurant in the north, he bought a ticket in a raffle and won first prize - around £150,000. He heard that the Auberge was for sale and the chance to be his own boss was too good to miss.

He is passionately devoted to the ingredients and recipes of his home territory, buying locally and in the valley itself if possible. Trout come from the ponds at Zérables, flour from the mill at Beussent, bread from the excellent baker at Montcavrel, jams and honey from farmers' wives, strawberries from Montechort, and of course chocolates from the famous chocolate factory down the road (see Beussent).

His 13.6€ menu is fairly limited - *terrine*, fillet of pork or fish of the day - but there are three other menus at 19.2, 24, 36€, on which you get the chance to sample *ficelle de l'auberge*, and *Potje vleisch*, both Flanders specialities, or the famous *truite au bleu*. *Crème brulée* comes *à la chicorée,* using the roots as subtle flavouring. The house speciality is a dish from a village near Lille, *tarte au Wambrechies*. Just right for a light lunch, I thought. Potatoes are piled into the flan, topped with *crème fraiche* and flavoured with juniper and a touch of gin.

Jean-Marc and his wife Laurence have actually reduced the price of their rooms. "I want people to come back," he says. And anyway, his love is in the restaurant not the hotel, so naturally he wants the bargain rooms to encourage people to eat there. They are unchanged since the tenancy of the former owner, are quite small but pleasant and well equipped. Two with shower cost 47€ and four with bath 59€. P.d. is 6.4€.

LAVENTIE 62840 Pas-de-Calais

33 km E of Lille

A rather grim little northern town in which to find such a treasure:

☆ **Le Cerisier** ⊠ **M**
3 rue de la Gare
tel: (0)3.21.27.60.59
fax: (0)3.21.65.35.85
closed: Sun. p.m. Mon. and Sat. lunch

Eric Delerue learned his trade with Marc Meurin at Béthune - see p.70 and it shows. He has been cooking in his own delightful little restaurant for 15 years now and has readily adopted the Meurin trademarks of impeccably fresh ingredients, local where possible, and imaginative flavour combinations. The noticeable difference is in the price. To be able to sample cooking like this for peanuts (lunch Tues.-Fri.) would alone merit a cross-Channel venture. Go on - it's just off the autoroute. Or at very least turn off on your way south in order to get the holiday off to a good start. Here's what to expect:

Only a gastronomic menu is served now; served in a pretty little room painted appropriately cerise and known as La Griotte. We took a *filet mignon* and *gratin dauphinois*, both perfect. Alternatively, there are, sensibly, just four entrées and four *plats* on the *à la carte* menu, costing 4.8€ and 8.8€ respectively. On the à la carte menu, all dishes range from 17.6-24€. Try the local dish *tourte au fromage* and top it up with a *mignon de porc à la moutarde*, or, if you're saving your appetite, order just one dish, even a starter, and there will be no raised eyebrows. A platter of good cheeses or a home-made dessert costs 9.3€.

The gastronomic restaurant, Le Cerisier, has a yellow theme and is as pretty and comfortable as its neighbour. This is where Eric can show off his talents without too much price restriction. Nevertheless the 26€ menu is astonishing value. A *ragout* of baby asparagus is served with orange hollandaise sauce, seabass is topped with grated truffle and served on a base of potato *purée* whipped with olive oil and garlic. Roast pigeon is twinned with breasts of smoked duck and *carré d'agneau* is basted with honey. Other menus at 38 and 54€. Exquisite desserts show off his skill as a *pâtissier*.

Don't go in a hurry because everything is cooked to order. Charming young Madame Delerue will help to make the waiting time fly.

Starred for excellent food of one-star-Michelin quality, with non-Michelin-star prices. Go soon.

LUMBRES 62380 Pas-de-Calais

42 km SE of Calais, 10 km SW of St. Omer

☆ **Moulin de Mombreux** 🛏 ⊠ L
rte de Bayenghem
tel: (0)3.21.39.62.44 and (0)3.21.39.13.13
fax: (0)3.1.93.61.34

There have been many changes in the road system around Lumbres and it is approaching spaghetti junction proportions. For the first time we approached the village from the south and discovered to our surprise quite a substantial small town. I had always imagined that it was just a factory complex.

The setting - grey dusty papermills belching grey dusty effluvia into the grey dusty Pas-de-Calais - makes arrival at the Moulin all the more sensational.

No trace of industry here except a few ducks working hard to combat the force of the fast-flowing river Bléquin. Even the ancient wooden mill-wheel is at rest. The building's venerable exterior is striped with honey brick and cream stone, its green lawn and wide terrace scattered with white recliners. All is very peaceful, very colourful - the antithesis of the activity down the valley and the busy network of roads above it.

The 24 bedrooms are in an annexe, pleasantly flowery, well equipped, french windows looking across to a photo-opportunity of the old mill. 96-109€. In the annexe is a comfy lounge, bar and breakfast room.

Back in the main building the reception area centres on another bar, huge, semicircular, stone, beyond which is an open log-burning fire just by the mammoth mill-wheel. Everything twinkles - glass, brass and polished flagstones. A corkscrew staircase leads up to the restaurant, a dignified room whose rough white walls are hung with Flemish tapestries.

The cheapest menu, at 37€, includes wine, and offers three choices in each course - e.g. a *terrine* of guinea fowl stuffed with pistachios and served with a *confiture* of red onions, then a breast of chicken from Licques (just down the road), and then any item on the dessert menu. The next one up is 59€, with more sophisticated fare, like home-made *foie gras* and seabass *en croûte*.

I have always eaten well at Le Moulin, but there have been one or two dissenters - chiefly about the price. The star is for the excellent cooking and the delightful setting.

LA MADELAINE-SOUS-MONTREUIL 62170

5 km W of Montreuil

A pleasant hamlet sheltering in a valley beneath the towering ramparts of Montreuil. The Canche flows wide and free here and there is usually a fisherman or two spending a patient hour on the banks.

☆ La Grenouillère ⇔ M ⊠ L
   tel: (0)3.21.06.07.22
   fax: (0)3.21.86.36.36
   closed: Tues.; Wed. o.o.s.; Jan.

At every available opportunity I find an excuse to visit The Froggery and its amiable chef-patron Roland Gauthier. I must stop describing him as youthful, since I see that he is now *quadragenaire*, but his welcoming smile is still decidedly boyish, as is his untiring enthusiasm for cooking and interesting ingredients.

For the first time I recently managed a July visit and I had been looking forward to dining on the terrace of his utterly charming whitewashed Picard erstwhile farmhouse. On previous out-of-season occasions it had understandably been impracticable but surely in July... alas, although the flowers bloomed bravely and the white tables and chairs were waiting for customers, the terrace was just as windswept as it had been in November.

So inside it had to be. No hardship whatsoever. Cosiness and warmth instead of chill. Even the frogs were smiling (for those unfortunates who have never visited La Grenouillère, the restaurant takes its name from the caricatures on the dark varnished walls of La Fontaine's fable of the frog who wished he were a bull and ate so much that he exploded, to the dismay of his lady frog companion - a recommendation for *nouvelle cuisine* if ever there were one).

Fresh flowers casually arranged as though they had just been picked, gleaming copper, uneven flagged floors, all add to the rustic ambience. There is nothing casual or rustic, however, about the place settings and the service - both highly polished, as is befitting a Michelin-starred establishment.

There are three menus: *Mer & Terre* for 48€, Dégustation for 67€ and *du Terroir* for 27€, which is such good value we rarely look elsewhere. I learned a new word - *Crème Froide à l'Ortie du Marais* is a chilled cream soup flavoured with nettles. Trust Roland to make good use of every conceivable ingredient that his beloved region can produce. The photograph on the front of his brochure depicts him hoeing his potager, and herbs and infantile vegetables are always prominent in his cooking.

Then the star course of the meal - a *Risotto aux Crustaces et Brunoise de Légumes de Saison*, a risotto perfumed with shellfish and served with tiny broad beans and carrots. Course three was sucking pig, skin caramelised, aromatic spices cutting the richness. Then, after a refreshing sorbet, a *millefeuille* of strawberries, which are a speciality of the region, cream scented with thyme.

This four-course menu - six if you count the *amuses bouches* and the *sorbet*, is obviously good value, but be prepared for a costly wine list, on which there is no opportunity to economise.

The value continues with the lodging. All four rooms were predictably occupied in July so I could not see the redecoration that Roland assured me had improved them still further. I hardly think it matters - they were all so attractive and comfortable last time I stayed there. There are two doubles at 72€, one with twins at 88€ and a flat which sleeps two adults with three children for 96€. All have luxurious bathrooms, so it's not surprising that you have to be quick off the mark to book one. It's an ideal combination with a memorable meal and breakfast, with any luck, on the terrace, to the sound of birds and rushing water. During the winter (not Saturday) you get a room thrown in if you tackle the 64€ menu.

☆ for some of the best cooking in the region.

☆ Auberge du Vieux Logis ⊠ S-M

pl. de la Mairie
tel: (0)3.21.06.10.92
closed: Wed.; 8 days in Nov.

This is where the locals go if they want an unpretentious evening out. It's an extremely pretty cottagey building dating from 1859, on the corner of a bend of the D139. Outside are plenty of tables, well-patronised in fine weather for drinks as well as meals. All very peaceful and countrified. Inside the tiny rustic dining room it's as archetypally French as you could wish for, with red-and-white checked table-cloths and low beams.

Véronique and Étienne Boutin are the owners here; Étienne likes to cook classical French dishes like his *cassoulet maison*, prepared every day. Menus from 18.4€ to 30€ feature veal kidneys, grills, and just a nod to more recent favourites like a *carpaccio* of raw fish. Nice atmosphere, nice people, all contribute to happy eaters.

MAINTENAY 62870 Pas-de-Calais.

2 km S of Montreuil, 40 km SE of Boulogne

To get in the right rustic mood, turn off the main road south from Montreuil and take the D139E through Écuires, Boisjean and Roussent past whitewashed farmhouses, through fields of corn and poppies, into dark woods, then turn left onto the D119, where lines of willow follow the river Authie.

Turn right to the Moulin, beyond the church, into an avenue of poplars festooned with mistletoe, past lakes on both sides and elegant Charolais cattle munching the rich pastures.

☆ **Le Moulin de Maintenay** ⊠ S
  tel: (0)3.21.90.43.74
  open 12-9 p.m.

The moulin has come up in the world since I first wrote about the enchanting scene of creaky waterwheel churning, lilies floating, and café serving lunchtime crêpes. Now it is altogether more sophisticated, in an artfully simple way. Pretty though the interior is, with all kinds of home-made goodies on sale in the shop, the terrace is the place to be. Here white tables, parasol shaded, directly overlook the water and nothing but that word idyllic will do for the scene.

Try one of Maître Paul's specialities, *Rhubarbois*, at 2.5€ a glass and snack elegantly on not only *crêpes* and *galettes* but quiches and *salades composées*. Just the thing for lunch on a hot day, but very agreeable too, early on a fine summer's evening.

Readers have enjoyed its unique charm, so a ☆.

There are organised tours of the 12C mill, describing its history from the time it belonged to the abbey at Valloires and its function. You can visit from 10-12 and from 2-9 p.m. for 3.8€ but phone first to check that there is not a group at the same time.

MARQUENTERRE Somme

60 km S of Boulogne, E of Rue, S of Fort-Mahon Plage

Marquenterre the sea (*mar*) that (*que*) enters (*ent*) the land (*terre*). Well-named indeed. Here the opalescent light that gives the Côte d'Opale its name does indeed have the effect of merging sea, land and sky. Sand dunes stretch to the horizon with no clear boundaries. Mud flats provide the perfect habitat for all manner of birds.

Parc Ornithologique du Marquenterre
St. Quentin-en-Tourmont
tel: (0)3.22 25.03.06

I strongly recommend an outing here for both bird-fanciers and beginners alike, especially for kids who might well become addicts after spotting spoonbills and cranes, using the hides that are dotted about the 5,000 acre reserve, and counting some of the 300 species that are known to drop in on their way to warmer/colder climes. Binoculars are provided and the whole enterprise is admirably well organised. Help-yourself restaurant on site.

Open daily 15-Mar. to 11-Nov., 9.30-7. Admission 9.6€; concessions 7.2€.

MARQUISE 62250 Pas-de-Calais

13 km NE of Boulogne
Market: *Thurs.*

For years I imagined that Marquise began and ended along the *nationale*. I now know that behind the Grand Cerf is a quieter Marquise, centred around a market square.

Le Grand Cerf ⊠ M-L

34, ave. Ferber
tel: (0)3.21.87.55.05
fax: (0)3.21.33.61.09
closed: Thurs. and Sun. p.m., Mon.

For serious eating by serious eaters. You do not drop in here for a snack. Echoes of le Grand Cerf's glorious past, when it justified a Michelin star, still remain. Generations of Englishmen have taken nourishment here before toiling down the old main route to the capital, ever since doors first opened as a *relais de diligence* - a posting stop for carriages. The place is very conscious of its illustrious past; the stone bench where Victor Hugo rested in 1837 is proudly in situ at the entrance.

Stéphane Pruvot too has an impressive past. His previous cooking experience was at the Côte St. Jacques in Joigny, of three-star fame.

Not surprising that his style is strongly traditional, but he insists on adding regional touches, like stuffed pancakes served with a beer-flavoured sauce, ox cheek again with beer, and chicory as a spice. This is what his customers ask for, but he is not afraid to experiment occasionally, with more exotic combinations, like his cauliflower mousse served with giant prawns gently curried. Fish, local of course, is predictably big - turbot is served with *petits gris*.

Menus start at 27€. This is high quality at reasonable prices, and if I do not award an arrow, perhaps it is because the establishment seems to lack a woman's touch - a touch of *tristesse* maybe. No feedback from readers hasn't helped. However, if you bring your own atmosphere and rate the cooking as of paramount importance, you will relish Le Grand Cerf.

MOLINGHEM 62330 Pas-de-Calais

9 km SE of Aire-sur-la-Lys by D188

All very confusing - Molinghem runs into Isbergues which runs into Berguettes. It is the station of Molinghem that you are aiming for.

☆ Le Buffet 🛏 S ⊠ M

22 rue de la Gare
tel: (0)3.21.25.82.40
closed: Sun. p.m.; Mon. 1 Aug. to 22 Aug.

Well, who would have thought it. This indeed was once the station buffet but that would be hard to guess in its reincarnation as one of the most attractive restaurants in the district. It has swapped dinginess for pastels - peach and almond green - white painted beams, and bleached wood, resulting in pleasing lightness and brightness.

With the aperitif white-jacketed waiters brought little stuffed cherry tomatoes and, during menu-perusal, a mouthful of delicate cauliflower soup sprinkled with crab in a tiny white porcelain pot.

For dinner, I had to go mad and fork out 17.6€ for three courses on the *Le Terroir* menu and husband staked even more on the *Le Gourmand* version at 27€ (there are two other menus at 35€ and 48€, and a la carte). I've noticed before that the youthful Thierry Wident has a penchant for *petits gris* (small snails); perhaps he knows where to find a good supply in his garden. Sure enough, here they were again, this time in a risotto. And very good too, with shreds of leeks and deep fried chervil as a garnish. The parmesan was the expensive fresh shaven kind not the dried stuff out of a plastic shaker. Husband's menu yielded very tender Licques chicken, braised with mushrooms and an unusually good selection of *petits farcis de l'été*, in other words seasonal vegetables stuffed with breadcrumbs and lots of garlic.

Christine Wident is a welcoming efficient hostess; she makes no bones about the fact that the restaurant is their first love and that the bedrooms are mere accessories. They are clean but very small and cost a modest 48€.

Readers have unanimously enthused about the set-up here, so the star stays.

MONTREUIL SUR MER 62170 Pas-de-Calais

38 km S of Boulogne
Market: *Sat.*

Hard to credit nowadays, when Montreuil, perched on an

escarpment, looks down on miles of fertile countryside, that indeed it was once 'sur mer'. In fact, in the days when the kings of France controlled very few provinces, it was France's only royal port. Now the estuary of the Canche has silted up and there are ten miles or so between sea and town.

A glimpse of the sea can still be snatched if you look hard enough in the right direction from the ramparts that surround the town, and a walk around them is a very good idea in any case. It takes 40 minutes to complete the circuit, high above the weathered roofs and cobbled streets, but there are numerous narrow alleys along the way, down which to escape if it's all a bit breezy up there. The view is over rolling farmlands, the valley of the Canche, the lighthouse marking the estuary, Le Touquet and Étaples and the old monastery of Notre Dame des Prés. Consider the cobwebs blown away.

With the advent of the autoroute there is now a choice of four roughly parallel roads approaching the town from the north. The coast road, the D940, runs through the sand dunes and forest of Hardelot and crosses the river at the old fishing village of Étaples; next comes the A16 which whisks you into Boulogne in no time, then the N1, which used to be lorry-loaded but might be relieved now, and then, for those who have time on their hands and enjoy the journey as much as the destination, the D127, following the valley of the Course (see p.109).

As you cross the river, wind up the steep hill to the town, and drive under the bridge, the oldest part of the town presents itself; the cavée St. Firmin, picturesquely cobbled with 17th-century cottages clinging precariously to its slopes, will be familiar from many a postcard.

First comes the little place Darnétal, flower-bedecked, fountain-spraying, tree-lined, and behind it the former church of St. Saulve, part 12th century, with flamboyant Gothic nave. Montreuil takes its name from the original monastery (monasteriolum) founded here in the 7C by St. Saulve, Bishop of Amiens.

Follow the Grande Rue to park in the Grande Place, where Douglas Haig, who had his WW1 headquarters here, is commemorated by a statue. And Grande the Place certainly is, spacious enough to accommodate the colourful Saturday market, which is just one more reason why Montreuil is a good weekend-break idea. Around the square are plenty of coffee/beer opportunities, and an excellent picnic-supplier, M. Vasseur. *"Outstanding range of delicious dishes are made on the premises every day. We tried two of M. Vasseur's pâtés, some mini-quiches and a local speciality, potje vleisch, a cold dish made from veal, chicken, pork and rabbit. The bread came from the Boulangerie Coulon in the Place Darnétal and delicious that was too".* Roger Davies.

A new chocolate, coffee, tea shop, l'Atelier du Gout, has just opened There are all kind of exciting chocolate drinks on offer - cinnamon, nutmeg and pepper among them.

The charm of this peaceful old town has always appealed to artists and writers, and anyone who has seen *Les Miserables* will know that Jean Valjean, having attained respectability, became mayor of Montreuil. Victor Hugo had visited the town in 1837 and it obviously impressed him so much that he decided to use it as the setting for one of the main episodes in his book. Laurence Sterne, author of *A Sentimental Journey through France and Italy*, lodged at the old coaching inn, the Hotel de France in the 18th century (see below).

Of recent years there have been many changes in Montreuil and nowadays it has become somewhat of a gastro-centre, with more than its share of hotels and restaurants to choose from. So near the beaches, so easily approached from the ports, on the way to Paris, in lovely countryside, it would be my No. 1 choice for a short break in the area.

☆ Château de Montreuil ⊨ ⊠ L

4 Chausée Capucins
tel: (0)3.21.81.53.04
fax:(0)3.21.81.36.43
Hotel and resturant closed: Mon (except holidays)
Restaurant closed: Tues lunch from Oct to May; Thurs lunch throughout the year.

How lucky we Brits are to have a luxurious bolthole like the Château de Montreuil waiting to pamper us just across the Channel. How lucky too that Lindsay and Christian Germain never rest on their considerable laurels but just go on making this little bit of paradise more and more heavenly. And in case you think this eulogy is totally o.t.t. (or that I'm being paid to write it!) I shall now get over and done with the single criticism that crops up is occasionally in the pile of praise - *i.e.* that the château is full of Brits. Just tell me how one could

Château de Montreuil.

avoid that, when it has been an Anglo-haven for so many years, even before the Germain regime, and word of mouth continues to do a better job than any advertising. It is, after all, far and away the most comfortable hotel in the region, with superb cooking thrown in, so what do you expect? Lindsay is very conscious of the problem and tries hard to get a continental mix, but with contented customers reserving a year ahead, she has her work cut out.

At least half the credit for the Chateau's popularity must be attributed to Lindsay, who looks after the hotel bit while Christian cooks. 'The English Rose' as the French guidebooks tend to describe her, provides not only the perfect reception - smiles, warm welcome for her new customers, remembering the names of old ones - but is also an extremely efficient housekeeper. No detail, however small, escapes her scrutiny, and, just as Christian runs cooking seminars, she could handle one on how to run the perfect hotel.

As usual, most of the rooms were occupied (book well ahead if you have a favourite), but she showed me round some of the newer (and cheaper) ones in the annexe, all of which were perfectly delightful. Good sized, furnished with Laura Ashley fabrics and pleasant furniture and with luxurious marble bathrooms. Then of course I had to peek at some of the old favourites - the one with the four poster and the copper-ceilinged bathroom is understandably the American's favourite. They are all different, but each one would stand up to the test - if you want to make sure your guests are comfortable try sleeping in the guestroom. I wouldn't put it past Lindsay to have done that.

Back at reception, an elderly couple, regular visitors, were departing. While his wife settled in the car, her husband nipped back for a farewell kiss from Lindsay.

The Château is a rare example of food perfectly complementing bed. Usually either the restaurant or the hotel dominates; here they are perfectly in harmony. Christian Germain, Roux protégé, continues to be in fine fettle. It must be hard to stay as passionate about one's metier for as long as he has but the cuisine shows no sign of fade. Insisting on the finest, freshest ingredients, as many as possible from local sources, he, experiments with new combinations and techniques, never resorting to clichés, as do so many traditional French chefs. I have never had a bad meal at the château and neither, according to my postbag, have any readers. You can rest assured that his cheapest menu, 54€ in the evening, 31€ inclusive of wine for lunch, will be a treat, but if you really want to see what he can do, go for the dégustation menu, where you trust the team to tease and delight your taste buds for 69€.

Some of my favourites: *tartare de concombre et huîtres de pleine mer, pressé de légumes de saison, vinaigrette de tapenade*, then for a main course *tronçons de lotte en croûte d'herbes sur palette de poivrons*, or *filet de canette de barbarie en croûte de sésame, jus aux navets et gingembre*. For dessert: *Minestrone de fruits glacés à la feuille destragon, sorbet au yaourt de brébis*, or *larme de chocolat blanc, abricot rôti à la vanille Bourbon, sauce amande amère*. All these feature on the 48€ Menu Carte.

The dining room, freshly decorated in blue and yellow, with swags of dried flowers, looks out on to the new swimming pool, surrounded by expensive recliners, and the terrace, where summer sipping is the perfect preface to the meal. The gardens are leafy and extensive, and like the building itself, in the *style Anglaise*. You could be in Weybridge, but I bet you're glad you're not.

13 rooms cost from up to 183€, demi-pension from 290-336€ per person, but there are all kinds of special deals, from two nights *gastronomique* break to a special mid-week out of season offer, which is particularly good value.

"We again stayed at the château, where we tend to go every six months, and it was absolutely fabulous. The service was absolutely

wonderful. I had the wonderful boulognnaise scallops as one of the courses on the menu gastronomique and they were the best scallops I have ever tasted. Also the foie gras was wonderful, the first night served with cabbage and red cherry beer and the second night with baby rhubarb. My wife has many allergies and she was looked after very well; this included croissants being made without any egg, no eggwash on the bread and on the menu gastronomique there were certain dishes prepared just for her, as she cannot eat any fish. There was no extra charge for this." Jonathan Paul Diamond.

☆ **Hotel de France** 🛏 **M**
rue Coquempot
tel: (0)3.21.06.05.36
closed: Jan., Feb.

Patronne Janie Hall has achieved the near-impossible. She has integrated herself into Montreuil society, from dustman to *duc*, and endeared herself to them so thoroughly that they are able to forget and forgive the fact that she is not French, and taken her to their hearts. Her cosy bar is the favoured rendezvous for *le tout monde*, and if there are Montreuil politics to be discussed (there usually are) she is there in the heart of the action.

It's not hard to see why Janie is so popular. She is warm and friendly and always has time for a chat. She tells me that her clients nowadays are 80% repeats. On my last visit there were a boisterous party of golfers, who stay with her at least twice a year, and a foursome who had got into the habit of dropping in whenever they flew their private plane from Birmingham to Le Touquet.

But here is a hazard warning. Do not even think of staying in the Hotel de France if your ideal is conventional mod cons, sanitised, sterilised and safe. This is a very idiosyncratic establishment, with Janie's somewhat bohemian personality stamped on every inch.

Take the décor for example. Not everyone warms to such an abundance of plastic flowers, red, orange and yellow, playing such a large part in the decoration, nor the daze of blue and gold painted walls embellished with pineapple stencils. In the huge breakfast room, appropriately equipped with a stage and piano, erratically paint-spattered canvas flaps, as though someone had lost inspiration halfway through. There are baubles, gold ivy leaves, stars on ceilings, posters, antlers, African drums, tambourines, and a hat-stand overflowing with assorted garments (whose? abandoned?).

Our friends described their loo as psychedelic and very pink with it (but were delightedly bemused with the whole set-up). Our shower curtain first resisted all attempts to draw and then came away in our hands, and the towels were off-white scratchy. Janice was horrified to read this and has remedied both.

But consider the positive touches - fresh flowers in all the bedrooms, mineral water and bon-bons, deep comfortable chintzy armchairs in the bar/lounge and above all Janie dispensing welcomes, smiles and alcohol.

A mural in the courtyard commemorates Laurence Sterne's stay in the old coaching inn. In summer, this is the place to sit with a glass or three, on the cobbles, among the miscellaneous pots and tubs full of colour. (Admittedly it wasn't looking quite so attractive during our April visit, when Janie hadn't quite got around to sorting out all the winter debris.) Sadly the useful connection with the restaurant across the courtyard has foundered and further association is doubtful, but there is no shortage of alternatives in the town.

This is a love-it-or-hate-it entry. Readers have been divided 80/20 in favour, but they did have my cautionary description to weed out the doubters in advance. I would advise choosing your room carefully, because some are on the bend of a noisy road and have only mediocre showers, while the best are quieter, lighter, and have bathrooms. You may have to book well in advance.

Rooms from 56-104€.

☆ for personality.

Les Hauts de Montreuil 🛏 ⊠ M

21 rue Pierre Ledent
tel: (0)3.21.81.95.92;
fax: (0)3.21.86.28.83

The oldest building in Montreuil, dating from 1537. Ridiculously picturesque in traditional black and white, with plentiful beams and flowers. Behind the façade is a modern hotel, the antithesis of the quirky Hotel de France. The rooms have been cleverly contrived round a courtyard, complete with fountain. We drew the short straw and got the one on the ground floor next to the tradesmen's entrance. Not much hope of sleep after dustmen, deliveries and laundry services started work at dawn. Tip! - avoid room no.1.

Parking is in the two narrow wings of the courtyard, involving some tricky manoeuvring if your car is parked first. It all worked out very smoothly during our visit, but it does assume a lot of goodwill from guests being asked to move their vehicles to allow access.

The rooms are excellent - surprisingly spacious and well-equipped with big double beds and a good bathroom. Breakfast is served in a converted stable, and a superb breakfast - or rather brunch; tuck into smoked salmon, pâté, ham, eggs, melon, strawberries, pineapple, compôtes of berries, cheeseboard, yoghurt, twenty different home-made jams and the usual pâtisserie and French bread and there should be little need for lunch expenditure. Only the mindless pop spoiled the perfect harmony. As every breakfaster was at least middle-aged (and British) I would have thought Ole Blue Eyes would have been more appropriate than youth-appeasing wail and thump.

The hirsute M. Gantiez is a hands-on *patron*, running his establishment with total efficiency and marketing it diligently. In the 16C caves beneath the hotel he offers wine-tasting (preferably followed by wine-buying) and a range of well-cared-for cheeses for sale, as are other *produits regionaux*, which guests can select as classy take-home presents. Fifteen wines are available by the glass (rare in France) so anyone like me, who thinks the perfect lunch is a platter of cheeses and a glass of red, will score here. The bar makes a cosy meeting place to partake of such a snack if the tables outside in the courtyard do not appeal.

The cheapest menu, termed *'Terroir'* is 26€, featuring *flamiche montreuilloise* - a pie filled with cheese, smoked breast of duck and leeks, or there is *l'assiette du saurisseur, tartare de brebis desgrange aux salicornes,* which should cause a few puzzled brows. Let me translate - a plate of smoked fish, with marinated kid and seaweed. An appealing third course option is a trilogy of regional farm cheeses served with a walnut salad. Other menus at 34 and 43€.

27 rooms cost 87€ (shower) or 96€ (bath). Breakfast is an additional 12€ per person, making this a pricey stop, but it is very popular with the Brits and booked well ahead.

Le Darnétal 🛏 ⊠ M

pl. Darnétal
tel: (0)3.21.06.04.87
fax: (0)3.21.86.64.67
closed: Mon., Tues. 1st week in July

Everybody loves the Darnétal, established on the corner of a pretty, be-limed, be-fountained, be-geraniummed square for over a century. It's all very neat, very freshly painted, very French, with brown shutters and overflowing windowboxes and tables outside for summer imbibing. Indoors not a lot has changed, thank goodness. There's still a lovely warm cosy atmosphere, generated by bright red tablecloths, lots of flowers and polished old furniture.

Chef-*patron* Jean-Paul Verney sticks with trad. French. Expect to find fresh local fish, plenty of oysters, hot and cold, ragouts, and good pastry on his menus, which start at 17€ (go for it), (not weekends). Others at 24 and 32€.

A relatively new innovation are the four bedrooms, each one different, furnished in vaguely Belle Epoque style. No telephone, no telly, just a lot of comfort, plenty of space and a good night's sleep after a satisfying meal. 35-48€.

☆ Le Clos des Capucins ⇤ ⊠ M

46 place du Général-de-Gaulle
tel: (0)3.21.06.08.65
fax: (0)3.21.81.20.45
closed: Sun. p.m.; Mon.

In the main square Jean-Luc Bigot and his wife have smartened up the hotel part of the old Les Remparts, and now the bedrooms are attractively furnished with cane beds and pastel floral prints and equipped with modern bathrooms. At the rear of the hotel is an unexpected sheltered terrace, a very pleasant spot for summer breakfasts.

Jean-Luc's skill in the kitchen is well-documented and now the combination of his culinary talents with comfortable bedrooms in the town centre merits a ☆.

Rooms at 54€. Menus at 16€, 27€ (recommended) and 35€.

☆ Le Coquempot ⊠ M

2 pl. de la Poissonnerie
tel: (0)3.21.81.05.61
fax: (0)3.21.86.46.73
closed: Wed., Thurs.

The responsibility was dreadful. Being asked to select the perfect venue for a friend's important birthday dinner is bad enough for

Auberge de la Foret   La Motte-au-Bois

anyone, but for those of us who claim to know a thing or two about French restaurants, it was asking for trouble. I need not have worried. Le Coquempot rose to the occasion admirably, as it rises to any occasion, from a romantic table for two amongst the flowers in the enchanting new terrace garden, to a boisterous party of twelve like ourselves.

I was delighted to find this delightful restaurant, with equally delightful young owners, just in time for the previous edition, and staked my reputation on guessing it would be a winner without any more back-up than my own instinct on good vibes. Since then the plaudits have amply supported the gamble. There have been a few changes, but all of them good ones, like the terrace. The young Poussets have gained in confidence; she is just as modest and retiring but even more quietly efficient at welcoming and taking orders, and he is not afraid to extend his repertoire.

The exterior of the tall 19th-century, typically French, house in the square is now softened by abundant geraniums trailing from nine window boxes. Inside the two dining rooms windows are high, oak floors are polished, napery, wallpaper and curtains are peachy. It remains a dignified gentleman's house, and perhaps first impressions are a touch stuffy, but Madame Pousset soon dispels any inhibitions.

We ate off the set 30€ menu (there's a cheaper 20.5€ menu, too) and every one of our party was incredulous at the modesty of the eventual bill. Each item on the menu was sampled - mussels and clams stuffed with sauerkraut and garnished with smoked salmon; marinated salmon flavoured with dill and Guérande salt; livers of chicken, duck and goose. Main courses were *'coq du cocquempot'* (Coquempot is a corruption of *coq au pot*), garlicky lamb *noisettes*, or cod cooked *en papillote*. Third course was cheeses, before a selection of desserts. Thumbs up all round.

A great pleasure to re-award this star, for fine cooking, pleasant surroundings, delightful owners, and good value.

LA MOTTE-AU-BOIS 59190 Hazebrouck Nord.

5 km S of Hazebrouck on the D946

The countryside around here is deep and green, with the Forest of Nieppe and the banks of the river Lys providing good picnicking/walking possibilities.

Auberge de la Forêt ⇔ ☒ M
   tel: (0)3.28.48.08.78
   fax: (0)3.28.40.77.76
   closed: Sun. p.m.; Mon.; 26-Dec. to 16-Jan.

There is an air of opulency about this large chalet-type building nowadays. The restaurant is very grand, with tapestry chairs, draped curtains, big stone fireplace and smart waiters. M. and Mme Bécu have been here for many years and have been steadily improving their property. The 12 bedrooms have all been agreeably renovated and cost a reasonable 53€. As they are nearly always fully booked, you should not arrive on chance.

The cheapest menu, now 23€ (not Sunday) offered *rillettes maison, contrefilet rôtie aux oignons* and dessert. There is also a midweek suggestion du jour for 10.4€. Other menus are 38€ and 48€.

"We have always had excellent service and they even kept the kitchen open for us late one night when we called to say we were stuck in a traffic jam", John Purrington.

NOEUX-LES-MINES 62990 Pas-de-Calais

5 km S of Béthune

As its name indicates, a mining town, with plenty of evidence, in the shape of surrounding slag tips, of the local industry. The main streets, however, seem prosperous and clean, with an astonishing preponderance of furniture and home decorating shops. Why should this be, I wonder?

Les Tourterelles ⇌ ☒ M
374 Route Nationale
tel: (0)3.21.61.65.65
fax: (0)3.21.26.98.98 R
closed: Sat. lunch, Sun. p.m. and fêtes

More astonishment to find an establishment called The Doves perched on the main road of a mining town, and more

Les Tourterelles.

astonishment again to find it peaceful and altogether charming.

The nice old white building is set well back from the traffic hazard in a sizeable, well-maintained garden. Inside are high ceilings and a sense of the elegance of the time it was built - a century or so ago I would guess. The dining room is welcoming and warm - panelled walls, pink cloths, and a white grand piano (but I forgot to ask when it got played). Chef Noel Verbrugge likes to introduce regional recipes and ingredients from Flanders and Artois on his menus at 30, 34 and 42€ but on the first we stuck to the more familiar avocado and shrimps and then salmon escalope and 'sorbet du jour'. The menus don't excite on first reading, but the quality is high and the portions generous. Good carafe wine.

There are 21 well-furnished and comfortable bedrooms, with a bathroom apiece, at 38-64€. Management is helpful and friendly and there is private parking. Altogether a good deal in an unexpected quarter.

PETIT FORT-PHILIPPE 59820 Pas-de-Calais

20 km E of Calais

On the eastern side of the estuary of the Aa. On the other side is Grand Fort -Philippe, with gravelly beach, benches for picnics, marshes, fish market and bizarre gabled lifeboat station. They were both named after King Philippe II of Spain. In 1557 his army had beaten the French troops at St. Quentin and in the following year they repeated their success at Gravelines and Henri II was forced to admit defeat. Philippe constructed the splendid lock in Petit Fort-Philippe and the twin towns took on his name.

On both sides of the estuary the walks are superb - miles of fabulous sand and endless skies. In P.F.P. walk out on the beach, along the prom, or out towards the often invisible sea on the breakwater - the best leg-stretch and ozone gulp imaginable. The sands are so firm that the local footballers have their pitch and goalposts thereon. There's another pleasant short walk along the river bank, good for watching the colourful boats. Plenty of benches for picnicking.

There's an important lighthouse here and I love the lighthouse-keeper's cottage, all spick and span and painted blue and white.

The keeper was digging his spruce little garden and planting out his vegetables. Not many lighthouse keepers can do that.

Appropriately along the river frontage is a series of fish restaurants, all very popular for a fine weekend outing, with tables outside to catch the sun. You can hardly go wrong with a plateful of moules or a fine sole, but the two special recommendations are:

L'Arlequin ☒ M-S
Bvd de l'Est
tel: (0)3.28.65.56.04
closed: Mon. o.o.s.

A tiny narrow restaurant, looking very fresh with its green-and-white banquettes. There are 12.8€ and 15.5€ menus but I preferred the 19.2€ *menu du poisson*, which produced an interesting *gratin de moules* with leeks, an immaculately fresh cod fillet in beurre blanc, a hot goat's cheese and salad and a good home-made apple tart.

PONT-DE-BRIQUES 62360 Pas-de-Calais

5 km S of Boulogne by D940

Boulogne sprawls all the way to Pont-de-Briques, which must once have been an independent village but is now virtually a suburb.

Hostellerie de la Rivière ☒ L
rue Gare
tel: (0)3.21.32.22.81
fax: (0)3.21.87.45.48
closed: Sun. p.m.; Mon. 16 Aug. to 6 Sept.

An unlikely spot to find a Michelin-starred restaurant, but it must work because the Martin family has been cooking here for two generations, and the accolades keep on coming. The recipe has been refined and improved over the years, with re-decoration of the restaurant and rooms; in the kitchen there has been acknowledgement of lighter culinary textures and even recognition of foreign influences and ingredients. The accent is on fish, fresh from the boats, with some sophisticated accents, like a celeriac *confit* with haddock, bass with bacon, but meat does get a look in -

witness one of the star turns - braised hare. Menus start at 27€.

The rooms are small but perfectly formed, and very comfortable, each one differently decorated, all with bath or shower. As this is emphatically a restaurant-with-rooms I would not advise trying to book a room without taking dinner but, that accepted, it would be very agreeable to have only the stairs to negotiate having done justice to M. Martin's cooking and wine list (not cheap).

Eight rooms cost 56€.

QUEND 80120 Pas-de-Calais

26 km S of Le Touquet, 29 km S of Boulogne

The setting is flat windswept dunes and vast skies, with most traffic turning off the main road towards the beaches and tourist facilities of Fort Mahon Plage. (Don't bother say I.)

Auberge le Fiacre 🛏 ☒ M

Route de Fort Mahon, Routhiaville
tel: (0)3.22.23.47.30
fax: (0)3.22.27.19.80

This old farmhouse, picturesquely timbered in black and white, has been converted into a luxurious hotel and upmarket restaurant. The new rooms are built round a well-kept garden, focussing on a white awning shading the many recliners tidily arranged to make the most of the sun. Lovely for al fresco breakfasts and evening drinks. Loads of charm here and in the raftered dining room, where high-backed rush-seated chairs accent the studied rusticity and expensive flowers add colour.

The bedrooms are lovely. All recently re-decorated in glazed chintzes, all with luxurious bathrooms, excellent value at 72€, with breakfast an additional 8€. In July, when most other hotels were heaving, there were still rooms available here, probably because it is so remote or perhaps because its recent upgrading has not been noticed yet.

The Fiacre would make a soothing oasis of calm after a busy day, or an excellent base for exploring the Marquenterre Ornithological Park, the abbeys of Valloires and St. Riquier, Crécy, and the often overlooked town of Rue. No reports, so the star goes. Temporarily I hope.

RECQUES-SUR-HEM 20 km S of Calais

Château de Cocove ⇔ ⊠ M
   tel: (0)3.21.82.68.29

This elegant 18C château was dropped from FE when the original owner sold out and his high standards declined. I was so disappointed at the loss of one of my favourites that I declined to go near it for several years. During that time it became popular with short-break brochures and English was the preferred language, all of which did not endear it to me. However, it is still a beautiful building in peaceful countryside, convenient for ferries. One reader has chided me for my neglect: *"As devoted followers of your French Entrée series, we must report back on some of our enjoyable experiences, among them. Le Château de Cocove. We make this a regular day return via the tunnel for a delightful leisurely lunch in the most beautiful and peaceful surroundings, only 30 minutes down the A26. A wonderful outing. You ought not to have dropped it "* Robert and Margret Pope-Rattersley.

   Perhaps one day I will cast aside my prejudices.

RUE 80120 Somme.

24 km NW of Abbeville, 54 km S of Boulogne

I never cease to wonder at the contrasts in the region covered in this book. There are some amazing one-offs - Cassel, Le Touquet, Bergues, Montreuil and Rue, all as different as chalk from cheese from one another and anything else. Rue is surprising simply because it is a typical French market town and there aren't many of them in this tourist/seaside/British-dominated area.

   It is the capital of the Marquenterre. No big deal you might say. But once, before 5 km of silt intervened between it and the coast, Rue was an important seaport and if I try hard enough I like to think I can still detect a salty flavour in the air. Stronghold of the Counts of Ponthieu, it also prospered as the site of a pilgrimage centred on the tomb of St. Vulphy and of a crucifix borne by an unmanned boat and said to have been discovered under the house of Nicodemus in Jerusalem. Rue's church is named after its benefactor-saint and the chapel of the St. Esprit on the north side remains a magnificent flamboyant Gothic gem, decorated with impressive statues of the evangelists, as well as more secular figures like Charlemagne and Charles VIII. Its double porch, whose doors were carved in the 15th century, is sculpted with scenes from the Passion and the Seven Sorrows of Mary. The cloister, equally rich, has statues of Louis XI and Isabeau of Portugal and carvings telling the story of the miraculous crucifix. In the interior, festooned with hanging bosses, are four nails - all that remains from the crucifix.

Whit Monday still sees a pilgrimage to the chapel. The pilgrims' hospice stands in the Grande Rue, dating from the 16C; the imposing Gothic Hotel de Ville's belfry has four round towers wearing witches' hats.

All this a few miles from the beaches! Not many people know that.

It's a surprisingly big town in this wild wind-swept corner, with wide main streets, and very important on Saturday morning when the market takes over, especially in the hunting season. Every man and boy in Picardy loves *la chasse* and shops to supply their needs are plentiful. Guns, nets, waterproofed clothing, bags and windowfuls of grey and green paraphernalia - can there really be enough huntsmen/poachers/fishermen/shooters to buy all that gear? Obviously yes. Local restaurants naturally follow the trend, especially:

Lion d'Or 🛏 ⊠M

> rue Barrière
> **tel:** (0)3.22.25.74.18
> **fax:** (0)3.22.25.66.63
> **closed:** Sun. p.m. o.o.s.; 20 Dec. to 10 Jan.

Very popular with the locals, and understandably so. Inside the black-and-white façade, past the bar, is to be found a surprisingly smart restaurant, raftered and furnished with light furniture and table settings. Good solid reliable cooking on menus from 14.4€, with quaffable carafe wine available. In season of course there is a *menu de chasse*, which is not to be missed, especially if you haven't eaten for days. 16 rooms (uninspected) cost 37– 51€.

ST AUBIN 62170 Pas-de-Calais

8 km SE of Touquet by D143 and D144E, 27 km SE of Boulogne

The new autoroute has sliced its concrete way through this triangle of unspoiled countryside between Montreuil, Le Touquet and Berck. I feared the worst, but once one has got used to the raw gash the aspect is still peaceful, flowery and surprisingly rural. St. Aubin is one of several pretty hamlets therein.

Otherwise:

Auberge du Cronquelet ⊨ ⊠ S.

> 3 rue de Montreuil
> **tel:** (0)3.21.94.60.76
> **open: 7** days a week.

Once the village forge, whose fireplace is still visible in the 'banquet room'. Now run by Véronique and Laurent Pérard, the latter a nephew of the more famous Pérard in Le Touquet

There are 8 rooms, pretty basic, 32€, and a restaurant serving menus from 12€-based on *cuisine du terroir*.

ST. JOSSE 62170 Pas-de-Calais

8 km SE of Le Touquet, 9 km W of Montreuil

One of the cluster of interesting dining possibilities in the pretty flowery villages in the rustic triangle south of the Canche. The D144 off the D143 is the easiest way to find it.

☆ Auberge du Moulinel ⊠ M-S

> 116 Chaussée Avant Pays
> **tel:** (0)3.21.94.79.03
> **closed:** Mon. and Tues. o.o.s. Otherwise open every day, last week of June; first 3 weeks in Jan.

An old village inn, purchased by Alain and Annique Lévy six years ago. Inside the wooden beams and open fireplace make for a warm and cosy atmosphere. Alain, who has cooked at three- and two-star Michelin establishments, insists on only fresh produce, makes his own bread and comes highly recommended by the head chef of the Westminster in Le Touquet, who should know what he's talking about.

The 25€ menu featured, for example, ravioli stuffed with *maroilles* cheese and served with cumin sauce, then the *queue de boeuf* for which Alain is rightly famous, then cheese or *crème brulée*. For 35€ you get an extra course thrown in - a judicious mixture of traditional and innovative. Other menus cost 40 and 47€.

"It was wonderful décor, food and service. There were seven of us with one small child who ordered the usual hamburger and chips and was served a very tender steak and sliced potatoes gently fried in butter, which impressed me no end. It's so nice to come across a restaurant which takes the same care catering for children and adults. I had the famous Parmentier of ox tail, which melted in the mouth. My 21€ menu more than fulfilled expectations." D. H.

That's just the kind of recommendation from a well-informed local resident that I like to confirm my ☆. Go catch it while you can.

Le Relais de St. Josse ☒ M-S

17 Grand'Place
tel: (0)3.21.94.61.75
closed: Mon.; Sun. p.m and every evening o.o.s.; no annual holidays

Fabienne and Etienne Delmer have been in this pretty little auberge in the village centre for seven years now and have built up a reputation for good traditional cuisine. Tables outside in the sunshine ensure a combination of good food and good gossip. Inside there are low beams, pink tablecloths and fresh flowers on the tables.

Weekday menus start at 13.6€, the 18.4€ version is entitled *Le Petit Royal*, the 26€ is *Régal du Palais* and 34€ *Gourmand de Relais*, but I don't think I could ever live up to that one.

ST. OMER 62500 Pas-de-Calai.

40 km SE of Calais.
Market: *Sat.*

An interesting, multi-facetted town, which does not reveal its charms easily; it took me several visits to appreciate it fully. Set at the junction of the Neufossé canal and the river Aa (whose name I'm told is the French crossword-deviser's delight), it is the heart of a complicated network of waterways, known by the Flemish word *watergangs*.

A pleasant interlude in a timetable of driving and sightseeing is to take a ride on one of the large flat-bottomed black boats typical of the region or on a more modern version. Among the possibilities are three trips starting from the canal on the D209: one goes to Arques as far as the unique hydraulic boat-lift at Fontinettes, one cruises the St. Omer *marais* and another explores the Aa to Houlle. Given a fine day, with a glitter to the ubiquitous wateriness, it's all very peaceful and miles away from the traffic tangle.

The banks of the *watergangs* are inhabited by sturdy market gardeners, who glide from their rich dark plot, intensively cultivated to yield several crops a year, to the market depots in time-warped flat-bottom punts laden down with fat cauliflowers, leeks, chicory and cabbages. At weekends the roadside to Clairmarais is lined with stalls selling their produce and people drive over from Lille to pick up the freshest vegetables in the region. The bungalows along the banks of the main waterways have mini-canals marking their borders, where small boys sit for hours, bemused, watching their fish floats drift on the water.

On Saturdays all this marais produce is displayed on stalls in the most important market in the area which takes place in a great splash of colour in the Grand'Place, the centre of the town. The dignified Town Hall is the focus; the tourist information is there currently, but not for long - it is destined to be housed in the new complex at the entrance to the town that was causing such muddy confusion at the time of my last visit. On the other side of the square is a disreputable collection of cafés leaning drunkenly one on another. This disparity of styles and moods is a feature of the whole town, with the ruins of the 15C St. Bertin, the ponderous Gothic cathedral of Notre Dame, the chapel of the Jesuits, and the elegant 18C Hotel Sandelin, in the rue Carnot, now a museum, full of treasures, including 2,000 pipes made in St. Omer (open from Wed. to Sun. 10-14 and 14-18 p.m.).

Hard to believe now that St. Omer was once a prosperous maritime town, Its rich merchants invested their profits in the substantial classical houses lining the wide streets. Those in quiet backwaters, like the rue Gambetta, have been sympathetically restored, revealing their

Cathédrale Notre Dame

honey-coloured stone and intricate ironwork. The town is a series of quiet and not so quiet squares, opening one out of the other, with one street off the square, the rue de Dunkerque, for everyday shopping and a more upmarket section in the pedestrianised area.

The best place to stock up for a picnic is the rue des Clouteries. Le Terroir, at no. 31, has an excellent range of cheeses, *foie gras* and *terrines*. They will even make up a picnic basket for you. You have a choice of the formal or informal in which to enjoy your purchases al fresco. St. Omer is rightly proud of its public gardens, built on the ancient ramparts of the town, where the neat beds and bedding make a colourful background for benches on which to consume a sandwich and a glass of whatever. For those who prefer to set up tables and chairs as the French do for a serious picnic, the nearby forest of Clairmarais is deep and green and silent. St. Thomas à Becket took refuge here in a Cistercian abbey, of which only the farm now remains. The lake of Harcelles is the haunt of modern fishermen just as keen to land a trout for supper as were the monks who first stocked the water.

A favourite visit from St. Omer is to the crystal factory at Arques, 2 km outside the town on the RN43. There is an audio visual presentation of the various stages of manufacture and a visit to the factory floor to see the molten glass transformed into the finished article. A Christmas booze cruise can profitably be combined with a visit to the factory shop, which offers a 20% discount on their wares and periodical special offers. Opening times are from Mon. to Sat. from 9.30-11.30 and 1400 to 16.30 by appointment. Entrance 5.6€. The shop is open to all from 9.30-18.30 from 2-Jan. to 31-Mar. and from 10.00-19.00 from 1-Apr. to 31-Dec. except Sundays and public holidays. Tel: (0)3.21.12.74.74.

Unfortunately all the hotels in St. Omer have to be in the 'Otherwise'category at present because of changes in management and lack of a strong contender.

Otherwise:

St Louis 🛏 ⌧ S-M
25 rue Arras.
tel: (0)3.21.38.35.21
restaurant closed: Sat. and Sun. lunch

The manager of my old standby has moved on to the Ibis and I know nothing of his successor. In a quiet street, five minutes walk from the town centre. 30 rooms; 54€ for two people. Menus from 14.4€.

Le Bretagne 🛏 ⊠ M

2 pl. Vainquai
tel: (0)3.21.38.25.78
Reataurant closed: Sat. lunch, Sun. p.m; 2 weeks in Aug.

On the other side of town, a solid modern building, with two eating possibilities, a restaurant and the Maeva grill. 75 functional rooms 58-77€. Meals from 14.4€.

Restaurants

Plenty to choose from, but reports vary wildly from exceptionally good to exceptionally bad. Only one that is consistent:

Le Cygne ⊠ M

8 rue Caventou
tel: (0)3.21.98.20.52
closed: Sun. p.m.; Mon.

The name is taken from the lovely stone swan that is the centrepiece of the fountain outside. It's an 18C house in a quiet square, with a smart ground floor restaurant all blue and yellow, and another pink version downstairs in the ancient cellars.

I suspect that Le Cygne might be suffering from the rush of new cheap restaurants in the town centre. Certainly its prices, which used to be a cause for complaint, seem to have come down and now compare favourably, considering that this is a quality restaurant of long-standing and high repute. There is a 12.8€ lunch menu, which offers a sensible choice of *entrée du jour* or quiche or salad, then *plat du jour* or *poulet sauté chasseur*, followed by dessert. Otherwise the 15.5€ menu offers excellent value - for example a game *terrine et ses légumes oubliés* (must try that one to find out what exactly are forgotten vegetables), then seabass with a horseradish sauce, and a trolley of either cheeses or desserts. Other menus go up to 42€. If this sounds a lot, you might like to know that it includes *foie gras*, lobster, beef fillet, cheeses and an *assiette gourmande de desserts*.

N.B. There is a particularly good charcutier, Mignot, just opposite the restaurant.

Otherwise:

Au Vieux Marché ⊠ S
tel: (0)3.21.98.29.39
closed: Sun.

A large restaurant divided by a straw-canopied central bar and decorated with engravings of St. Omer's old market *halles*. Cane chairs and a bistro atmosphere.

The value looks amazing – 10.4€ includes a drink. Can't answer for the cooking because I have yet to try it, but a sample of what was on offer would be chicken liver pâté, fish of the day (or guinea fowl or pork), and dessert. At that price it's not surprising that the place was heaving. They also do pizzas and a good range of grills and the pastry-based desserts looked good. Certainly this is where I shall head next time but in the meanwhile all reports would be valuable for a main entry.

Le P'tit Montmartre ⊠ M
11 Place Pierre Bonhomme
tel: (0)3.21.98.33.33
closed: Sat. lunch; Wed.

I really didn't have much luck in St. Omer one way and another. This was one restaurant I really wanted to try, after several readers' recommendations and no, it wasn't Monday, but a *fermeture exceptionnelle* barred the way. All I can tell you therefore is that menus start at 14.4€ and that the 22€ one looked most interesting. Another at 27€.

Au Vivier 🛏 ⊠ M
22 rue Louis Martel
tel: (0)3.21.95.76.00
fax: (0)3.21.95.42.20
closed: Sun. p.m.

It says a lot for my beautiful nature that I even mention Au Vivier, the scene of the worst crisis of my last round-up. We had prudently reserved a room there, knowing that St. Omer tends to be full year-round, and after a long day trailing round in torrential rain, decided that the late afternoon would be better spent putting our feet up than getting them even more sodden. The road is pedestrianised, so we got saturated scuttling with suitcases to the door. Which was firmly locked. Banging and shouting got us nowhere and the lady in Le Terroir told us that the hotel was never opened until the evening staff for the restaurant came on duty at 18.30. Two hours to go. We tried every hotel in town and the only room available was overlooking the main road at Les Frangins. Sleepless night guaranteed. I am still waiting for a letter of apology from Au Vivier.

I couldn't bring myself to eat there after that experience, but I have to admit it looks good. On that dismal dank evening the rain did not prevent the terrace restaurant, covered with green-and-white awning, from being full. Fish is the speciality and no doubt when the memory fades a bit I shall be able to report further. Menus start at 15.5€ and if you don't mind not having access to your room before aperitif time, the seven rooms cost 46.4€.

L'Entrecôte ⊠ S
1 rue Henri Dupuis
tel: (0)3.21.98.14.38
closed: Sun.; Thurs. p.m.

Mainly for carnivores but fish too is grilled over a charcoal fire. Meat grills cost around 14.4€ and fish grills around 12.8€.

Chlorophylle ⊠ S
3 Place Maréchal Foch
closed: Mon.

An antidote to all that meat is this little vegetarian restaurant/*salon de thé* serving tarts, savoury and sweet.

LA COUPUL
5 km from St. Omer, access from the autoroute by exits 3 or 4, well-signed.
tel: (0)3.21.93.07.07
closed: the second week in January. Otherwise open every day from 09.00-19.00. from 1-Apr. to 31-Oct., and from 10.00-18.00 from 1-Nov. to 31-Mar.

The publicity describes this new 'attraction' as "From the war to the moon", and indeed this sums up the two aspects. It is a contemporary exhibition of aspects of WW2, when this was the most important subterranean base for the V2 rockets, constructed in a giant bunker built by Russian and Polish prisoners. The conquest of space is the other theme, re-living the first steps on the moon by Neil Armstrong. There are two cinemas, 18 audio-visual films and more than three hours of projection. That should keep quiet on a wet day.

Admission 8.8€ for adults and 6.4€ for children.

ST. VALERY-SUR-SOMME 80230 Somme

49 km S of Boulogne

A tablet on the quayside by the canal commemorates the fact that William the Conqueror set off from St. Valery in 1066 for the conquest of England, taking with him some bare essentials: a sword to fight with, wine to fortify him and a bishop to give him absolution. Joan of Arc stopped here on her way to Rouen. Layers of history, illuminative details of past encounters, add richness to what is in any case an utterly delightful town, probably the most interesting along the whole littoral.

St. Valery's position at the mouth of the Somme, the natural guardian against invasion, led to its being pillaged by the Vikings, occupied by the English during the Hundred Years' War, sacked by the Spanish under Charles of Austria, and passed to and fro between the Catholics and the Huguenots. A walk up the cobbled streets to the Vieille Ville, around the ramparts, is the best way to soak up the old-time atmosphere. This second, fortified town, secluded behind massive wooden gates, with flowery beamed houses and a freedom from traffic, comes as a pleasant shock after the bustle of the port and shopping street down below (pleasant though these are). Take the camera to record the astonishing views across the estuary to Le Crotoy.

The approach to the town is from the Abbeville road, across the flat marshes; then as you cross the bridge, the prospect becomes more enticing, with the photogenic masts of yachts lined up in the canal. In the port fishing boats unloading their catch accentuate the salty flavour. Essential to walk along the tree-shaded walks by the water's edge, where the expanse of river, marsh and sky ahead, stretching for ever towards the Somme's mouth, can best be appreciated. Great picnicking: benches, shade, views, calm.

Or not so calm - after a while it strikes you that it is in fact rather noisy. The volume comes not from engines and people but from the millions of birds in colonies across the water, their chatter vying with the bleating of the picturesque sheep dotted about the marshes. The salty vegetation they are so innocently cropping will ultimately prove their undoing. *Pré-salé gigôts*, naturally flavoured, are greatly prized by French gourmets.

Bathing depends on the tide; there is a little beach at the end of the quays, but when the tide recedes literally for miles, swimming is cancelled. This is the opportunity to walk over the sea lavender or along the path towards Le Hourdel, admiring the opalescence of the light and understanding why this is a favourite artists' haunt.

Among the manifold attractions of St. Valery, there are few modern manifestations. Fitting therefore that the preferred method of transport should be 70 years old; the best way to appreciate the bay scenery and to visit Le Crotoy, Noyelles and Cayeux is to take the *Chemin de Fer de la Baie de Somme*, proudly twinned with the Kent and East Sussex Railway. The engine driver leans out of his cabin to check the single track is clear, pulls his whistle and with an impressive hiss, off puffs No. 3714, across fields, past leafy lanes and willow-lined streams.

The train runs every day from 15-Mar. to 15-Nov. Reservation office fax. (0)3.22.26.95.66. In April there is a steam gala, with other trains joining in, and a model railway exhibition and just before Christmas there is a departure from the Christmas market stalls in St. Valery as far as Noyelles, with a special night-time journey on the Saturday night. Fares are from 6.7-10€ depending on how far you travel.

Le Relais Guillaume de Normandie 🛏 ☒ M-S

Quai du Romerol
tel: (0)3.22.60.82.36
fax: (0)3.22.60.81.82
closed: Tues.; 21 Dec. to 5 Jan.

Rising six storeys high from its own valley between port and the old town, Le Relais could have been a Disney fantasy. Half-château, half villa, with towers and turrets and balconies and curlicues, brown peeling paint, quintessentially French. It was actually built a century or so ago by an eccentric English milord as a romantic lovenest-by-the-sea for his mistress.

The view that he chose for her can now be enjoyed by diners in the first-floor restaurant. The food prepared by chef-*patron* Thierry Dupré is copious and good and greatly appreciated by the French on Sunday lunchtimes. He makes full use of local fish and the saltmarsh lamb. Menus from 14.4€, with carafe wine available.

The rooms vary greatly. If you get a dud one you might just as well not bother about a sea view - some are dark and overcast by the trees outside. On the other hand if you are lucky enough to book No.1, with its own charming little terrace, or No. 7 with its Picard furniture, you're on to a winner. 14 rooms at 51-56€. Good value.

Otherwise:

The **old Hotel de Port** and **des Bains** might look shabby, but readers have continued to report favourably on the value on offer here.

Excursion: Take a drive to the tip of the promontory that marks the extremity of the estuary; in the little harbour of **Le Hourdel** is a good bistro, **La Pointe du Hourdel**, serving 120 beers from all over the world. Nice terrace, good place to eat a simple fish lunch.

STE-MARIE-CAPPEL 59670 Nord

3.5 km S of Cassel

Just a name on a sign on the nationale the D916.

Le Petit Bruxelles ☒ Ṁ
rte Nationale
tel: (0)3.28.42.44.64
closed: Sun. p.m.; Mon.; Tues. p.m. and Wed. p.m. o.o.s.; Feb. hols

There was a special menu on offer when I last visited, celebrating fifteen years of M. and Mme Desnave's tenure. They are kindly hosts who have made a lot of friends, including several French Entrée readers. Their restaurant is typical comfortable bourgeois, serving copious helpings of well-cooked food guaranteed to keep out the northern chill.

Entrées include home-made *foie gras* (15.5€) and S*alade royale de homard* (23.7€). Fish features strongly and here the guilt can be assuaged, because all the fish and vegetables are *cuits à la vapeur* which sounds much more agreeable than 'steamed'. Mind you the accompanying sauces are not so virtuous. Fish are around 18€ and meat dishes not far off - lots of duck, roast lamb and fricassées - all traditional stuff. There are special menus de la mer (40€) and, it being autumn when I visited, 'gibier'; the menu du terroir sounds good value costing 23.7€ and including aperitifs, beer and coffee with the three courses.

"We lunched at Le Petit Bruxelles. Not the cheapest, but for a special occasion the delicious food, attractive surroundings and the delightful Mme Desnave in attendance make this worth every centime." Red and Ann Harvey.

M. Desnave also sells attractive take-home presents in the shape of jams and conserves. 14 different varieties of *pâtés* cost around 10.4€ a pot, enough for three to four persons. Jams are around45f. For a special present a basket *"terroir"* would be a good idea, containing one duck *pâté*, one chicken fricassée, one local beer and the decorated basket for 39€.

The Desnave family have also opened a restaurant run by their son, Nicolas, **l'hazewinde Estaminet** (Pl. du Village de St Sylvestre Cappel), about 2km from Le Petit Bruxelles. They have a large beer selection; simpler and cheaper menus (10.8-18.8€); and a children's menu at just 5.6€.

SAULCHOY 62870

16 km SE of Montiér, 17 km SW of Hesdin

On the north bank of the Authie, probably the largest village along the river valley, with a central grassy square lined with plane trees, on one side of which is to be found:

☆ Val d'Authie ⊠ S-M
tel: (0)3.21.90.30.20
closed: Thurs. o.o.s.; 2 Sept. to 16 Sept.

Madame Pottier undoubtedly works hard. Just look at the closing hours to establish that. During the rest of the week she is keeping her pretty little restaurant spotless, welcoming her guests and doing all the cooking. She proudly showed me a rhubarb tart that had just come out of the oven, and very tempting it looked too, even soon after breakfast.

Her dining room (always full on Sunday and often on other days too, so book) is now hung with black flowered curtains in a pink and burgundy colour scheme. The dresser is polished like a mirror, the fireplace is wide and often in use and the grandfather clock has stopped at 3 o'clock.

The cheapest menu at is a snip, bearing in mind that every course is not just thrown-together but the result of great care and attention. Choose, for example, the generous *hors d'oeuvres*, featuring items that originated in Madame Pottier's kitchen not in the local delicatessen, an excellent lasagne with local vegetables, and a slice of her signature fruity tarts. The price includes a carafe of house wine (good stuff) or beer.

For 21€ you could sample Madame's version of the Picardy dish, *ficelle* (like a pancake), go on to *coquilles St. Jacques, gigôt d'agneau*, cheese and dessert, and for 25€ you get yet another extra course. They have just the two menus now.

Splendid value and ☆ of course.

An added asset is that you can bed down just up the road in the Pottiers' *chambres d'hôtes*, 575 rue de Haut, tel: (0)3.21.81.57.21.

It is a comfortable modern villa set in a well-tended garden. One room has bathroom and loo and the other just washbasin and loo; both have T.V. Use of a salon with log fire, and garage, all add up to a good deal for 38€, including breakfast.

TILQUES 62500 Pas-de-Calais

6 km NW of St. Omer, 30 km SE of Calais, sighposted off the N43

Château Tilques 🛏 ☒ M
    tel: (0)3.21.88.99.99
    fax: (0)3.21.38.34.23
    open: all year

"Why don't you include Château Tilques?" I get asked. The answer has been because it's so well-known, in the brochure of every tour operator, including the ferries, in every other guidebook, almost exclusively patronised by fellow-countrymen, I thought there was hardly any point.

But then I wondered if there was a degree of pique in all this (I found it first, sucks boo, when it was being converted from Le Vert Mesnil) and never let it be said.... So I went to have another look and have to confess that it is a lovely building (well, inside anyway), with high ceilings, light and cheerful, helpful reception staff, wide terrace, pleasant bedrooms overlooking the grounds, charming restaurant in the old stable block.

Not a lot has changed here, but there is now new management - French taking over from British - so the food might be improving and the atmosphere becoming a touch more gallic. It is always full, with either conferences or individuals, so make sure you book if you are not on a package deal, which is often better value here. If not, rooms cost a hefty 120-168€ and dinner 35-56€.

For the first time I wandered past the château into the watery world beyond. I discovered that you could hire rowing boats on which to explore the inlets and canals on whose banks weekend gardeners grow giant vegetables on the fertile soil. Or you can opt for a ride on one of the traditional flat-bottomed black boats of the *marais*, the *bacoves*. There are a couple of little cafés too, but even in September they were firmly shut for the season.

TORCY Pas-de-Calais

43 km SE of Boulogne

Take the D341 to Dèsvres, D343 to Maninghem, D108 to Lebiez and finally the D130. Some of the prettiest countryside in the whole area; the valley of the Creqoise is particularly picturesque, with quiet villages like Embry, where a white shrine to Our Lady looks out over a surprisingly hilly terrain. Royan, where the river flows alongside the road is another village to plan a picnic around.

Le Baladin
tel: (0)3.21.90.62.51

Le Baladin, in the centre of the village, is a name that cropped up repeatedly from local advisers on where to go, what to see, what to do, where to eat and drink. I have tried repeatedly to work it into my schedule but it just never happens, so here is the hearsay. A fun place to be on Friday or Saturday evenings or Sunday lunchtimes (those are the only times it's open!) for lovers of jazz and crêpes. The food is basic, simple and cheap. It's the atmosphere you go for. Everyone does a double take when they enter for the first time, since the furniture is on the ceiling! A piano, tables, chairs, you name it, are all upside down, suspended in space. Definitely different. Reports please.

LE TOUQUET 62520 Pas-de-Calais

32 km S of Boulogne
Market: Sat., Thurs.: Marché Couvert year-round; from 19th May to Sept. Mon., Thurs., Sat.

The oddball in the Côte d'Opale. Quite different from any of the other resorts and in many ways quite different from anywhere else in France. It has echoes of some of the spa towns, Biarritz perhaps, hints of past elegance, but proximity to England exerts a strong influence on its character. After all it was an English businessman who, at the end of the 19th century, fell in love with the perfect site of dunes, forest and sea and founded the Touquet Syndicat to develop the area attractively, build hotels and initiate tourism from across the Channel. Drive around today some of the quiet leafy side streets where expensive burglar-proofed villas are set back in gardener-intensive grounds and boards proclaim names like Byways, Wood End and Low Wood Manor, where the late lamented P.G. Wodehouse lived until he was snatched away to a German jail, and Weybridge or Sevenoaks spring to mind.

Between the wars the development accelerated rapidly but the town's heyday was in the Twenties and Thirties, when Le Touquet-Paris-Plage was about as chic as you could get for both Parisiens and Brits. The first casino was actually built as early as 1913, just in time to shut down for WW1; it reopened in 1919 and soon established itself as one of the major casinos in France, attracting the British aristocracy, including the Prince of Wales, and stars of stage and screen. A full orchestra played every day at "Le teatime". Le Touquet became known as "Part of England on French soil". To gain entry to the casino dinner jackets or tails were required for the gentlemen and for their shingled flapper companions here was the chance to air the most dashing frocks, furs, and fol-de-rols. Until quite recently the balls held here were strictly dress-to-kill affairs and James Bond would have been quite at home. Today the thrill of roulette takes second place to the largest slot machine room, the widest choice of games and Le Jumbo, the biggest "Slot" in France. Dress code somewhere between trainers and jeans and d.j.s and diamonds.

The Casino is open every evening. Take your passport. Telephone (0)3.21.05.01.05 for more information. You don't have to play, but it's worth while checking out this intrinsic part of the Le Touquet atmosphere. A White Lady cocktail on the summer terrace sets the scene perfectly.

Our grandparents, as children, sat on the beach with their nannies, and when they grew up came back to build eccentric villas on the sea front. A few of them remain, pinnacled, balconied, mock-beamed and large (the villas, not the grandparents). Too large for modern holiday homes, alas. Bulldozers attack them, one by one, and yesterday's hole in the ground becomes today's undistinguished and indistinguishable apartment block, so that in order to catch even a sniff of past character it is necessary to retreat further and further away from the beach.

And what a beach! Miles of firm golden sands, stretching into infinity left, right and, when the tide recedes, centre. Such an abundance of sand in fact that a large slice of it was covered with concrete and turned into a car park, and still left more than most resorts could dream of. A stroll along the prom still gives a taste of briny but it's better to gaze out to sea these days than be bored with the seafront architecture. There is every amusement a child could wish - beach clubs, sand yachting and the Aqualud complex, a very present help in times of inclement weather, especially for those who like their water heated and no sand between their toes. Here, under a glass pyramid the temperature all year round is a comfortable 29 degrees. Giant toboggan, rivers, wave pool, jacuzzi, cost 8.3€ for three hours, up to 11.2€ for a full day. Sauna and café extra.

The main street, the rue St. Jean, runs for half a mile or so from the floriferous, wooded, upmarket Westminster/Casino end of town, past the most expensive shops, designer labels, antiques and wickedly beguiling children's clothes, to the more popular, more crowded, T-shirted, seafront conclusion. In between, because, praise be, this is France after all, there is still space and customers for praiseworthy *chocolateries, pâtisseries*, cafés and restaurants. Le Chat Bleu is famous for its hand-made chocs;

However as the everyday food shops are being squeezed out of the main drag, the side streets, like the rue de Metz, take over, becoming more animated in the process, Here are good fruit and veg shops, butchers, and *charcutiers*, and that not-to-be-missed

Le Manoir
Le Touquet.

Touquetois institution, Pérards, part restaurant, part fish shop, where the inevitable take-home buy is a jar or two of their fish or crab soup and accompanying *rouille* and *croûtons*. Many a hostess has lied about the provenance of her, 'home-made', first course, bought thus.

The rue de Londres, another up-and-coming cross street, leads to the wide circus of the distinctive Art Deco covered market, built in 1927. Be there early for the best fish, on sale every day.

In summer the flowers are astonishing, I've never seen a town use them more lavishly and it great to sit outside the numerous restaurants and bars, but Le Touquet prides itself on being a year-round resort. It may not look its best when the sky lowers and the sea pounds in winter storms against the prom, but there are indoor attractions to compensate somewhat. Gambling aside, the casino is the scene for winter concerts, an international music festival and entertainments - and of course golfers are used to defying the weather. Golf is BIG, Le Touquet Golf Club is one of the largest golf set-ups in France and organises many prestigious competitions. 45 holes cover more than 250 hectares. Apart from the two famous courses, La Mer, established in 1931 and La Forêt in 1904, there is now Le Manoir, a nine holer, where beginners are welcome.

Le Manoir hotel, overlooking the fairways, is still dedicated to the sport that used to be played stylishly here in tweed plus-fours and brogues. It offers special golfers' rates, including green fees, from 142€. (It does do special reservations for golfers but it is the same price.) Telephone (0)3.21.06.28.28; fax: (0)3.21.06.28.29.

In summer the town regularly wins prizes for its flowers, and they are the first thing that strikes you as you turn the corner after the forest and approach the casino, spilling over from tubs, baskets, boxes and beds in Technicolor profusion. It's a very well-groomed, well-organised town altogether, and hard to beat in the area for the combination of sea air, shopping and walking.

The eating/lodging scene in Le Touquet has changed recently. Whereas the town was strong on restaurants and weak on hotels, the reverse is now true. It is particularly gratifying at last to have found a couple of budget hotels I can recommend.

And soon there will be another new possibility, a three-star hotel in a lovely old building called L'Hermitage. Who will be the first to report back to me?

Hotels

Le Westminster ⛺ ⌧ L

ave. du Verger
tel: (0)3.21.05.48.48
fax: (0)3.21.05.45.45
restaurant closed: Tues.; all Jan., Feb., Mar.

Le Touquet's Grande Dame, Le West, has seen its share of celebrities since the palmy thirties when it was built and good casino customers were billeted gratis here, where they had just the road to cross before getting on with the serious business of losing money. Its transition into contemporary comfort and requirements has been skilful, and unashamedly luxurious. The spacious bedrooms have not been chopped into two, but have had en suite bathrooms attached, with marble basins, deep deep baths and fleecy bathrobes to wear en route to the indoor swimming pool. Good news, as is the retention of

179

the original birdcage lifts that come clanking to your command.

The fortunes of the gastro restaurant, **Le Pavilion** decline or ascend with the incumbent chef. Menus start at 42€, including drinks and coffee; the wine list is reasonable considering the high standards. A more modest alternative is the Coffee Shop, where menus start at 20€, and expertise is just as high.

The Westminster has some particularly interesting *forfaits*, i.e. special offers, available throughout the year. The *Forfait* 3 nuits for example suggests three night's B&B, cocktails, one dinner in the Pavillon, one dinner in another posh Touquet restaurant, two hour's tennis, and - here is the unusual bit - two days instruction in char-à-voile (sand yacht racing) from the World Champion, all for 98€ per person per day.

"We stayed six nights in a very good room and the whole ambience was one of high-class professionalism. Everything required was provided without fuss. I enjoyed several swims in the pool, which was scrupulously clean. We ate once at the Pavillon and enjoyed some inventive dishes. We also ate once in the busier Le Coffee and found the standard of preparation as good, with the simpler fare and the prices very acceptable." Pat and John Corbett.

No doubt that if you feel like a pampering weekend in Le Touquet, Le West will fill the (considerable) bill.

113 rooms from 158 to 222€.

Red Fox 🛏 M

    rue Metz
    tel: (0)3.21.05.27.58
    fax: (0)3.21.05.27.56

A good middle-of-the-road choice, with the slightly high charge justified by this being popular Le Touquet, with an accommodation shortage in this bracket. On the corner of the main street, with the entrance in the rue Metz and parking available. The owner, who seems to be permanently behind the reception desk, night and day, is helpful and efficient. Rooms are nondescript - good sized, quite pleasantly decorated, but lacking in any memorable character. Bathroom ditto. Breakfast an averagely good buffet. It was not the Red Fox's fault that we elected to stay there on the night that France won their semi-final of the World Cup and the partying went on all night under our window, but I imagine that in any circumstances it would be a good idea to ask for a room at the side, rather than over the rue St. Jean. 48 rooms 77€ breakfast is an extra 7.2€.

Les Embruns 🛏 S

89 rue Paris
tel: (0)3.21.05.87.61
fax: (0)3.21.05.85.89
closed: Christmas week

A great find - a young couple have been working hard to restore this old hotel and now the atmosphere is light, bright and cheerful. They had seven newly decorated rooms out of a total of 19 when I visited and are working their way systematically redecorating the rest to the same high standards.

Prices are 42-56€ for two, or 56€ for three, with two rooms specially adapted for the handicapped.

Artois 🛏 S

123 rue Paris
tel: (0)3.21.05.17.09
fax: (0)3.21.05.33.61

A similar story. M. and Madame Barlet are the proprietors in this case, and have finished decorating 15 rooms. A terrace roof garden is the next project (though since work still hasn't started on this, it's still 'the next project') but meanwhile breakfast is taken in a cheerful ground-floor dining room. 51-61€.

☆ Flavio's ⊠ L

1 Ave de Verger
tel: (0)3.21.05.10.22
fax: (0)3.21.05.91.55
closed: Mon. o.o.s.; 10 Jan. to 10 Feb.

Flavio is dead. Long live Flavio's. The influence of the late lamented Flavio was felt right up to his death in 1995, when at 85 he was still in the habit of chatting to his guests. The influence is still felt, especially by his daughter Daniele Delmotte, who has capably taken on her father's colourful mantle. It helped that she married the chef. Guy Delmotte has been cooking here since 1968, but has somehow managed to retain enthusiasm and passion for his craft, as well as marrying the boss's daughter.

The restaurant, next to the Westminster, opposite the casino, has always attracted the rich and famous. It is almost an annexe to Le

Flavio's.

West, with the hotels clients booking up at Flavio's, where they know they can rely on consistently high standards. It has an air of well-manicured prosperity, with expensive chairs outside on the lawn, coloured awnings, lavish fresh flowers, well-upholstered seats, pristine napery, sparkling glass, and perfect service from waiters who know how to smile as well as bow, and an unfaultable maître d', Laurent. They even managed not to make us feel unwanted when we booked for the night when France was playing in the World Cup and the rest of the restaurant and town were deserted. (We did the decent thing, ate up, declined a brandy, and allowed them to catch the last half hour.)

Daniele is an efficient hostess, who really cares about her customers, and as her son Xavier helps out too, it is still very much a family concern.

If all this sounds expensive, well it can be, but not necessarily. Imagine a lunch in an English restaurant of equivalent standing for £15 including wine and service! The evening menus start at 31€; *Le Privé* depends on *la retour du marché*, three superb courses, topped up by *amuse-bouches* and including wines and service. Call that expensive?

The specialities appear on *La Découverte* at 67€: *Langoustines rôties aux épices et soupe de truffes, Meunière de volaille de Licques aux baies de genièvre fraîches, caramel de bière et petits ragoût de légumes*, but as this menu does not include wine, you can expect a considerable additional outlay, since the wine-list is famous for its prices as well as its range. Guy combines new ideas with traditional dishes and local ingredients, like the very local potatoes originating in Le Touquet, regrettably called rattes. And very delicious they are too. Order them whenever an opportunity arises.

Superb value if you stick to the menu, and starred accordingly.

"The restaurant is very comfortable and the tables are well spaced. I liked the extremely civilised atmosphere and the friendly but polished service of the efficient waiters. The cheapest menu is certainly the one to go for as it includes a bottle of red wine (Anjou and very acceptable). The wine list is outrageously expensive - even half a bottle of Sancerre was 30€. We ate a delicious little crab soufflé in a ramekin and smoked salmon, served with wonderfully fresh rolls, followed by fillets of sole, lightly sautéed in court bouillon. Breast of duck came next, served with a good selection of fresh vegetables including some unusually delicious cabbage. The dessert was a sort of superior apple turnover with beautifully light pastry, nicely garnished with fresh orange slices and raspberry coulis. I thought the package represented good value."

☆ Café des Sports ⊠ S-M

22 rue St. Jean.

tel: (0)3.21.05.05.22.

Open: all hours, and that means 24 hours in high season.

From outside Les Sports looks just like any of Le Touquet's dozens of other brasseries. Less attractive than many in fact in summer, because it is one of the few that lacks tables outside. Inside too, the maroon plastic benches are instantly familiar from many a clone. The difference lies in the food. Where other lesser brasseries sell fast food cheap, prepared by anyone they can lure into their kitchens, Les

Sports employs three live chefs to cook the freshest of ingredients in no-corners-cut dishes.

All the traditional Parisien-style brasserie dishes are here, like pigs trotters, home made terrines and rillettes, tête de veau and jambon persillé. Oysters galore, in eleven different styles and sizes, simple grills and pan-fried fish. Nothing special about that, but here the emphasis is on home-made and fresh. Even old-fashioned dishes like egg mayonnaise are featured, but with golden-yoked farm eggs and of course unctuous home made mayo.

Brasseries are the answer for the whole family. If mother's not hungry she could settle for moules (10.5€) or a salad (5€), while Dad tucks into the whole three course menu du jour for 10.6€ and the little darlings wolf down their croque Monsieurs and chips. (3.2€). The couple on the table next to ours were consuming the plat du jour, an enormous cous cous (8€). They told us that they came over from Kent several times a year, stayed at the Westminster and ate at Les Sports twice a day.

The emphasis on fresh seasonal food extends to a herring festival in November. Everything from simple fillets in oil, to more elaborate dishes like harengs en papillote are on offer. I was glad to see that 'le kipper' featured and that dish belatedly discovered in France pommes de terre en robe des champs (baked potatoes to you),

A ☆ for honest, good value cooking.

Otherwise:

Fierval (C d'H)L
6. Ave Leon Garet
tel: (0)3.21.05.10.22

The Delmotte hospitality has recently been extended. Daniele has put her father's old villa in a quiet residential area near the restaurant to excellent use as a B&B. It is luxuriously furnished in 1930s comfort, with the guests invited to use the deep deep armchairs and other solid furniture in the salon and dining room. At present there are four bedrooms, three with bathrooms attached, but Daniele is planning to open up another floor shortly, which will enable all her rooms to have their own baths/showers. The 72€ includes a lavish breakfast, with bacon and eggs, since this is an English enclave (Daniele speaks the language fluently), and a 10%

discount on meals at Flavio's. Daniele is an exceptionally kind hostess, who will ensure her guests enjoy their stay.

La Dune Aux Loups ⊠ M

ave. de la Dune aux Loups
tel: (0)3.21.05.42.54
fax: (0)3.21.05.51.68
closed: Tues. p.m. Wed. 15 Nov. to 6 Dec.

Where other Touquetois restaurants seem to be on a downward slope, reports from La Dune are the reverse. Down in the forest something is stirring. Delve deeply through the trees into a quiet residential area to find this rustic hideaway. It's all very Hansel and Gretel, exposed beams and bricks outside, but indoors it gets more sophisticated with smart covers and efficient waiters. There's a leafy garden bordering an equestrian centre.

Arnaud Pannier, chef, dispenses mostly traditional dishes, like *blanquette de veau* and *meringue glacé* on his menus that start at 21€. Inexpensive wines result in an affordable bill.

Café des Arts ⊠ M

80 rue de Paris
tel: (0)3.21.05.21.55
fax: (0)3.21.84.64.20
closed: Tues. and Wed.

Local reports are disappointing on my erstwhile favourite. The décor was the only thing I disliked about the little restaurant and that has been changed. It's now very bright red and very bright yellow in and out. Eye-catching anyway. You can eat outside on the terrace, given fair weather. Jerome Pannis' cooking continues to be imaginative - witness his lobster with artichokes and green apples, or sole with grapefruit.

We stuck to the cheapo 16.5€ menu (not available on Saturday evenings where the next menu up is at 26€) and enjoyed our *moules à la biere*, *confit de porc à la Flamande* and *crème brulée à la Cassonata*, so I need some more reports to see who is right, but meanwhile the ☆ will have to go.

Chez Pierrot, ⊠ M,

rue Grande,
tel: (0)3.21.05.30.30.

The owner, Pierre, runs a very successful restaurant in Lille and is a well-known local character on TV, writing recipes in magazines and so on. He likes to chat to the customers and I'm told that the atmosphere in both his restaurants is warm and lively.

He likes to cook typical dishes of the area, like os à moelle, ficelle picard but more than that I don't know since I only discovered his little restaurant just behind the covered market as this guide was going to press. More details would be most welcome.

☆ Pérard ⊠ M

67 rue de Metz
tel: (0)3.21.05.13.33
closed: never.
No cards, no cheques

It's strange that there are not more good fish restaurants in Le Touquet, but perhaps they know that they could never compete with the famous Pérard, whose reputation gives him a headstart. Serge Pérard's fish soup sells all over the world; you can buy it here in the fish shop entrance to the bustling brasserie style restaurant.

There has been a recent change of management here and the Pérard family are no longer in charge. The menu is exactly the same as ever.

Le Diamant Rose ⊠ S

110 rue de Paris
tel: (0)3.21.05.38.10
closed: Wed.

If there is one restaurant that is constantly recommended by locals and readers alike it is Le Diamant Rose. I have never seen it written up in any guidebook, it is not glitzy, nor dirt-cheap, but continues to offer excellent value with friendly service. Here is a view that sums it all up:

"No faltering of standards here and as popular as ever. Menus at 16€ and 22€ both very good. Moules marinières were ten times better than at Pérard. Well prepared, fresh ingredients and excellent friendly service. Passes the acid test - very popular with French extended families coming for their end of holiday blow-out." Jim Taylor.

LE WAAST 62142 Pas-de-Calais

19 km E of Boulogne

Well marked from the N42. Turn north on the D127 through an attractive rural area, the Parc Regional squeezed between the autoroute and the nationale.

Château des Tourelles ⊯ ⊠ M
    tel: (0)3.21.33.34.78
    fax: (0)3.21.87.59.57

The 'château' is hardly recognisable nowadays as the rather run-down manor house that Serge and Michelle Feutry took on as a base for Serge's excellent cooking abilities. Extensions have sprouted all over the place, tacked on to the old grey stone. Breakfast is served in a glassed-in extension into the garden at the rear. There is a new dining room, seating 70, one extension has rooms at 46.4€, with bath or shower room, and yet another add-on - the most radical yet - was still being completed last time I visited. This one is approached

Hostellerie du Château des Tourelles

187

by a grandiose sweeping iron-railed staircase in an imposing new hall. There's a lot of mock walnut about. The new bedrooms here cost 67€ and demi-pension runs between 43€ and 51€ depending whether you choose old or new section.

The new dining room sports an open kitchen, where Serge has a team of sous-chefs and commis working for him. His 13.6€ menu changes every day, according to season and markets. For example: pan-fried cod with a coulis of leeks, roast beef and dessert. Other menus are from 21-40€.

'Improvements' and extensions are still going on. A family suite in the rafters of the latest add-on costs approx. 88€.

The Feutrys have worked hard to achieve this considerable success and it is great to see their daughter carrying on the good work behind the reception desk.

WIERRE EFFROY 67200 Rinxent. Pas-de-Calais

5 km S of Marquise by D238, 21 km NE of Boulogne

The hamlet of Wierre Effroy is well marked from the main roads that encircle it. Just as well, because, in the middle of nowhere, it is not easy to locate on the map. Michelin lines the lanes that approach it in green (signifying particularly attractive countryside), and rightly so. Oddly enough, in the heart of this gently rolling, unspoiled farming land, there are two establishments, at opposite ends of the hamlet, that merit an inclusion here:

Ferme du Vert ⊨ ⊠ S

tel: (0)3.21.87.67.00
fax: (0)3.21.83.22.62
restaurant closed: Sun., Mon. lunch. Open only p.m. o.o.s.

No longer an undiscovered farmhouse with a few beds but a Logis-de-France that publicises its existence prominently with numerous signs. The same family, the friendly Bernards, still run the business, now with valuable input from their grown-up son. The farm complex centres on a large cobbled yard. Beside the front door is a shop selling home-produced cheeses, *terrines, quiches* and other farm produce. The dining room takes up another wing and the bedrooms the rest.

A reader chastised me for describing the rooms as monastic, so I went to look again. I stick by my view. They are small, whitewashed and furnished extremely simply. True, the en suite cons are immaculately mod, but the whole feeling of the ensemble is of peace and removal from daily cares.

The cooking is strictly based on local produce, usually their own, and the recipes are regional. Fillet of pork is cooked with juniper berries and the duck legs are braised in beer. There are the farm's own cheeses of course and a choice of five home-made desserts. The 21€ menu has three courses and the 24 and 37€ versions merit one extra. *Plâteaux de fruits de mer* are available too if you remember to order ahead.

Rooms cost between 56-112€.

Ferme Auberge de la Raterie 🛏 ☒ S
tel: (0)3.21.92.80.90
closed: Sun. p.m.; Mon.

Draw in your mind's eye a picture of a typical picture-postcard-pretty unspoiled farm and the reality will not disappoint. The *auberge*, though nowadays more concerned with people than animals, still looks like a farm - low and rambling, rough stone walls, wooden shutters, courtyard, set among pastures - but with far more geraniums in pots, baskets and troughs, fresh white paint and white benches around from which to admire the view than the average farmer would have time for. At the rear is a surprisingly large flowery garden, with very un-farmer-like recliners scattered about for exhausted tourists.

Inside the farmhouse there is no evidence of the usual farm clutter, but all the best bits of the atmosphere remain. Low beams, flagged floors, log fires, pine panelling, swinging lamps, and an old grandfather clock gleaming with polish.

The Coquerelle family team has been depleted by the departure of their daughters but Christophe's commitment to the *auberge* has been affirmed. He pointed out to me that they are now officially registered as *'Les Coquerelles, et leur fils'*. He injects a new generation's enthusiasm for sharing their adorable home. I am sure that it was the women in the family, though, who were responsible for choosing the furnishings of the prettiest bedrooms imaginable. They are all decorated in fresh and simple country style fabrics and wallpapers, with white frilly curtains and lace bedspreads. The older ones, up a steep polished wooden staircase, have hand-painted porcelain washbasins but have to share a bathroom with three other rooms. In two years' time they will all have their en-suite bathrooms and will no doubt cost more but at present the bill is 40€. In the new block running along the garden, the bathrooms are in situ and the cost is 57-69€.

The dining room is as charming as the rest of the house. Farmhouse ingredients are used in menus from 17.4€. The next one up, at 25€, offered five courses, vegetable soup, *terrine*, roast chicken or ham, cheese, pudding.

Now, I have a problem. I thought on this last visit that the whole charming countryside set-up should have a star. On consulting my files however, I find a dichotomy. On the one hand: *"The cheapest evening meal was soup, roast chicken and burnt rhubarb tart. A total of 107€ for a night stop for two makes La Raterie expensive and not deserving of an arrow"*, and

"The rooms were spotless and nicely decorated, but very cold with no heating on when we arrived. The dinner was extremely dull and the wine list impossible. Madame appeared to be away and we only ever saw one daughter who was not very welcoming. The Labrador was the only friendly being there." And on the other hand:

"Sensational! The rooms at 48€ were certainly pricey for that sort of thing but excellently furnished and beautifully set out. But it was the meal that persuaded us that Mme Coquerelle should receive an arrow. Glorious gammon, falling off the bone, preceded by a huge tureen of home made cream of vegetable soup and a quite superb Delice de Licques. This local delicacy, of onions, cream and chicken in a delightful little lidded pot was sensational and all on a menu costing just 22€. The hardworking family Coquerelle deserve all the praise we can give them". Mike Souter.

And:

"Excellent meal. A very thick potato soup followed by roast pork. The pork was large slices (no portion control) that had been roasted with garlic. Tarte aux pommes was also good. Their house wine was not very good but we felt the final bill was good value. Hearty French farmhouse cooking". Mark Girling.

Ah... put all these valuable opinions together and a clearer picture emerges. The simple farmhouse fare is always going to include thick vegetable soup for starters, then chicken or ham and a fruit tart. The two correspondents on the more expensive menu felt they had better value than those on the lowest-priced. But as all four had roughly the same menu, what happens if you stay for several nights? All agree that the wine is dicey - either not very good house, or expensive. I have to admit that 48€ is plenty for a *ferme auberge* room, but personally I thought it justified because it was so exceptionally atmospheric. However, if they cannot be bothered to switch on the heating when visitors are expected, it does not look so attractive a deal.

I have a feeling that things are looking up with Christophe's involvement, but there is obviously room for improvement. As things are it would seem that a bit of cashing-in is taking place, and the star disappears. It would be good to see it reinstated on the basis of more favourable reports.

WIMEREUX 62930 Pas-de-Calais

6.5 km N of Boulogne
Market: *Tues., Fri.*

Once upon a time, when white flannels were *de rigueur seaside* gear for the gentlemen, and parasols and shady hats for the ladies - and I do mean gentlemen and ladies - Wimereux was *the* place to go for a naughty (but nice) weekend. A breath of sea air, a stroll along the promenade, and a delicious dinner of food unheard of back home was a very pleasant little escape. Abroad but not too far abroad. The Atlantic Hotel dominated the sea front then, as it does today.

With Boulogne suffering from a shortage of hotels and a surfeit of traffic, it makes good sense to head along the coast road and stay in Wimereux. The little town retains its sleepy old-fashioned air, even if the main through road is usually too congested for agreeable shopping. More tranquil is the Tuesday morning market by the river, which gave its name to the town

Given fair weather it is still very agreeable to stroll along the wide *digue*, where children pedal furiously, mothers push buggies and stout, elderly couples take their constitutionals. There's a wide and wonderful beach to explore when the tide recedes and none at all when it is high. If that coincides with a strong wind, the waves pound against the seawall and kids play dodge-the-spray along the prom. A wall of boulders keeps the seawater in a permanent pool for those disinclined to walk the considerable distance to the water when the tide is at its lowest. I enjoy the town in winter too, when I have to share the whole expanse of beach with only with a few muffled figures and the prom is populated by poodle-walkers wrapped up in furs.

☆ Hotel Atlantic and Restaurant La Liègeoise 🛏 ☒ M
Digue de Mer
tel: (0)3.21.32.41.01
fax: (0)3.21.87.46.17
restaurant closed: Sun. p.m., Mon. lunch
hotel and restaurant closed: Feb.

It was a very good day for the little resort when Alain Delpierre decided to sell his restaurant in Boulogne and put all his eggs in the Wimereux basket. The legendary Atlantic was looking sad and shabby before he set about restoring it to the standard of its heyday. Now the Art Deco façade gleams with paint, cream, peach and blue; a focus that the town can be proud of is intact.

There are surprisingly few hotels or restaurants capitalising on sea views in the Pas-de-Calais. Without doubt the Atlantic has the prime site along the whole Côte d'Opale. It makes the most of them. A seat by the panoramic windows of the restaurant Liègeoise makes you feel you could be on an ocean liner, cresting the waves. This, understandably, is not only my favourite restaurant, but that of a good many locals, looking for a treat or a business extravaganza, so make sure you book.

Not surprisingly, fish is the star turn on the menus. The 30€ version (not weekends) features Alain's home-smoked salmon, fish *'selon l'arrivage du jour'*, and dessert. For 40€ you could choose six oysters or fresh crab with a shellfish sauce, followed by roast monkfish with mushrooms and Basmati rice, but there are carnivore alternatives - *magret* or fillet of beef for example. On the carte a sole cooked with *langoustines* costs 17.5€ or turbot on a bed of spinach and leeks 29€. You don't come here for gastronomic fireworks, but rather for the freshest fish cooked simply to perfection.

Downstairs is a more modest *brasserie* which spills out onto the wide terrace in fine weather. Blue and white canvas director's chairs spell out the marine theme, windbreaker glass screens extend the season. This has to be the most agreeable outdoor eating in the area. Or drinking for that matter, since this is also a bar/*salon de thé*.

Seafood and salads are the fare, and it is perfectly acceptable to order just a platter of oysters - a dozen *fines* cost 16€, or 12 *langoustines* with the kind of mayonnaise that begs to be mopped up with some home-made bread (14.4€). If you have the afternoon to spare the *plâteau de fruits de mer* at 34€ should take care of that nicely.

This is primarily a restaurant with rooms, rather than a hotel with food, but the Delpierres have decorated all ten bedrooms, each in a different colour, and hung co-ordinating flowery curtains, laid new carpets and installed modern bath/shower rooms. Decisions have to be made - a larger room facing the side, or a smaller one with sea-view. They all cost 78€. More recently, there have been added some more luxurious rooms at 120€.

Ask before you book if there are any special offers - *forfaits* - going. Alain often arranges out-of-season-bargains.

It would be hard to find shortcomings with the new-style Atlantic - sea views, fine cooking, comfortable rooms, and best of all an exceptionally warm welcome from Alain and Beatrice Delpierre. Starred on all counts.

Otherwise:

☆ La Goëlette (Ch'd)M
13 Digue de Mer
tel: (0)3.21.32.62.44

In summer you have to delve behind the beach huts on the prom to find this 1930s villa freshly painted in blue and cream, bay trees primly in pots on the balcony; in winter the huts vanish, folded up like a pack of cards. Be thankful that this building at least, erected in the resort's prime, escaped the developers who, as in Le Touquet, have vandalised so many charming eccentricities in favour of apartment blocks, empty for most of the year.

La Goëlette is certainly not empty for most of the year. Mary Arvot's very special b. and b. is so popular that I curse the day I ever wrote about it. Now I can't get in. If you are planning a weekend visit you should book weeks ahead. But it's worth a bit of juggling with dates to lie in bed and listen to the waves, or to look out of the tall windows to the marine panorama that has made at least one reader feel she is sailing on a big and very comfortable ship.

Mary is not your average landlady. Young, attractive, warm and friendly, she has converted four bedrooms with style. They are vaguely Scandinavian in character, with polished wooden floors, lots of blue and white, and expensive linen. Any severity is softened by antique pine furniture, and the bathrooms are efficient and modern. The two front rooms (80€) are the ones to aim at, though the two 'garden' rooms (64€) are pretty nice too, even without the seaview. At weekends and holidays there is a 16€ supplement to encourage you to spread the load.

Breakfast is unusually good, with cereals and yoghurts as well as the usual croissants and several kinds of bread and proper jam. The little bar and sitting area is now up and running, though Mary has not yet persuaded the authorities to give her a drink licence.

The ☆ is reinforced.

"The wonderful La Goëlette has become of our favourite places and I cannot commend it and Mary Avots welcome enough." Alison Kerrigan.

Alison Kerrigan also recommends Le Bar de la Mairie in the town, where she says the wine is particularly good value.

☆ L'Epicure ⊠ M
1 rue de la Gare
tel: (0)3.21.83.21.83
fax: (0)3.21.33.53.20
closed: Wed p.m.; Sun.; Christmas holidays

The youthful chef-patron Philippe Carée continues to cook the best food in town and, for my money, probably the best on the Côte d'Opale. His restaurant is tiny - just six tables - and one wonders how he can possibly make it work; however, it is evident that he cooks because that is what he loves to do, not to make a huge commercial success, and perhaps this is the size that he and his wife Claudette can handle best.

Fish, of course, features prominently - his salad of scallops and oysters is to die for but whatever he is cooking is enhanced by his magic touch with herbs and spices. Not for him the expensive cuts that anyone could dish up, but the old neglected favourites like ox cheek and pigs trotters lovingly cajoled into juicy tenderness and enhanced by appropriate vegetables (rare in France these days).

I felt absolutely safe in choosing the cheapest no-choice menu, at

22€. With a chef of this calibre, you can put yourself in his hands and enjoy a bargain. You may even discover an interesting new dish that you might not have chosen for yourself. For me it was a confit of rabbit, as flavoursome and tender as I could wish, and a fillet of cod encased in a herby crust and sitting on a puree of endives. Not for Philippe the out-of-season veg and fruits that most restaurants are not ashamed to serve. In winter he finds new ways of using root vegetables, chicory, leeks, each one designed to enhance the main ingredient but a lovingly conceived dish in its own right.

Dessert was another French rarity - a plate of fruit. Here were mangos and pink grapefruits in an orange coulis, fresh and tart, with no unnecessary embellishment. Nevertheless Phillipe is a skilled pâtissier, so count yourself lucky too if a more sophisticated dessert features for you.

I'll stick my neck out and forecast a Michelin star here, and the ☆ remains, but there is a caveat. You come here for the food, not the atmosphere. Not a lot of smiles around. And no concessions made to non-French speakers.

Le Centre 🛏 ⊠ S

78 rue Carnot
tel: (0)3.21.32.41.08
fax: (0)3.21.33.82.48.
Restaurant closed: Sun. o.o.s. and Mon.

One of those archetypally French hotels that have been in the centre of the little town as long as anyone can remember, with the nice Boulanger family at the helm. The food makes no concession to fashion fads and is as resolutely substantial and traditional as anyone nostalgic for unfussy, seasonal fare could wish for. Better perhaps in winter than when the sunshine beckons, always packed, dark and intimate with the cheerfulness coming from the chatter of French families who know what they like and know too that they will find it here. Mary Avot (see La Goëlette) says that it is the favourite Wimereux restaurant of all her clients, who find it *'adorable' 'romantique'* and *'vivant'.*

Menus start at 17€ (e.g. *moules marinières, lapin en gelée maison, crème brulée*, then for 28€ you could choose *coquille St. Jacques, pavé de boeuf*, cheeses and *profiteroles. Plats du Jours* could be steak *tartare* at 12€, *confit de canard*, 10.8€ or *moules en casserole* 10.4€. An *omelette aux champignons* at 6.8€ would make an excellent lunch served with good frites. Plats du Jour vary in price, but start at 9.6€.

Hotel du Centre

It is for the food that you would choose Le Centre but there are 25 rooms, 40-51€ with bath or shower. Ask for one at the rear, overlooking the courtyard, rather than those on the main road. Parking available.

Cap Nord ⊠ S

Digue de Mer
tel: (0)3.21.33.78.23
closed: Thurs. o.o.s.; 1 Oct. to 20 Oct. and 12 Jan. to 31 Jan.

A new brasserie on the promenade run by Jean-Marc and his sister Catherine Boulanger, with Catherine in charge. On days when sitting outside is not a good idea, even with the glass windshields, it is no hardship to retreat into the interior; the décor here is bright and cheerful, adopting a Scandinavian-look open-plan. A large galleon-shaped bar adds considerable character. With a family dedicated to good food it is not surprising that Catherine knows a thing or two about cooking and presentation. While the *brasserie carte* enables customers to eat exactly what they fancy throughout the day, the main menu concentrates on local produce, especially fish, with the chef delighted to show off his specialities. Two menus, both with three courses, cost 15€ and 20€.

In fact there is truly something here for everyone - breakfast by the sea, afternoon *pâtisserie*, *apéritifs*, full Monty. In summer there is a special light menu with lots of salads and in winter the kind of satisfying calorific fare, like *raclette, choucroute and fondue, 'pour rendre les soirées d'hiver encore plus conviviales'* to quote Jean-Marc.

A very welcome addition to the Wimereux scene.

WIMILLE 62200 Pas-de-Calais

2 km SE of Wimereux

Take the D233 that leaves Wimereux by the river and dives under the bridge. Stick with it till you see a church ahead, turn right and the Relais is on the left-hand corner. No hardship if you get lost - the surrounding countryside is particularly attractive and well worth exploring.

La Brocante ☒ L-M
   2 rue Ledinghen
   tel: (0)3.21.83.19.31
   fax: (0)3.21.87.29.71
   closed: Sun. p.m.; Mon.

When the respected Gault et Millau guide looked for a chef to represent the best regional cooking in the North of France, it was to Jean-Francois Laurent of La Brocante that they turned, awarding him 16 points out of a theoretically possible 20. He is a one-off in the region - more innovative than any other. If your idea of a good meal is steak with a daring touch of béarnaise, head elsewhere.

He has been cooking for 12 years now in the untouristy situation of a sleepy village centre, in the former presbytery next to the church. It later became a canteen for the local school and then an antique shop - hence the name Jean-Francois chose for his restaurant - La Brocante.

Le Relais de la Brocante

The old building has been converted to give a feeling of intimacy and cosiness to counter the severity of the cold stone walls. Fresh flowers, polished antiques, a grandfather clock, deep leather armchairs all help to dissipate any restaurant formality. And it's tiny - so book.

Jean-François' enthusiasm for ingredients that have spent the least possible time between farm/sea and his kitchen encourages him to cycle round the neighbourhood searching out likely suppliers. His passion is researching old recipes and re-creating them with regard to today's tastebuds. He could not have chosen to live in a more favoured region. The Boulogne fish is some of the best in France and the countryside is rich and fertile. Whatever he fails to find growing there, he cultivates himself in his *potager*.

Combining unlikely ingredients is another signature theme. From Licques, famous for its poultry, he chooses a plump guinea fowl and adds to the casserole a secret ingredient that you know is there but can't quite put your finger on. Coffee. Just a grain or two to add that *je ne sais quoi*. Liquorice is another taste-teaser - he grates a shred or two of the root into one or two appropriate desserts, and only the true gourmet would know what it was that gave the extra punch. His star turn I sampled on my last visit - *galette de kipper aux oignons, fleur de thym et jus de poule*. In other words a kipper cake. The base of thin potato roundels is neatly arranged in circles, the onions are cooked in local beer, flavoured with thyme and alternated with the kipper flakes, and the chicken *jus* is pepped up with just a touch of... coffee.

Menus start at 27€ and reach 61€.

Otherwise:

La Bonne Idée ⊠ S
68 rue de l'Aiglon
tel: (0)3.21.31.49.36

This has been highly recommended and sounds just my kind of place. There are only 25 covers and you must book. Great atmosphere I'm told. Tell me more. There was a change in management two years ago. They are now open seven days a week and menus are 11.2€ and 17.6€.

WIRWIGNES Pas-de-Calais

12 km SE of Boulogne on the D341

Mémère Harlé ⊠ S
Route de Dèsvres
tel: (0)3.21.87.34.87
open: only for Sunday lunch

Drive through the Forêt de Boulogne and on the corner of a crossroads stands an establishment that has changed little since 1919. Here is the legend of Granny Harlé:

"Once upon a time, in a small village deep in the Boulonnais countryside, with a name difficult to pronounce - Wirwignes - there was an admirable woman, an honest Christian and an excellent cook, who made the best Tarte au Papin in the whole area. A marvellous tart with thick sides as golden as a halo, as creamy as the milk of springtime and with the perfume of a girl from the islands. People would travel to this place just to come for a taste of this tart whose pastry captured the smell of the different woods burned in the oven while cooking the casing and whose cream, made from the very best milk, had the creaminess of a smile from His Eminence."

Yes, well. The amazing thing is that Guy Louchez and his wife still serve the best Tarte au Papin in the whole area, made from the original recipe. Not a lot else has changed either. The dining room is as pretty as an old picture, with mauve periwinkle tiles. The menu formula is exactly as it always has been - soup, tongue, garden vegetables, roast leg of lamb, gratin of potatoes, flageolet beans, cheeses from Philippe Olivier and of course the famous tart, cooked on a wood fire as always.

This feast costs 19.2€ and is served for Sunday lunch only on reservation. Predictably the place is packed.

WISSANT Pas-de-Calais 62179

17 km S of Calais
Market: *Wed.*

In a superb position between the two sheltering arms of the two Caps, Blanc and Gris, Wissant has arguably the finest beach of all the fine beaches of this coastline. It would be a finicky child indeed who was not enchanted by the choice of sand, wet or dry, rocks, pools, and puddles. Sand yachts provide extra animation. Great for walkers too, with wonderful cliff-edge paths in both directions.

Unusually, the centre of Wissant is not the beach but some way back, around a distinctive hotel, the black and white Normandy, where there are seats for conversation and plenty of drinking opportunities. This is where to find:

Le Vivier 🛏 ☒ S-M

pl. de l'Eglise
tel: (0)3.21.35.93.61
fax: (0)3.21.82.10.99
website: www.levivier.com
closed: Tues., Wed.

This has appeared briefly in FE before and there have been considerable changes, it is now a hotel as well as a restaurant. Two hotels in fact, under the same management. Le Vivier 1. is in the centre of the village; Le Vivier 2, a villa, is in the rue Victor Hugo, same telephone number. The latter has views over the bay, and all rooms have garden, terrace or balcony, baths or showers, for 56-88€, breakfast included .

The original Vivier is easy to spot because of the old fishing boat full of flowers outside its doors. Here the rooms are light and airy and good sized, at the same price, but without the view. There is a little garden at the back. The pleasant restaurant downstairs predictably majors on fish, but there is a good range of meat and poultry dishes too, with fresh local produce used throughout. Menus 17.6-32€.

With friendly, helpful proprietors, who will arrange transport to stations or ferries, this would be a good choice for a family holiday, especially as there are kitchenettes provided in some rooms in the new building. Lock up garages are another asset, and there are special weekly rates throughout the year.

Wines and spirits

by John Doxat

> *Bonne cuisine et bons vins, c'est le paradis sur terre.*
> (Good cooking and good wines, that is earthly paradise.)
>
> King Henri IV

Outline of French Wine Regions

Bordeaux

Divided into a score of districts, and sub-divided into very many *communes* (parishes). The big district names are Médoc, St Emilion, Pomerol, Graves and Sauternes. Prices for the great reds (châteaux Pétrus, Mouton-Rothschild, etc.) or the finest sweet whites (especially the miraculous Yquem) have become stratospheric. Yet 'château' in itself means little and the classification of various rankings of châteaux is not easily understood. Some tiny vineyards are entitled to be called château, which has led to disputes about what have been dubbed 'phantom châteaux'. Visitors are advised, unless wine-wise, to stick to the simpler designations.

Bourgogne (Burgundy)

Topographically a large region, stretching from Chablis (on the east end of the Loire), noted for its steely dry whites, to Lyons. It is particularly associated with fairly powerful red wines and very dry whites, which tend to acidity except for the costlier styles. Almost to Bordeaux excesses, the prices for really top Burgundies have gone through the roof. For value, stick to simpler local wines.

Technically Burgundies, but often separately listed, are the Beaujolais wines. The young red Beaujolais (not necessarily the over-publicised *nouveau*) are delicious when mildly chilled. There are several rather neglected Beaujolais wines (Moulin-à-Vent, Morgon, St Amour, for instance) that improve for several years: they represent good value as a rule. The Mâconnais and Chalonnais also produce sound Burgundies (red and white) that are usually priced within reason.

Rhône

Continuation south of Burgundy. The Rhône is particularly associated with very robust reds, notably Châteauneuf-du-Pape; also Tavel, to my mind the finest of all still *rosé* wines. Lirac rosé is nearly as good. Hermitage and Gigondas are names to respect for reds, whites and rosés. Rhône has well earned its modern reputation - no longer Burgundy's poorer brother. From the extreme south comes the newly 'smart' dessert *vin doux naturel*, ultrasweet Muscat des Beaumes-de-Venise, once despised by British wine-drinkers. There are fashions in wine just like anything else.

Alsace

Producer of attractive, light white wines, mostly medium-dry, widely used as carafe wines in middle-range French restaurants. Alsace wines are not greatly appreciated overseas and thus remain comparatively inexpensive for their quality; they are well placed to compete with popular German varieties. Alsace wines are designated by grape - principally Sylvaner for lightest styles, the widespread and reliable Riesling for a large part of the total, and Gerwürtztraminer for slightly fruitier wines.

Loire

Prolific producer of very reliable, if rarely great, white wines, notably Muscadet, Sancerre, Anjou (its rosé is famous), Vouvray (sparkling and semi-sparkling), and Saumur (particularly its 'champagne styles'). Touraine makes excellent whites and also reds of some distinction - Bourgueil and Chinon. It used to be widely believed - a rumour put out by rivals? - that Loire wines 'did not travel': nonsense. They are a successful export.

Champagne

So important is Champagne that, alone of French wines, it carries no AC: its name is sufficient guarantee. (It shares this distinction with the brandies Cognac and Armagnac.) Vintage Champagnes from the *grandes marques* - a limited number of 'great brands' - tend to be as expensive in France as in Britain. You can find unknown brands of high quality (often off-shoots of *grandes marques*) at attractive prices, especially in the Champagne country itself. However, you need information to discover these, and there are true Champagnes for the home market that are *doux* (sweet) or *demi-sec* (medium sweet) that are pleasing to few non-French tastes. Champagne is very closely controlled as to region, quantities, grape types, and is made only by secondary fermentation in the bottle. From 1993, it is prohibited (under EU law) to state that other wines are made by the 'champagne method' - even if they are.

Minor regions (very briefly)

Jura - Virtually unknown outside France. Try local speciality wines such as *vin jaune* if in the region.

Jurançon - Remote area; sound, unimportant white wines, sweet styles being the better.

Cahors - Noted for its powerful *vin de pays* 'black wine', darkest red made.

Gaillac - Little known; once celebrated for dessert wines.

Savoy - Good enough table wines for local consumption. Best product of the region is delicious Chambéry vermouth: as an aperitif, do try the well distributed Chambéryzette, a unique vermouth with a hint of wild strawberries.

Bergerac - Attractive basic reds; also sweet Monbazillac, relished in France but not easily obtained outside: aged examples can be superb.

Provence- Large wine region of immense antiquity. Many and varied *vins de pays* of little distinction. Best known for rosé, usually on the sweet side; all inexpensive and totally drinkable.

Midi - Stretches from Marseilles to the Spanish border. Outstandingly prolific contributor to the 'EU wine lake' and producer of some 80 per cent of French *vins de table*, white and red. Sweet whites dominate, and there is major production of *vins doux naturels* (fortified sugary wines).

Corsica - Roughish wines of more antiquity than breeding, but by all means drink local reds - and try the wine-based aperitif Cap Corse - if visiting this remarkable island.

Paris -Yes, there is a vineyard - in Montmartre! Don't ask for a bottle: the tiny production is sold by auction, for charity, to rich collectors of curiosities.

Hints on spirits

The great French spirit is brandy. Cognac, commercially the leader, must come from the closely controlled region of that name. Of various quality designations, the commonest is VSOP (very special old pale): it will be a cognac worth drinking neat. Remember, *champagne* in a cognac connotation has absolutely no connection with the wine. It is a topographical term, *grande champagne* being the most prestigious cognac area: fine champagne is a blend of brandy from the two top cognac sub-divisions. Armagnac has become better known lately outside France, and rightly so. As a brandy it has a much longer history than cognac: some connoisseurs rate old armagnac (the quality designations are roughly similar) above cognac.

Be cautious of French brandy without a cognac or armagnac title, regardless of how many meaningless 'stars' the label carries or even the magic word 'Napoleon' (which has no legal significance).

Little appreciated in Britain is the splendid 'apple brandy', Calvados, mainly associated with Normandy but also made in Brittany and the Marne. The best is *Calvados du Pays d'Auge*. Do taste well-aged Calvados, but avoid any suspiciously cheap.

Contrary to popular belief, true Calvados is not distilled from cider - but an inferior imitation is: French cider (cidre) is excellent.

Though most French proprietary aperitifs, like Dubonnet, are fairly low in alcohol, the extremely popular Pernod/Ricard pastis-style brands are highly spirituous. Eau-de-vie is the generic term for all spirits, but colloquially tends to refer to local, often rough, distillates. Exceptions are the better *alcools blancs* (white spirits), which are not inexpensive, made from fresh fruits and not sweetened as *crèmes* are.

Bringing Back Those Bottles

When thinking of what to bring back from France in the way of wines and spirits, apart from considerations of weight and bulk, there are a few other matters to bear in mind. Within the theoretically unlimited import for personal consumption of products which have paid any national taxes in the country of origin, there are manifest practical as well as some semi-official restrictions.

Wine: to choose sensibly is not inevitably to go for the least expensive. Unless you envisage having to entertain a lot of relatives, beware the very cheapest of French table wines! Though France produces many of the world's greatest, her prolific vineyards also make wines to which no British supermarket would allocate shelf-space. Quality does count along with value. Primarily what you are saving by purchasing in France is the comparatively high excise duties imposed in Britain against the minimal ones in France. However, the British tax is just the same on a bottle of the most ordinary *vin ordinaire* as on the rarest of vintage claret. When it comes to the latter, buying fine vintage wines in France does not automatically mean obtaining a bargain, unless you are an expert. There are not that many specialist wine merchants in France, a commerce in which Britain excels.

To summarise: it is undoubtedly sound, middle range wines that are the most sensible buy.

If you like those famous liqueurs, such as Bénédictine, Chartreuse, the versatile Cointreau, which are so expensive in Britain, shop around for them: prices seem to vary markedly.

I have briefly dealt elsewhere with French spirits. If you are buying Scotch whisky, gin or vodka, you may find unfamiliar names and labels offering apparent bargains. None will harm you but some may have low, even unpleasant, taste characteristics. It is worth paying a trifle more for well-known brands, especially de-luxe styles. Though they are little sold in Britain, former French colonies distill several excellent types of rum (rhum).

I deem it a good idea to make an outline list of intended purchases, after deciding what you can carry and how much you wish to spend. As to wines, do you want mainly red, or only white, or what proportion of both types? Can you afford champagne? Best to buy that in visiting the region where you should have the opportunity to taste and possibly find a bargain. What about other sparklers? What do you require in dessert wines, vermouths, liqueurs, spirits? Does your list work out at more cases (12 bottles) than you can easily transport? A conspicuously overloaded vehicle may be stopped by police as a traffic hazard. Now you have a list of sorts. What about cost? For essential comparisons, I would put against each item the maximum (per bottle) I would be prepared to pay in Britain.

Basic glossary of French wine terms

Alsace - See Wine Regions (page 202)

Abricotine - Generic apricot liqueur: look for known brands.

Alcool blanc- Spirit distilled from various fruits (not wine); not fruit-flavoured cordials.

Aligoté - Light dry Burgundy.

Anis - Aniseed, much favoured in pastis (Ricard/Pernod) type aperitifs.

Anjou - See Loire, Wine Regions (page 202)

Aperitif - Literally 'opener': any drink taken as an appetiser.

Appellation (d'origine) Contrôllée - or AC wine, whose label will give you a good deal of information, will usually be costlier - but not necessarily better - than one that is a VDQS 'designated (regional) wine of superior quality'. A newer, marginally lesser category is VQPRD: 'quality wine from a specified district'. Hundreds of wines bear AC descriptions: you require knowledge and/or a wine guide to find your way around. The intention of the AC laws was to protect consumers and ensure wine was not falsely labelled - and also to prevent over-production. Only wines of reasonable standards should achieve AC status: new ones (some rather suspect) are being regularly admitted to the list.

Armagnac - See Hints on Spirits (page 205)

Barsac - Very sweet Sauternes of varying quality.

Basserau - A bit of an oddity: sparkling red Burgundy.

Beaumes-de-Venise - Well-known vin doux naturel; see Provence, Minor Regions (page 204)

Beaune - Famed red Burgundy; costly.

Bergerac - Sound red wine from south-west France.

Blanc de Blancs - White wine from white grapes alone. Sometimes confers extra quality but by no means always. White wine made from black grapes (the skins removed before fermentation) is Blanc de Noirs - Carries no special quality connotation in itself.

Bordeaux - See Wine Regions (page 202).

Bourgeuil - Reliable red Loire wine.

Bourgogne - Burgundy; see Wine Regions (page 202).

Brut - Very dry; description particularly applicable to best sparkling wines.

Brut Sauvage - Dry to the point of displeasing acidness to most palates; very rare though a few good wines carry the description.

Cabernet - Noble grape, especially Cabernet-Sauvignon for excellent, if not absolutely top grade, red wines.

Cacao - Cocoa; basis of a popular crème.

Calvados - See Hints on Spirits (page 205).

Cassis - Blackcurrant; notably in crème de cassis (see Kir).

Cave - Cellar.

Cépage - Indicates grape variety; e.g. Cépage Cabernet-Sauvignon.

Chablis - See Burgundy, Wine Regions (page 202). Fine Chablis are expensive.

Chai - Ground-level storehouse, wholly employed in Cognac and sometimes in Bordeaux and other districts.

Champagne - See Wine Regions (page 202). Also specialty note Méthode Traditionelle below.

Château(x) - See Wine Regions, Bordeaux (page 202).

Châteaneuf-du-Pape- Best known of powerful Rhône red wines.

Chenin-blanc - Grape variety associated with many fine Loire wines.

Clairet - Unimportant Bordeaux wine, its distinction being probable origin of English word Claret.

Clos - Mainly a Burgundian term for a vineyard formerly (rarely now) enclosed by a wall.

Cognac - See Hints on Spirits (page 205).

Corbières - Usually a sound south of France red wine.

Côte - Indicates vineyard on a hillside; no quality connotation necessarily.

Côteau(x) - Much the same as above.

Crème - Many sweet, sometimes sickly, mildly alcoholic cordials with many local specialities. Nearer to true liqueurs are top makes of crème de menthe and crème de Grand Marnier (q.v.). Crème de Cassis is mixed with white wine to produce kir or a sparkling white wine to produce kir royale.

Crémant - Sparkling wine with strong but rather brief effervescence.

Cru - Literally 'growth'; somewhat complicated and occasionally misleading term: e.g. grand cru may be only grower's estimation; cru classé just means the wine is officially recognised, but grand cru classé is most likely to be something special.

Cuve close- Literally 'sealed vat'. Describes production of sparkling wines by bulk as opposed to individual bottle fermentation. Can produce satisfactory wines and certainly much superior to cheap carbonated styles.

Cuvée - Should mean unblended wine from single vat, but cuvée spéciale may not be particularly special: only taste will tell.

Demi-sec - Linguistically misleading, as it does not mean 'half-dry' but 'medium sweet'.

Domaine - Broadly, Burgundian equivalent to Bordeaux château.

Doux - Very sweet.

Eau-de-vie - Generic term for all distilled spirits but usually only applied in practice to roughish marc (q.v.) and the like.

Entre-deux-Mers - Undistinguished but fairly popular white Bordeaux.

Frappé - Drink served with crushed ice; viz. crème de menthe frappée.

Fleurie - One of several superior Beaujolais wines.

Glacé - Drink chilled by immersion of bottle in ice or in refrigerator, as distinct from frappé above.

Goût - Taste; also colloquial term in some regions for local eau-de-vie (q.v.).

Grand Marnier - Distinguished orange-flavoured liqueur. See also crème.

Haut - 'High'. It indicates upper part of wine district, not necessarily the best, though Haut-Médoc produces much better wines than other areas.

Hermitage - Several excellent Rhône red wines carry this title.

Izarra - Ancient Armagnac-based liqueur much favoured by its Basque originators.

Juliénas- Notable Beaujolais wine.

Kir - Well-chilled dry white wine (should be Bourgogne Aligoté) plus a teaspoon of crème de cassis (q.v.). Made with champagne (or good dry sparkling wine) it is Kir Royal.

Liqueur - From old liqueur de dessert, denoting postprandial digestive. Always very sweet. 'Liqueur' has become misused as indication of superior quality: to speak of 'liqueur cognac' is contradictory - yet some very fine true liqueurs are based on cognac.

Loire - See Wine Regions (page 202).

Méthode Traditionnelle- Most widely-used description of superior sparkling wine made as is champagne, by fermentation in bottle, now that any labelling association such as 'champagne method' is banned.

Marc - Mostly coarse distillations from wine residue with strong local popularity. A few marcs ('mar') - de Champagne, de Bourgogne especially - have achieved a certain cult status.

Marque - Brand or company name.

Meurseult - Splendid white Burgundy for those who can afford it.

Minervoise- Respectable southern red wine: can be good value as are many such.

Mise - As in mise en bouteilles au château ('château-bottled'), or ... dans nos caves ('in our cellars') and variations.

Montrachet - Very fine white Burgundy.

Moulin-à-Vent - One of the rather special Beaujolais wines.

Muscadet - Arguably the most popular light dry Loire white wine.

Muscat - Though used for some dry whites, this grape is mainly associated with succulent dessert-style wines.

Nouveau - New wine, for drinking fresh; particularly associated with now tiring vogue for Beaujolais Nouveau.

Pastis - General term for powerful anis/liquorice aperitifs originally evolved to replace banned absinthe and particularly associated with Marseilles area through the great firm of Ricard.

Pétillant - Gently, naturally effervescent.

Pineau - Unfermented grape juice lightly fortified with grape spirit; attractive aperitif widely made in France and under-appreciated abroad.

Pouilly-Fuissé - Dry white Burgundy (Macon); sometimes over-valued.

Pouilly-Fumé - Easily confused with above; a very dry fine Loire white.

Porto - Port wine: usually lighter in France than the type preferred in Britain and popular, chilled, as an aperitif.

Primeur - More or less the same as nouveau, but more often used for fine vintage wine sold en primeur for laying down to mature.

Rosé - 'Pink wine', best made by allowing temporary contact of juice and black grapes during fermentation; also by mixing red and white wine.

Sauvignon - Notable white grape; see also Cabernet.

Sec - 'Dry', but a wine so marked will be sweetish, even very sweet. Extra Sec may actually mean on the dry side.

Sirop - Syrup; e.g. sugar-syrup used in mixed drinks, also some flavoured proprietary non-alcoholic cordials.

Supérieur(e) - Much the same as Haut (q.v.) except in VDQS.

VQRPD. - See AC above.

Vin de Xeres - Sherry ('vin de 'ereth').

Glossary of cooking terms and dishes

This basic glossary provides an introduction to the terms you are most likely to encounter. For a more complete guide, see the companion pocket-sized book French Entrée *Companion to Food and Drink in France* (ISBN 1-904012-05-1) that provides a comprehensive bilingual menu dictionary together with all the useful phrases that will help you make the most of French food and restaurants.

Aigre-doux	bittersweet
Aiguillette	thin slice (*aiguille* - needle)
Aile	wing
Aiolli	garlic mayonnaise
Allemande (à l')	German style, i.e.: with sausages and sauerkraut
Amuse-gueules	appetisers
Andouille	large uncooked sausage, served cold after boiling
Andouillettes	(as per Andouille) but made from smaller intestines, usually served hot after grilling
Anglaise (à l')	plain boiled. *Crème Anglaise* - egg and cream sauce
Anis	aniseed
Argenteuil	with asparagus
Assiette Anglaise	plate of cold meats
Baba au rhum	yeast-based sponge macerated in rum
Baguette	long, thin loaf
Ballotine	boned, stuffed and rolled meat or poultry, usually cold
Béarnaise	sauce made from egg yolks, butter, tarragon, wine, shallots
Béchamel	white sauce flavoured with infusion of herbs
Beignets	fritters
Bercy	sauce with white wine and shallots
Beurre blanc	sauce from Nantes, with butter, reduction of shallot-flavoured vinegar or wine
Beurre noir	browned butter
Bigarade	with Seville oranges
Billy By	mussel soup
Bisque	creamy shellfish soup
Blanquette	stew with thick, white creamy sauce, usually veal
Boeuf à la mode	braised beef
Bombe	ice-cream mould
Bonne femme	with root vegetables
Bordelais	Bordeaux-style, with red or white wine, marrowbone fat
Bouchée	mouthful, *e.g.* vol-au-vent
Boudin	sausage, white or black
Bourride	thick fish-soup
Braisé	braised
Brandade (de morue)	dried salt-cod pounded into mousse
Broche	Spit
Brochette	skewer
Brouillade	stew, using oil
Brouillé	scrambled
Brûlé	burnt, e.g. *crème brûlée*
Campagne	country style
Cannelle	cinnamon
Carbonnade	braised in beer

GLOSSARY OF GASTRONOMIC TERMS

Cardinal	red-coloured sauce, e.g. with lobster, or in *pâtisserie* with redcurrants
Cassolette or cassoulette	small pan
Cassoulet	rich stew with goose, pork and haricot beans
Cervelas	pork garlic sausage
Cervelles	brains
Chantilly	whipped sweetened cream
Charcuterie	cold pork-butcher's meats
Charlotte	mould, as dessert lined with sponge-fingers, as savoury lined with vegetables
Chasseur	with mushrooms, shallots, wine
Chausson	pastry turnover
Chemise	covering, i.e. pastry
Chiffonnade	thinly-cut, e.g. lettuce
Choron	tomato Béarnaise
Choucroute	Alsatian stew with sauerkraut and sausages
Civet	stew
Clafoutis	batter dessert, usually with cherries
Clamart	with peas
Cocotte	covered casserole
Compôte	cooked fruit
Concassé	e.g. *tomates concassées*-skinned, chopped, juice extracted
Confit	preserved
Confiture	jam
Consommé	clear soup
Coque (à la)	e.g. *oeufs* - boiled eggs
Cou	neck
Coulis	juice, purée (of vegetables or fruit)
Court-bouillon	aromatic liquor for cooking meat, fish, vegetables
Couscous	N. African dish with boiled grains of millet, served with chicken or vegetables

Crapaudine	involving fowl, particularly pigeon, trussed
Crécy	with carrots
Crème pâtissière	thick custard filling
Crêpe	pancake
Crépinette	little flat sausage, encased in caul
Croque-Monsieur	toasted cheese-and-ham sandwich
Croustade	pastry or baked bread shell
Croûte	pastry crust
Croûton	cube of fried or toasted bread
Cru	raw
Crudités	raw vegetables
Demi-glâce	basic brown sauce
Doria	with cucumber
Émincé	thinly sliced
Entremets	sweets
Étuvé	stewed, e.g. vegetables in butter
Farci	stuffed
Feuilleté	leaves of flaky pastry
Fines herbes	parsley, thyme, bayleaf
Flamande	Flemish style, with beer
Flambé	flamed in spirit
Flamiche	flan
Florentine	with spinach
Flûte	thinnest bread loaf
Foie gras	goose liver
Fond (d'artichaut)	heart (of artichoke)
Fondu	melted
Forestière	with mushrooms, bacon and potatoes
Four (au)	baked in the oven
Fourré	stuffed, usually sweets
Frais, fraîche	fresh and cool
Frangipane	almond-cream *pâtisserie*
Fricadelle	Swedish meat ball
Fricandeau	veal, usually topside
Fricassé	stew (usually of veal) in creamy sauce
Frit	fried
Frites	chips

Friture	assorted small fish, fried in batter
Froid	cold
Fumé	smoked
Galantine	loaf-shaped chopped meat, fish or vegetable, set in natural jelly
Galette	Breton pancake, flat cake
Garbure	thick country soup
Garni	garnished, usually with vegetables
Gaufre	waffle
Gelée	aspic
Gésier	gizzard
Gibier	game
Gigot	leg
Glacé	iced
Gougère	choux pastry, large base
Goujons	fried strips, usually of fish
Graine	seed
Gratin	baked dish of vegetables cooked in cream and eggs
Gratinée	browned under grill
Grecque (à la)	cold vegetables served in oil
Grenadin	nugget of meat, usually of veal
Grenouilles	frogs: cuisses de grenouille – frogs' legs
Grillé	grilled
Gros sel	coarse salt
Hachis	minced or chopped
Haricot	slow cooked stew
Haricots	beans
Hochepot	hotpot
Hollandaise	sauce with egg, butter, lemon
Hongroise	Hungarian, i.e. spiced with paprika
Hors-d'oeuvre	assorted starters
Huile	oil
Île flottante	floating island - soft meringue on egg-custard sauce
Indienne	Indian, i.e. with hot spices
Jambon	ham
Jardinière	from the garden, i.e. with vegetables
Jarret	shin, e.g. jarret de veau
Julienne	matchstick vegetables
Jus	natural juice
Lait	milk
Langue	tongue
Lard	bacon
Longe	loin
Macédoine	diced fruits or vegetables
Madeleine	small sponge cake
Magret	breast (of duck)
Maïs	sweetcorn
Maître d'hôtel	sauce with butter, lemon, parsley
Marchand de vin	sauce with red wine, shallots
Marengo	sauce with tomatoes, olive oil, white wine
Marinière	seamens' style e.g. moules marinière (mussels in white wine)
Marmite	deep casserole
Matelote	fish stew, e.g. of eel
Médaillon	round slice
Mélange	mixture
Meunière	sauce with butter, lemon
Miel	honey
Mille-feuille	flaky pastry, (lit. 1,000 leaves)
Mirepoix	cubed carrot, onion etc. used for sauces
Moëlle	beef marrow
Mornay	cheese sauce
Mouclade	mussel stew
Mousseline	Hollandaise sauce, lightened with egg whites
Moutarde	mustard
Nage (à la)	poached in flavoured liquor (fish)
Nature	plain
Navarin (d'agneau)	stew of lamb with spring vegetables
Noisette	nut-brown, burned butter

GLOSSARY OF GASTRONOMIC TERMS

Noix de veau	nut (leg) of veal
Normande	Normandy style, i.e. with cream, apple, cider, Calvados
Nouilles	noodles
Onglet	beef cut from flank
Os	bone
Paillettes	straws (of pastry)
Panaché	mixed
Panade	flour crust
Papillote (en)	cooked in paper case
Parmentier	with potatoes
Pâté	paste, of meat or fish
Pâte	pastry
Pâte brisée	rich short-crust pastry
Pâtisserie	pastries
Paupiettes	paper-thin slice
Pavé	thick slice
Paysan	country style
Périgueux	with truffles
Persillade	chopped parsley and garlic topping
Petit pain	bread roll
Petits fours	tiny cakes, sweetmeats
Piperade	peppers, onions, tomatoes in scrambled egg
Poché	poached
Poêlé	fried
Poitrine	breast
Poivre	pepper
Pommade	paste
Potage	thick soup
Pot-au-four	broth with meat and vegetables
Potée	country soup with cabbage
Pralines	caramelised almonds
Primeurs	young veg
Printanier (printanière)	garnished with early vegatables
Profiteroles	choux pastry balls
Provençale	with garlic, tomatoes, olive oil, peppers
Pureé	mashed and sieved
Quenelle	pounded fish or meat bound with egg, poached
Queue	tail

Quiche	pastry flan, e.g. *quiche Lorraine* - egg, bacon, cream
Râble	saddle, e.g. *râble de lièvre*
Ragoût	tew
Ramequin	little pot
Râpé	grated
Ratatouille	Provençale stew of onions, garlic, peppers, tomatoes
Ravigote	highly seasoned white sauce
Rémoulade	mayonnaise with gherkins, capers, herbs and shallots
Rillettes	potted shredded meat, usually fat pork or goose
Riz	rice
Robert	sauce with mustard, vinegar, onion
Roquefort	ewe's milk blue cheese
Rossini	garnished with foie gras and truffle
Rôti	roast
Rouelle	nugget
Rouille	hot garlicky sauce for *soupe de poisson*
Roulade	roll
Roux	sauce base -flour and butter
Sabayon	sweet fluffy sauce, with eggs and wine
Safran	saffron
Sagou	sago
Salade niçoise	salad with tuna-fish, anchovies, tomatoes, beans, black olives
Salé	salted
Salmis	dish of game or fowl, with red wine
Salpicon	meat, fowl, vegetables, chopped fine, bound with sauce and used as fillings
Sang	blood
Santé	lit. healthy, i.e. with spinach and potato
Saucisse	fresh sausage
Saucisson	dried sausage
Sauté	cooked in fat in open pan

Sauvage	wild
Savarin	ring of yeast-sponge, soaked in syrup and liquor
Sel	salt
Selle	saddle
Selon	according to, e.g. *selon grosseur* (according to size)
Smitane	with sour cream, white wine, onion
Soissons	with dried white beans
Sorbet	water ice
Soubise	with creamed onions
Soufflé	puffed, i.e. mixed with egg-white and baked
St-Germain	with peas
Sucre	sugar (*sucré* - sugared)
Suprême	fillet of poultry breast or fish
Tartare (sauce)	mayonnaise with capers, herbs, onions
Tartare	raw minced beef, flavoured with onions etc. and bound with raw egg
Tarte Tatin	upside down (apple) pie
Terrine	pottery dish/baked minced, chopped meat, veg., chicken, fish or fruit
Thé	tea
Tiède	luke warm
Timbale	steamed mould
Tisane	infusion
Tourte	pie
Tranche	thick slice
Truffes	truffles
Tuile	tile, i.e. thin biscuit
Vacherin	meringue confection
Vallée d'Auge	with cream, apple, Calvados
Vapeur (au)	steamed
Velouté	white sauce, bouillon-flavoured
Véronique	with grapes
Vert(e)	green, e.g. *sauce verte*, with herbs
Vessie	pig's bladder
Vichysoisse	chilled creamy leek and potato soup
Vierge	prime (virgin) olive oil
Vinaigre	vinegar (lit. bitter wine)
Vinaigrette	wine vinegar and oil dressing
Volaille	poultry
Vol-au-vent	puff-pastry case
Xérès	sherry
Yaourt	yoghurt

FISH - Les Poissons, SHELLFISH - Les Coquillages

Alose	shad
Anchois	anchovy
Anguille	eel
Araignée de mer	spider crab
Bar	sea bass
Barbue	brill
Baudroie	monkfish, anglerfish
Belon	flat-shelled oyster
Bigomeau	winkle
Blanchaille	whitebait
Brochet	pike
Cabillaud	cod
Calamar	squid
Carpe	carp
Carrelet	plaice
Chapon de mer	scorpion fish
Claire	oyster
Coquille St-Jacques	scallop
Crabe	crab
Crevette grise	shrimp
Crevette rose	prawn
Daurade	sea bream
Écrevisse	crayfish
Éperlan	smelt
Espadon	swordfish
Étrille	baby crab
Favouille	spider crab
Flétan	halibut
Fruits de mer	seafood

GLOSSARY OF GASTRONOMIC TERMS

Grondin	red gurnet
Hareng	herring
Homard	lobster
Huître	oyster
Julienne	ling
Laitance	soft herring-roe
Lamproie	lamprey
Langouste	Dublin Bay prawn
Lieu	ling
Limande	lemon sole
Lotte de mer	monkfish
Loup de mer	sea bass
Maquereau	mackerel
Merlan	whiting
Morue	salt cod
Moule	mussel
Mulet	grey mullet
Ombre	grayling
Oursin	sea urchin
Palourde	clam
Pétoncle	small scallop
Plie	plaice
Portugaise	oyster
Poulpe	octopus
Praire	large clam
Raie	skate
Rascasse	scorpion-fish
Rouget	red mullet
Sandre	zander
Saumon	salmon
Saumonette	rock salmon
Seiche	squid
Sole	sole
Soupion	inkfish
St-Pierre	John Dory
Thon	tuna/tunny
Tourteau	large crab
Tortue	turtle
Truite	trout
Turbot	turbot
Turbotin	chicken turbot

FRUITS - Les Fruits, VEGETABLES - Les Légumes, NUTS - Les Noix HERBS - Les Herbes, SPICES - Les Épices

Abricot	apricot
Ail	garlic
Algue	seaweed
Amande	almond
Ananas	pineapple
Aneth	dill
Arachide	peanut
Artichaut	globe artichoke
Asperge	asparagus
Avocat	avocado
Banane	banana
Basilic	basil
Betterave	beetroot
Blette	Swiss chard
Brugnon	nectarine
Cassis	blackcurrant
Céléri	celery
Céléri-rave	celeriac
Cêpe	edible fungus
Cerfeuil	chervil
Cerise	cherry
Champignon	mushroom
Chanterelle	edible fungus
Châtaigne	chestnut
Chicorée	endive
Chou	cabbage
Chou-fleur	cauliflower
Choux de Bruxelles	Brussels sprouts
Ciboulette	chive
Citron	lemon
Citron vert	lime
Coing	quince
Concombre	cucumber
Coriandre	coriander
Cornichon	gherkin
Courge	pumpkin
Courgette	courgette
Cresson	watercress
Échalote	shallot
Endive	chicory
Épinard	spinach
Escarole	salad leaves
Estragon	tarragon
Fenouil	fennel
Fève	broad bean
Flageolet	dried bean
Fraise	strawberry
Framboise	raspberry
Genièvre	juniper
Gingembre	ginger

GLOSSARY OF GASTRONOMIC TERMS

Girofle	clove
Girolle	edible fungus
Grenade	pomegranate
Griotte	bitter red cherry
Groseille	gooseberry
Groseille noire	blackcurrant
Groseille rouge	redcurrant
Haricot	dried white bean
Haricot vert	French bean
Laitue	lettuce
Mandarine	tangerine, mandarin
Mangetout	sugar pea
Marron	chestnut
Menthe	mint
Mirabelle	tiny gold plum
Morille	dark brown crinkly edible fungus
Mûre	blackberry
Muscade	nutmeg
Myrtille	bilberry, blueberry
Navet	turnip
Noisette	hazelnut
Oignon	onion
Oseille	sorrel
Palmier	palm
Pamplemousse	grapefruit
Panais	parsnip
Passe-Pierre	seaweed
Pastèque	water melon
Pêche	peach
Persil	parsley
Petit pois	pea
Piment doux	sweet pepper
Pissenlit	dandelion
Pistache	pistachio
Pleurote	edible fungi
Poire	pear
Poireau	leek
Poivre	pepper
Poivron	green, red and yellow peppers
Pomme	apple
Pomme de terre	potato
Prune	plum
Pruneau	prune
Quetsch	small dark plum
Radis	radish
Raifort	horseradish
Raisin	grape
Reine Claude	greengage
Romarin	rosemary
Safran	saffron

Salsifis	salsify
Thym	thyme
Tilleul	lime blossom
Tomate	tomato
Topinambour	Jerusalem artichoke
Truffe	truffle

MEAT - Les Viandes

Le Boeuf	Beef
Charolais	is the best
Chateaubriand	double fillet steak
Contrefilet	sirloin
Entrecôte	rib steak
Faux Filet	sirloin steak
Filet	fillet
L'Agneau	Lamb
Pré-Salé	is the best
Carré	neck cutlets
Côte	chump chop
Epaule	shoulder
Gigot	leg
Le Porc	Pork
Jambon	ham
Jambon cru	raw smoked ham
Porcelet	suckling pig
Le Veau	Veal
Escalope	thin slice cut from fillet
Les Abats	Offal
Foie	liver
Foie gras	goose liver
Cervelles	brains
Langue	tongue
Ris	sweetbreads
Rognons	kidneys
Tripes	tripe

POULTRY - Volaille, GAME - Gibier

Abatis	giblets
Bécasse	woodcock
Bécassine	snipe
Caille	quail
Canard	duck
Caneton	duckling
Chapon	capon
Chevreuil	roe deer
Dinde	young hen turkey
Dindon	turkey

GLOSSARY OF GASTRONOMIC TERMS

Dindonneau	young turkey	Pluvier	plover
Faisan	pheasant	Poularde	chicken (boiling)
Grive	thrush	Poulet	chicken (roasting)
Lièvre	hare	Poussin	spring chicken
Oie	goose	Sanglier	wild boar
Perdreau	partridge	Sarcelle	teal
Pigeon	pigeon	Venaison	venison
Pintade	guineafowl		